Basic Reading Skills

REVISED EDITION

FOR HIGH SCHOOL USE

by Marion Monroe, Gwen Horsman, and William S. Gray

Special acknowledgment is made to:

MILDRED A. DOUGHERTY for her helpful advice on the selection,
organization, and gradation of materials in this book and for her practical suggestions
in light of classroom use. (Teacher, Ahrens Trade High School, Louisville, Kentucky;
formerly, teacher in Western Junior High School, Louisville.
Fellow, Fund for the Advancement of Education.)

CHARLES G. SPIEGLER for his careful selection and annotation of the books
suggested in the section "Books You May Like." (Chairman, Academic Subjects,
Food Trades Vocational High School, New York, New York; Lecturer, Queens College of
New York and City College of the City of New York. President,
International Reading Association [Manhattan Chapter].)

Scott, Foresman and Company

Chicago   Atlanta   Dallas   Palo Alto   Fair Lawn, N.J.

Contents

You Can Improve

As you have discovered, one of the greatest differences between high school and the upper grades or junior high school is the increased amount of homework you are expected to do. And homework means *reading*—not just a page or two, but whole chapters and entire books. Frequently you are asked to prepare written as well as oral reports on the reading you have done. You are perhaps finding, too, that you need to spend more and more time in the library working on assignments. Often you may carry home not one book, but an armload of books that you need for your homework.

The world of serious study is opening up before you. The amount of reading you will need to do may sometimes seem unreasonable to you, but it is only a preview of what you will need to do as a high-school senior or as a college student. From now on, the largest part of your education at school will come to you through the printed page. There are not enough hours in the day for your teachers to *tell* you all you need to know. You have to dig information out of books for yourself.

Of course, you will want to do your best with your studies, for you realize that one of the re-

wards of good work in high school is a good job in adult life. If you can read well, you will take your studies in your stride.

But many high-school students, for one reason or another, find that they do not read as well as they should to keep up with all their assignments. Here is a comment made by one freshman: "I thought I was a good enough reader when I was in the grades. But now I find that I'm really slow—so slow I can't keep up with the others. To finish my homework, I have to begin to read early and I'm still at it late at night! If only I could read better, it would make all the difference in the world to me!" Don't feel discouraged if this comment describes you too. You have plenty of company. Just look around you. There are many students—smart ones, at that— who do not read as well as they would like to.

Now is the time to take stock of your ability to read. Ask yourself the questions that are printed below. You don't need to discuss your answers with anyone—just be honest with yourself. Put a mental check mark beside any of these questions that you think apply to you.

Do you dread being called on in class to read a passage aloud?

Do you stumble over words, finding many that you can't pronounce?

When you read silently, do you often find that you are only saying the words to yourself without really getting the meaning of the text?

When you are assigned a passage to read during class, do you find that others finish before you are even half through?

Do you find many words whose meanings you do not understand? If so, do you skip these words?

If you use a dictionary, do you find it difficult to understand the definitions given there?

Is it hard for you to figure out the pronunciation of words from dictionary symbols?

Do you put off reading your homework assignments as long as possible, doing everything else before you settle down to study?

Now, here are some more questions. Answer these questions just as honestly as you did the other ones.

Have you ever been so wrapped up in a book that you sat up most of the night finishing it?

When you are reading a book, does the story "come alive" in your mind so that you "see" the action clearly?

When you come to a sad part in a book that really "reaches" you, do you sometimes find yourself blinking back a tear? (Don't be ashamed—even football heroes have confessed to doing this.)

Do you ever wish that you could meet and talk with the author of a certain book?

Do you ever use your library card during summer vacations?

Do you enjoy reading about famous people?

Do books about science fascinate you?

Do you understand the meaning of most of the words you meet in reading?

Do you find it easy to pronounce new words, and are you usually sure that you have pronounced them correctly?

Do you find yourself using new words you have come across in reading?

Do you sometimes prefer the story of a book you have read to the movie or TV version of the story?

Do you find it easier to follow printed directions than to have someone tell you the directions orally?

Do you like to have a record player or the TV turned on while you are reading?

Does your mind wander a lot while you read?

Is it hard to remember what you have read?

Do you have trouble finding the main idea of a paragraph or making an outline of a chapter in a book?

Do you find books too boring to read?

If you answered "yes" to several of these questions, you are not getting as much out of reading as you should. Reading isn't much fun for you, is it? In fact, if you answered "yes" to even one question, you may need to improve your reading.

If you answered "yes" to some of the questions in the second set, you have found that reading can be fun, and you are probably doing a lot of it just for pleasure.

Now for the last and most important question to ask yourself: *Do you want to be a better reader than you are?*

If your answer to this question is "yes," then you are ready to apply yourself to *Basic Reading Skills for High School Use.*

If you think you can learn to read better and really want to improve your reading, *Basic Reading Skills* will (1) help you learn what your strong and weak points in reading are; (2) provide the practice you need to improve your ability to read; and (3) guide you in finding books that you can read and enjoy.

What does Basic Reading Skills *do to help you learn what your strong and weak points in reading are?* On pages 172-176 of this book, there are several tests called "Survey Tests." After you have taken these tests you may discover that you need to improve your reading vocabulary or your ability to attack new words. On the other hand, you may find that your chief difficulty is in getting the meaning of what you read. These survey tests are for your information, and they will help you know which reading skills you lack and which ones you need to strengthen.

How can Basic Reading Skills *help you improve your ability to read?* You will find that the book is divided into sections that stress different reading skills. Some of these sections may be quite easy for you, but you may need to study other sections much more carefully. Your teacher will help you correct your mistakes, suggest various ways for you to overcome your difficulties, and help you get more practice of the kind that you need.

Remember, everyone in your group is trying to improve, too. This is not the time to be shy. Ask all the questions you wish. By asking questions, you will help not only yourself but your classmates clear up some confusions.

Although *Basic Reading Skills* offers many practice pages, there is one rule you should always remember as you read and mark each page. *Never let your mind wander from the meaning of the page.* The pages are not long, but they do require your complete attention. If you discover yourself dreaming, make an X at the spot on the page where your mind wandered. As you work through the book, try to reduce the number of X's you have on the pages. Remember, you can't improve your reading until you are able to think about what you read with your whole mind. Each page is planned to hold your interest and to make your review of the basic reading skills as much fun as possible. But you must give each page your full attention. You can always daydream some other time.

How can Basic Reading Skills *help you find books you can read and enjoy?* At the back of this book there is a section called "Books You May Like." The books in this list were chosen because they are not too hard to read and because high-school students have liked them. You may find books there that you will like too.

There are brief comments about each book in the list. Try to find a book that is easy for you to read and that is interesting to you. If you find it is hard to get interested in a book, remember that you can't tell too much about a story until you've read the first chapter. So give the book a chance by reading that far before making up your mind. Your teacher may be able to help you select a book, if you will tell her about your likes and dislikes.

Each book you read and like will make the next book easier to read. Don't read a book that is too hard, however. If you stumble over more than three or four words on a page, try something easier. You want to practice good reading; you do not want to practice making mistakes. So try out a book by reading several pages to see if the book "fits" your ability to read. You may find in this list of books just the right book to get you started. Here's hoping!

As you try to improve your reading, think about the things that have happened in the past—things that may have kept you from being the good reader you want to be. If you have any physical trouble such as poor vision, have it corrected, if you can. You may have had a bad start in a school because of illness or moving from one school to another. If so, all you may need is just the chance to review some of the reading skills you missed in the grades. You can do this as you read and work the pages in *Basic Reading Skills for High School Use.*

Perhaps you have become discouraged and wonder whether you are as smart as some of your friends who are good readers. You will be comforted to know that many poor readers are just as intelligent as good readers. Since these poor readers have not been able to do much reading, they have missed out on a lot of the information that makes good readers more capable in school. When a person improves in reading, his grades usually improve too. He also gains self-confidence and ability to do many other things well.

Don't waste your energy blaming yourself or other people for the fact that you are a poor reader. Whatever got you off to a poor start probably happened long ago. Instead, try to understand yourself, for it helps to know why you are as you are. And hold fast to the knowledge that *you can improve.* That improvement is worth your best efforts.

And He's Not Telling

by Richard Armour

Consider the lowly, downtrod worm:
His walk is a groveling, servile squirm,
He wears no clothes and he bears no fur,
And it's hard to distinguish a him from a her.

Though he passes his days in toiling for us
By making the ground all nice and porous,
We either are quite unaware he is near
And tread him into a dark-brown smear
Or show him our thanks and our warm good wishes
By casting him out to attract the fishes.

But the worm in at least one way is smart,
He can grow at will a replacement part.
If his head's cut off, he can sprout another
As good as the one he got from mother;
If his tail's detached, a new one will burgeon
Without any help from nurse or surgeon.

Now this is a trick that men of science
Would like to pass on for the use of their clients,
But its secret they ruefully grant is known
To the lowly, downtrod worm alone.

From which it may readily be discerned
That at long, long last the worm has turned.

The subject matter of this poem was suggested by a newspaper headline. Underline the headline that you think inspired the poet to write "And He's Not Telling."

New Life Expectancy for Lowly Worm

Foresee Possible Wiping Out of Earthworm Population

Renewed Hope for Headless Worms

Worm Turns and Bites Hand That Feeds Him

Science Finds Answer to Riddle of the Ages

New Bait for Fishermen

Science Seeking Worm's Secret of Self-Repair

Celebrate Be-Kind-to-Earthworms Week

From *Yours for the Asking* by Richard Armour; copyright, 1942, by Bruce Humphries, Inc.

Remote-Control Classroom

Mrs. Dana and her out-of-town visitor, Mrs. King, were chatting over a cup of coffee in the kitchen. In the middle of a sentence, Mrs. King gave a startled jump. "What in the world is going on upstairs? I thought you said Jimmie was alone, but I just heard somebody say 'Hi, Jimmie,' and then more people talking and chairs being pushed around."

Mrs. Dana set down her cup of coffee and smiled mysteriously. "Come up and see."

The two women started up the stairs. Since a bus accident five years before, Jimmie had been unable to leave his bed. In all that time, he had not been in a schoolroom.

As the women neared Jimmie's room, they heard gusts of laughter. Then a woman's voice inquired, "Jimmie, do you agree with Mary's answer?" Jimmie replied, "No, Miss Cord. A boneshaker isn't something to use in the gym. It's an old-fashioned bi——" He stopped as he saw his mother and her guest.

Mrs. King's eyes were fairly popping out of her head as she looked around the large room. "But . . . but——" she sputtered, "there isn't a soul here!"

Jimmie grinned at her. "No, just my two-way intercom speaker," he replied, pointing to the device on the table beside his bed.

Today hundreds of bedfast boys and girls like Jimmie Dana are attending school regularly by means of special telephone communication between the home and the classroom.

The apparatus consists of a speaker-microphone device that carries sound over a telephone wire. The student at home has one such box near his bed. Connected with it by telephone hookup is another box at the school that can be plugged into a special telephone outlet and moved from one room to another.

By flipping a switch, a bedfast student can hear everything his teachers and classmates at school say. When it is his turn to speak, he presses a button and his voice is carried back to the schoolroom. The box at school carries sounds both ways without the use of a switch.

It costs from fifteen to twenty-five dollars a month to rent this equipment, depending upon the distance between the home and the school and the number of classrooms that are hooked up. In some states the school and the state government share the cost between them.

For bedfast pupils, absence from school doesn't need to mean dropping behind in their studies. Many boys and girls who attend "push-button classrooms" become honor students. In fact, some get better grades than they did in school. Perhaps they achieve more because there is less to disturb them at home. Moreover, being "on the air" is a challenge to their pride.

Check the statements below that best give the main idea of this article.

---- Modern devices enable ill or handicapped students to continue their school work.

---- Radio and television are important in the classroom.

---- In recent years many schools have participated in home-study plans.

---- Modern machines are helping to solve unusual problems.

---- Standard transmitting devices are being used in both schools and homes.

---- Absentees can make up class work.

---- Pupils who attend "push-button classrooms" often become honor students.

When the Bleachers Rocked

by Vincent Edwards

Baseball through the years has had sidesplitting moments. Without intending to, players and umpires have made the stands rock with laughter.

In Cincinnati, long ago, the bleacherites had a habit of jumping over the railing and moving closer to the infield just before the ninth inning. The first time Umpire McFarland came to Cincinnati, he got a shock. He thought that he had done a good job behind the plate, for he had heard no loud complaints. Then, in the eighth, he received a scare that was enough to knock him out of five years' growth.

Suddenly, like an advancing army, fans swarmed over the barriers and onto the field. McFarland thought his time had come. From his post behind home plate, he took a quick look at all those men moving in his direction. The next instant, without bothering to ask questions, he tore off his mask, threw it on the ground, and dashed through the players' gate. He hustled down the passageway under the stands, swept through the turnstile, and then, still on the run, made a record-breaking leap onto a passing streetcar.

That fast getaway became a favorite story with the fans. The crowd never got over how their umpire had run out on them, for no apparent cause.

Sometimes players produce just as big a laugh. In Chicago, in 1894, the Giant outfielder, Foster, made a sensational catch. The only trouble was that he failed to catch the right thing. A Chicago batter had taken a tremendous swing at the ball but merely tipped it. The ball rolled toward the shortstop, who put the runner out. But Foster didn't see what happened. The shadow cast by the late afternoon sun made it hard for him to see the ball after it left the bat. He saw the mighty swing and saw the batter run like mad. Looking into the sky, he beheld a dark object coming in his direction.

His back was to the grandstand, but he thought he heard encouraging shouts. Foster uncorked his well-known speed and beat the object to the fence. He took one glance into the sun to make sure the thing was coming his way, then leaped high in the air. His gloved hand shot out and closed around—an English sparrow!

The crowd in the stands hadn't missed a thing. After seeing the runner put out at first, they stared in astonishment at Foster's unexpected sprint. But when people saw the descending bird and the outfielder's catch, they let out such a hilarious roar that the stands must have been shaken to their foundations.

Even when the ball is real, it has cut up some surprising capers. Once when Duffy of Boston was playing center field, McAleer of Cleveland slammed one over his head. Duffy went for the ball, but just as he was ready to close on it, it bounced into an old tomato can. Duffy tugged and tugged, but got nowhere. The ball was stuck fast. All this time McAleer was rounding bases.

There was only one thing to do, and the fielder did it. He picked up that canned ball and heaved it to Nash at third. Nash caught the can, looked at it in wonderment for a second, and then relayed it to Bennett, who was waiting at the plate. Bennett managed to catch it and tagged McAleer as he ran in.

But the umpire had ideas of his own. He called McAleer safe. No arguments could convince him that a runner was out because he was tagged with a rusty tomato can, even if the ball was inside!

One of the headlines below might have appeared over a newspaper story describing each of these incidents. Choose the best headline for each incident and put the number in the margin beside it.

1. Sensational Catch Puts Runner Out

2. Umpire Makes Home Run

3. Catch As Catch Can

4. Crowd Mobs Umpire

5. Baseball Player Gets the Bird

What's in a Name?

Many unusual place names in the United States grew out of incidents that happened at the spot. Match each incident with the correct place name from this list:

Hoosick	Mount Misery	Mount Joy	Noah's Brig
Flagstaff	Independence Creek	Nags Head	Smackover
Bone Venture	Superstition Mountain	Council Bluffs	Bride Brook

Along the coast of North Carolina is a spot where, according to local legend, "land pirates" in early days deliberately tried to wreck ships. On stormy nights the pirates would tie a lantern to the neck of an old horse and then ride him slowly along the beach. Ships would mistake the light for a beacon and be lured to the dangerous reefs along the shore, where they were boarded and looted by the crafty pirates. This spot is now known as _____

On July 4, 1876, a party of scouts camped near a spring in Arizona. To celebrate the holiday, the men stripped a lofty pine of its branches and, with suitable ceremony, fastened an American flag to it. This giant flagpole later became widely known, and travelers began stopping overnight near this landmark. Before long a town grew up there, called _____

In early days in Pennsylvania, two explorers wandered away from their camp and became lost. Cold and hungry, they stumbled along the slopes of a mountain most of the night. As daylight was breaking, however, they made their way across a creek and climbed another height of land. Lo and behold, in the distance they spied their camp! Later they named the first mountain _____ _____ They called the second mountain _____

On a mountain in Arizona are rocks that resemble human figures. An Indian legend says they are Indians who sought refuge there from a great flood and were warned not to make any sound until the waters had gone down. They disobeyed and were turned to stone. Other stories are associated with this mountain, including tales of a mysterious lost mine that seems to bring bad luck to everyone who tries to find it. The mountain is _____

On the borders of a stream in New York State, tradition says, formerly lived a good old lady who was always curious about her neighbors' affairs. Whenever she saw the doctor drive by, she called to him, "Doctor, who's sick?"

Finally the doctor began to call the neighborhood where the old lady lived "Who's Sick," and when asked by his neighbors, "Which way are you riding today, Doctor?" he would reply in fun, "I'm going to Who's Sick." Gradually people began using this name, and in time the stream and surrounding country came, by a slight change in spelling, to be called _____

Toward the end of winter in 1646, two young people in Connecticut decided to get married. As the magistrate in their town was away, they sent word to Governor John Winthrop at New London that they would ride there to have him perform the ceremony. He decided to ride to meet them. Both he and the wedding party, however, had to stop when they reached a stream near the town, for the water was so high that no one could get across. But the marriage took place just the same. The governor on his side pronounced them man and wife, and they on the other side promised to love, honor, and obey. Since then the stream has been called _____ _____

One foggy day a certain captain was going down the Hudson River with a fleet of rafts. Suddenly he sighted a dark object apparently riding on the waters. It looked like a two-masted ship under full sail. "Brig ahoy!" he shouted. No answer. "Brig ahoy! Answer, or I'll run you down!" Still no reply. The captain kept to his course. Suddenly there was a crash, and keel crunched on rock. The captain had mistaken two trees on a rocky island for masts with sails set. The island is now called _____

Most animal behavior is based on instinct, not on reasoning as is the behavior of human beings. However, there are many instances in which animals seem to behave more like people than like unreasoning creatures. Described below are several incidents that illustrate this kind of "human" behavior.

Animal Coöperation

1. One day a member of the Texas Game Commission was mystified to see a bluejay bringing some food to another adult jay that was sitting on a bough of a fir tree. This was surprising because usually only baby birds are fed this way. The wildlife expert took his field glasses and studied the two jays more closely. The puzzle was solved. The jay being fed had a broken beak and could not pick up food for itself. Its "friend" seemingly had taken the responsibility of feeding it.

2. African elephants often seem surly and vengeful. These massive creatures strongly resist capture and when confronted by man will attempt to save themselves at almost any cost. But hunters have seen these elephants, in immediate danger of capture, stop beside a wounded comrade and carefully lift him with their trunks and tusks so that he might get away safely.

3. In a test, a scientist raised three groups of kittens. One group remained with their mothers and learned how to kill rats. The second group did not learn about killing rats until the kittens were several months old. The third group was raised in the same cage with baby rats. Most of the first group became rat-killers. Less than half of those in the second became rat-killers. In the third group the kittens lived contentedly with their cagemates and never at any later time showed signs of wanting to harm rats.

4. In another experiment a scientist discovered that white mice isolated in cages do not grow nearly so fast as mice that are grouped two, three, or four to a cage. Goldfish eat more and grow faster when grouped. Even an ant digging a nest will move more dirt when working with a company of ants than when working alone.

5. Once a man who was an authority on apes gave a chimpanzee a box of delicious-smelling food. However, the lid of the box had a very intricate latch. When the chimp found that he could not figure out the complicated latch, he went to find another chimp. He tapped the other chimp on the shoulder and gestured for help. The two worked together to open the latch and happily settled down to share their dinner.

6. A favorite food of the coati, a raccoonlike animal of Central and South America, is the iguana, a large lizard. But the iguana is too big for a coati to tackle alone. The hunting coatis therefore split up into two groups. One band goes up into the trees and routs the iguanas that are sleeping on the branches. The second group, that is waiting on the ground beneath, pounces on the iguanas that fall. Then all the coatis have a meal together.

Each sentence below summarizes the main idea of one of the paragraphs. Number the sentences to match the incidents. Some statements will fit more than one incident.

_____ Animals coöperate with surprising cleverness when working together on their food-getting problems.

_____ There is evidence that the strong do not always prey upon the weak.

_____ In many circumstances animals seem to show a sense of sympathy and responsibility for the care of others.

_____ It has been proved that many animals thrive best when they are with those of their own kind.

Danger Detectives

by Lawrence Lader

The telephone calls kept coming in to the foreman's office at a large manufacturing plant. First one girl called to report that she was "sick"; then three more women employees phoned. By the end of the week forty women were victims of the same mysterious malady—their blonde hair had turned green overnight.

The plant manager put in a frantic call to the chief safety engineer of the plant's insurance company. The safety engineer took air-pollution samples and examined every machine in the plant. A staff of doctors analyzed the hair of every girl. In two days the crisis was solved.

The shampoo used by the girls had combined with fumes in the plant to play a fantastic trick with the color of their hair. The safety engineer immediately installed a large new ventilating system to dispel the fumes and directed the girls to change their shampoo. Their hair soon turned blonde again.

Working behind the scenes in factories, office buildings, construction jobs, or any spot where accidents may lurk, safety engineers are a new kind of detective. They not only battle such strange industrial hazards as green hair, but also save the country thousands of lives and millions of dollars yearly. Their objective is to locate mechanical dangers, analyze past accidents, hunt for their causes, and then develop means to prevent accidents.

These engineers have marshaled the resources of science behind them. Their staffs employ chemists, physicists, and doctors, backed up by huge research laboratories. Many of the most successful safety engineers, however, have had no special training in schools. They simply possess keen minds.

From a tiny clue, a safety engineer must often track down a hazard that could eventually cause more accidents. In a large coffee warehouse, for instance, a large stack of coffee bags fell on a watchman and killed him.

There seemed to be no reasonable explanation. The bags were properly piled and protected by guardrails. Then the safety engineer found one bag from which half the coffee beans had spilled. The imbalance thus created had caused the entire stack to topple. The bag itself wasn't defective, but there were several odd slashes in it.

The only clue to the cause of the slashes was a few tiny pieces of fatty substance around the slashes. For hours the engineer walked around the plant and questioned workers. Then he told the manager: "All I know is that the culprit is of Italian origin and doesn't go home for lunch. Come to the warehouse at noon and you'll see him."

At noon a workman came into the warehouse and sat down near a stack of bags. From his lunch box he pulled a long Italian sausage, sliced it with a knife from his pocket, and jabbed the knife into a coffee bag a half-dozen times to clean the blade. It was this thoughtless knife jabbing that had caused the stack to collapse.

An understanding of human nature is also an important tool of the safety engineer. For example, there was the case of the stairway in a department store that had become a mysterious accident trap. Salesgirls tripped and fell on it continually, suffering a succession of bruises and broken bones. The safety engineer could find nothing wrong. The treads, handrails, and lighting were good. The landing was wide and covered with a nonslip surface. Then he noticed a full-length mirror on the landing.

"Get rid of that mirror," the safety sleuth said, "and the ladies will watch their feet instead of their faces." As soon as the mirror was removed, the accidents stopped.

Why is "danger detective" a good name for a safety engineer? _____

_____

What is the most important job of a safety engineer? _____

Which "mysteries" mentioned in the article did a safety engineer solve by using good sense and knowledge of human nature? _____

_____

_____

In which case did the engineer need to use scientific tests, too? _____

_____

Conquering the Wilderness

1. In pioneer days, the first thing a settler did when he reached his new home was to clear a spot of land big enough for a cabin and garden patch. This was no small task in country where trees stretched as far as the eye could see. Trees less than a foot and a half around were cut down. The larger ones were girdled by deep ax cuts or burned about the roots. In time these trees fell. On appointed days neighbors came for logrollings and made great fires of the logs that they could not use.

2. In preparing his land for crops, the frontiersman used crude tools. Many were made entirely of wood. Iron tools were so rare that they were highly prized and were loaned back and forth. Plowing was difficult because of the logs, stumps, and roots everywhere. A hoe was the most useful tool for breaking up clods. With it the settler could work around the stumps and logs. After the land was finally ready, the grain was sown by hand. The hoe was used again to fight the weeds that grew up almost overnight.

3. The men and boys spent much time in the woods seeking game. Boys were taught at an early age how to shoot and how to imitate the calls of birds and beasts. Patience was needed by all hunters. Sometimes they had to sit for hours repeating at intervals the cluck of a wild turkey before they were rewarded by the sight of one. When streams overflowed, hunters often had to wade in cold water up to their waists.

4. Herds of deer wandered into the fields, and the pioneers had to drive them out to save the crops. In some places wolves were so numerous that it was almost impossible to raise sheep or pigs. The woods swarmed with squirrels and raccoons that found the young corn choice eating. Foxes killed the lambs and little pigs. Sly opossums sneaked into henhouses and ate the eggs. Snapping turtles in the ponds preyed on geese and ducks. Bears and panthers killed the cattle. The pioneers had to be constantly on the watch.

5. Because the pioneer had no sugar, he was very much interested in wild bees. After locating a bee tree by following a bee he had caught and dusted with flour, he marked the tree with his ax. Such a mark was always respected by other pioneers. In the fall the frontiersman cut down the tree after smoking the bees out. He might be badly stung, but he would get several gallons of honey for his trouble.

6. Toward the end of summer neighboring pioneers went from one field to another reaping and shocking the summer's yield. The boys, eager to become expert workers, often staged contests of skill and endurance. The women tried to outdo one another in the preparation of good meals, and everyone ate well and long. The delicious food repaid the settlers for their hard work, and all the hardships of the past months were forgotten. For a short time life was as gay as the bright autumn colors of the forest.

One sentence in each pair below summarizes the main idea of a paragraph above. Number the correct sentence to match the paragraph.

____ Hunting was more than a sport; it was grim necessity accompanied by hard work.

____ It took an amazing amount of patience to lure a wild turkey within shooting range.

____ Fall was the most beautiful time of the year.

____ In spite of the long days filled with hard labor, autumn was a season of rejoicing.

____ It was a difficult task to clear the land in areas that were heavily forested.

____ A great deal of wood was wasted by the pioneers, who burned it to get rid of it.

____ Smoking out bees was a dangerous business for the frontiersman.

____ Bees were important to the frontiersman because they furnished sweetening for his food.

____ The frontiersman had to be on guard to protect his crops and livestock from wild animals.

____ Wild animals wandered into the fields.

____ Preparing the soil and raising crops were no easy tasks for the pioneers.

____ Wood was very important to the frontiersman because he made farm tools with it.

The Main Idea

*The situations below call to mind well-known sayings, or proverbs. After
each section, write the number or numbers of the proverbs that apply.*

Betty nudged Olive's arm. "Look at Ann," she whispered. "Do you suppose she tries to look unattractive, or is it just accidental?"

Olive giggled nervously. It was true that Ann often wore clothes that didn't suit her, but there was no sense hurting her feelings.

Fortunately, Ann did not hear the remark. Her mind was racing ahead of her footsteps, planning how she could entertain her younger brother Pat who had been bedridden for more than a year.

"Pat!" she called dramatically as she entered his room. "I have here the very first autumn-colored leaf that's dropped to the ground this year. And it's all yours!"

Pat grinned and reached out a thin arm. "It's beautiful, Ann—just like you." _____

"I vote to drop Tom from our Radio Club," Doug announced indignantly. "After all, the rest of us made our own radios from old parts. If Tom goes out and buys a radio, he's cheating, and there's no room for cheats in this club!"

"I don't know," said Jim Hogan, the president. "We didn't say *not* to buy a radio, because none of us had enough money to buy one when we started the club. Personally, I'm willing to let Tom stay in the club."

"I'm not," muttered Doug, even while the vote showed that the rest of the boys disagreed with him.

On the way home, Doug continued to complain. Finally Jim interrupted with, "Have you finished the report for class tomorrow?"

Doug stopped in his tracks. "I forgot! And I can't get to the library today! Say, lend me your notes. I'll write a report on them. No one will know about it. Come on, Jim, please." _____

"So anyway, Dad," Steve announced, "I've decided to enter the science contest at school. But I'm not going to have my own exhibit. I'm going to help Dave Miller with his."

Mr. London was silent for a minute. At last he said, "I'm glad you've decided to enter the contest, but why with David? I thought you were going to do an exhibit by yourself."

"Well, I did think of one," Steve admitted, "but when I told Dave about it, he said he thought the idea was much too elementary. The project he's working on is sure to win because it's so unusual. Dave and I have always done things together, and it seems silly for me to waste time on my own exhibit when I can help him with one that will win a prize." _____

"All right, now," Frank said to the boys at the table. "We have to put on a round-table discussion tomorrow. So let's talk about what we've found on our topic and decide how to present it."

"There's only one way to do it," said Jack, "and everything I've read supports my point of view."

The others looked startled. "What books and articles did you find?" someone asked.

"I didn't find any *one* book," said Jack. "But everybody around here feels the same way I do."

"You mean you went around and asked people? A good idea—getting the opinion of the man on the street! How many people did you ask?"

"Well, I didn't really ask anybody. But I'm certain my whole family feels just as I do."

"Even your brother?" asked Frank in surprise.

"Well, I didn't ask my brother. But I'm positive he would agree with me. There's no other right way to think!" _____

1. He who lives in a glass house shouldn't throw stones.
2. Paddle your own canoe.
3. Beauty is often in the eye of the beholder.
4. Don't cry over spilled milk.
5. He who knows nothing is always sure of everything.
6. He travels fastest who travels alone.
7. Empty barrels make the most noise.
8. He must be pure who would blame another.

Stories to Illustrate a Point

Abraham Lincoln often used stories to emphasize a point or make his ideas clear.
At the left below are some situations that caused Lincoln to tell a story. On the right
are the stories he told. Number each story to match the right situation.

1. Lincoln sometimes disagreed with members of his cabinet. One day he remarked, "No matter how wrong a person is, he can always think of some defense." Then he told this story.

2. On the day of the trip to Gettysburg, where Lincoln was to give the address that later became so famous, his carriage waited a long time to take him to the station. When he finally appeared, it was rather late, and someone remarked that there was no time to lose. This was Lincoln's reply.

3. In 1856, Lincoln addressed a meeting of Illinois newspaper editors. He told the audience that since he was not an editor, he felt somewhat out of place. Then he told this story.

4. Once Lincoln and his political associates were discussing the day's happenings in the legislature. "I sometimes wonder," mused Lincoln, "whether members who get into a tight place in debate do not often wish they could dismiss the House until the next day and then take a new start." Then he told a story.

5. During the crucial war years, when Lincoln was spending anxious days and sleepless nights trying to deal with the problems of the great conflict, a farmer once buttonholed the president at a public reception. He told Lincoln that Union soldiers had helped themselves not only to his hay, but to his horse. He insisted that Lincoln personally see to it that the proper government officer pay him immediately for his loss. The president answered by telling this incident.

6. In one lawsuit, the lawyer opposing Lincoln talked long and loudly, making many reckless and unfounded statements.

Lincoln had a wry smile on his face as he rose to answer. Turning to the jury, he said, "My friend on the other side would be all right if it were not for a certain peculiarity. He reminds me of something I observed in my youth."

____ "Back in the days when I was working as a boatman, I made the acquaintance of a trifling steamboat that used to bustle and wheeze and puff about in the Sangamon River. It had a five-foot boiler and a seven-foot whistle, and every time it whistled the boat stopped."

____ "One day when my son Tad and I were lunching together, I said sternly, 'Don't eat your fish with your knife, my boy. It's not polite.'

" 'But, Father,' said Tad, 'is it polite to stare at folks when they're eating?' "

____ "This happened while I was a captain in the Black Hawk War. One day I was marching with twenty men in a line across a field, when we came to a gate. For the life of me I couldn't remember the proper word of command to get my company 'endwise' so they could pass through the gate. So as we came near the gate, I shouted: 'This company is dismissed for two minutes, when it will fall in again on the other side of the gate.' "

____ "As I was riding in the woods one day, I met a woman and stopped to let her pass. She stopped, too, looked at me intently, and said, 'I believe you're the ugliest man I ever saw.'

" 'Madam,' said I, 'you probably are right, but I can't help it.'

" 'No,' she replied, 'but you *could* stay home.' "

____ "I feel the way a condemned criminal in one of our Illinois towns felt when he was going to the gallows. As he passed along the road with the sheriff, the people, eager to see the hanging, kept crowding and pushing past him. At last he called out, 'Boys, you don't need to be in such a hurry. There won't be any fun till I get there!' "

____ "Jack Chase was the best pilot on the Illinois River. Once his boat was plunging and wallowing in the rapids, and Jack had to exercise the utmost care to keep it in the narrow channel. At that moment a boy pulled his coattail and said, 'Say, Mr. Captain! Please stop your boat a minute. I've lost my apple overboard!' "

Cooled with Kerosene

Selling an icebox to an Eskimo probably no longer represents the ultimate in salesmanship. Nowadays you can find refrigerators, fueled by kerosene, in many an unlikely place. In wind-swept Patagonia at the icy tip of South America, for instance, such refrigerators have been remarkably successful. One salesman explained it thus: "I just remind these people how much they hate to go outside during the winter. Of course, they've got to go out if they keep their food outdoors. And then I remind them that bacteria like to be warm, too, and crowd into the kitchen to spoil food that has been brought in."

The kerosene refrigerator looks much like an electrical refrigerator and makes the same sort of ice cubes. Evaporation of ammonia forms the ice. Since no gas or electrical connections are required, this mechanism can be utilized wherever kerosene is available.

Its chief use, naturally, is in the less industrialized parts of the tropics. At evening, along steaming rivers in Sumatra, exploration parties come back to camp and raid the kerosene refrigerator for cold drinks. Photographers working in remote places use it for storing photographic chemicals. In jungle hospitals it preserves perishable drugs.

The great usefulness of refrigeration in the wilderness makes one of these machines worth much trouble and expense. A 500-pound refrigerator may have to be moved in pieces on strong backs over jungle trails or flown in sections in light planes to its destination. By the time transportation costs are paid, it may cost a purchaser twice what he would have paid in the United States. Nevertheless, in Venezuela, for example, some 30,000 kerosene refrigerators were sold between 1946 and 1956.

In Central America a salesman made a suggestion to the owner of a rural store: "Set aside an empty kerosene tin to hold the pennies which children will pay you for sweetened ice cubes. At the end of the month, you will have enough to meet the payment on the refrigerator." This proposal worked. Ice cubes, colored and flavored with cane syrup or fruit juices and garnished with a toothpick, have become a delicacy in this part of the world.

The kerosene refrigerator makes its greatest impression where ice has never been seen before. One incident is told by the Rev. John Morrison, an American missionary in Africa. When the Morrison family first went to the Congo region some thirty years ago, they lived "out of cans" and on such vegetables as they could grow. After the invention of the kerosene refrigerator, they ordered several for use in their home and in their clinics. The fame of the "box of coolness" spread rapidly among Congo tribes, and a former cannibal chief, King Bope, came to inspect the new wonder.

Mr. Morrison presented King Bope with an ice cube. It stuck to his hand, "burning" painfully, but his dignity would not permit him to show any sign of discomfort. However, he soon handed the cube to an attendant, instructing him to wrap it up to take home to the royal wives.

The missionary thought quickly. The king's house was about twenty-five miles away, and he was traveling by hammock. No telling what might happen when he arrived home and found that the ice cube had disappeared! Accordingly, Mr. Morrison hastened to explain in some detail how the coldness comes—and goes.

The refrigerator has not yet come into general household use in the Congo, but it has won a place—after the foot-treadle sewing machine, the wind-up phonograph, and the bicycle—on the list of mechanical wonders that families hope some day to own.

Check the generalizations below that you think are brought out in this article.

What a person thinks of as a "modern wonder" depends on what he is accustomed to.

Kerosene refrigerators have become outmoded since the invention of electric refrigerators.

A variety of ingenious new inventions will soon make life in the tropics more comfortable.

Many people both in hot and cold regions find kerosene refrigerators useful.

Which Word Is It?

Underline the word that you think answers each question correctly.

Which is a young horse—colt, bolt, volt?

Which would you catch in a pond—mirrors, minnows, minerals?

Which could you hear sing—lard, lack, lark?

Which are bundles of wheat—sheaths, sheaves, shelves?

Which is a means of transportation—trick, truck, truce?

Which would have a spicy taste—cinder, center, cider?

Which is a piece of jewelry—necklace, negative, neighbor?

Which does a laundry bag full of clothes do—bugles, bungles, bulges?

Which would you like to see on TV—spurts, sports, spots?

Which is an apparatus for signaling—semaphore, metaphor, sophomore?

Which is used in a laundry—beach, bleach, bleak?

Which is a loud, harsh sound—squeak, squeal, squawk?

Which breathes through gills—trout, trowel, trunk?

Which would be found in a snowstorm—flames, floats, flakes?

Which is a mob—horse, horde, hurdle?

Which would you hang on a wall—phonograph, photograph, photographer?

Which is best for fishing—steam, seam, stream?

Which is a part of a horse's harness—bridge, bridle, burble?

Which comes from wet soap—letter, latter, lather?

Which drips from a candle—tallow, talcum, talon?

Which can be written on with chalk—state, stale, slate?

Which would you find in a motor—pickle, pistol, piston?

Which can you do with a pen—white, write, wilt?

Which is a very strong wind—gate, goal, gale?

Which might be fluttering in the sky—kit, kilt, kite?

Which would you see on a roof—vase, vane, vale?

Which would a magician wave—wart, ward, wand?

Which is a boat—skiff, sniff, shift?

Which would have a hot taste—peplum, pepper, pebble?

Which is a doctor who treats animals—vegetarian, vacationist, veterinarian?

Which is a musical instrument—orange, organ, orphan?

Which is electricity in the sky—lighting, lighter, lightning?

Seeing Words Clearly

Some words look much like other words. They may have the same letters but the letters may not be in the same order. Or they may look alike except for one or two letters. Look carefully at the three words above each paragraph. Then complete the paragraph by writing the correct words on the dotted lines.

form   forum   from

The band will march _____ the goal line to the center of the football field. There the band members will play the school song as they _____ a triangle.

expect   expert   except

You would _____ a larger crowd to turn out for the homecoming game at the stadium, _____ in unusually bad weather.

layer   relay   early

Tom won the final _____ race of the year. Since he was no longer in training, he could eat the fudge _____ cake his mother baked for him.

dial   daily   laid

As soon as Doris rushed into the house, she _____ down her books and ran to the television set. To get the news bulletin, she quickly turned the _____ .

seen   seem   seer

That morning Jim had _____ several flocks of geese flying south. Snow had been falling in the mountains and winter began to _____ near.

though   thought   through

As Jerry was walking _____ the woods, he _____ he saw rabbit tracks.

lunged   longed   lounged

The freshmen admired the tall seniors who _____ near the candy machine. They _____ for the time when they would be seniors.

bought   bough   brought

After Janet had saved her allowance for a long time, she _____ a record player. Her father _____ home four new records the next night.

quit   quiet   quite

Jane was _____ sure she had really heard something rattling in the kitchen, but when she went there to investigate, all was _____ .

them   than   then

With more _____ ten pages of science to read for homework, Richard studied late. He went to bed _____ and dreamed of summer vacation.

easel   lease   sealer

The artist stood at his _____ , putting the finishing touches on a painting. The next step would be to cover the fresh paint with a _____ .

very   every   ever

Bob wondered why he _____ thought it would be fun to eat both pie and cake _____ noon instead of lunch.

What Is the Correct Word?

*In each sentence below there is a misused word.   Underline
it and write the correct word in the blank at the right.*

A going rang to announce that visiting hours in the infirmary were over. ----------------

Before leaving the house, Becky tied a banana around her head. ----------------

Following the mother duck were five fuzzy yellow dunkings. ----------------

Vic was horrified to see that he had knocked down a nest of honests. ----------------

Mr. Putnam bought a load of black loan for his garden. ----------------

The fireplace had a beautiful marble mental. ----------------

The windows rattled as the sleek beat on them. ----------------

Al was hungry, so he went to the kitchen to get a midnight slack. ----------------

Mrs. Smith decided that her pearls needed to be stung on a new string. ----------------

Hearing the immense chorus sing was a trill for the students. ----------------

First prize in the slogan contest was a wicked basket full of groceries. ----------------

Tim studied so long his mine no longer seemed to be working. ----------------

As the famous pianist began to play, a hash fell over the recital hall. ----------------

Helen discovered that her new pleated dress needed to have the hen shortened. ----------------

The Kimberley family decided to move to a new distinct of the city. ----------------

The explorers spent nearly two years in the African juggle. ----------------

Anita wove a scarlet rug on her loon. ----------------

A policeman gave Jerry a ticket for not putting a nickel in the parking meteor. ----------------

When Rebecca saw the box of chocolate candy, the scrawl on her face vanished. ----------------

Smoke poured from the ship's funerals as it left the port. ----------------

Cedars, birches, firs, and populars grew on the estate. ----------------

The man was sent to prism for committing the robbery. ----------------

The United States is one of the largest counties in the world. ----------------

The dampness of the air caused a mole to appear on the loaf of bread. ----------------

Mrs. Kane put a fresh batch of soup to summer in the kettle. ----------------

Some Words Have About the Same Meaning

*Underline the word or words below each sentence that could be substituted
for the italicized word without changing the essential meaning of the sentence.*

Sandy watched the long *shafts* of light filter
through the tree.

rays	plumes	wedges
sheets	beams	stalks

It is a difficult climb to the mountaintop, but
travelers are always *entranced* by the view.

insulted	impressed	delighted
charmed	enlarged	spellbound

The acrobat was *whirling* around the stage
with unbelievable speed.

fluttering	sagging	zigzagging
spinning	sliding	pivoting

Six climbers ascended the high cliff, *trudging*
steadily up the narrow trail.

wandering	tramping	plodding
sauntering	skipping	walking

As the hunters stared, great *screeching* birds
rose from the swamp.

yelping	shrieking	threatening
squealing	squawking	cheering

The *panic-stricken* boy took to his heels when
he saw the angry bees swarming around him.

cowardly	frightened	terrified
fortunate	horrified	pitiful

Carl hit the *protruding* root of a tree with his
power lawn mower.

splintered	jutting	sunken
attached	jagged	mossy

Tom dug up a small *weather-beaten* pine tree
that was growing near the shore.

stunted	smooth	withered
lanky	scraggly	snow-laden

The *incessant* roar of the storm kept everyone
awake during the night.

loud	continuous	ceaseless
constant	frequent	unusual

July 4, 1776, is a *significant* date in the
history of the United States of America.

remarkable	minor	important
numerical	social	meaningful

Jim tripped on the top step and went *tumbling*
all the way down the flight of stairs.

hurtling	soaring	toppling
lolling	loping	somersaulting

When Jack was *completely* convinced that his
plan would not work, he asked for help.

almost	partly	thoroughly
actually	nearly	entirely

The hunted animal moved *quietly* through the
tall jungle grass.

swiftly	silently	noiselessly
expertly	busily	aimlessly

The driver was surprised when he came to
an *abrupt* turn in the road.

absurd	sudden	cloverleaf
narrow	broad	unexpected

There was *confusion* near the ticket window
on the night of the big game.

silence	commotion	disorder
order	loitering	uproar

Thomas Edison, maker of the first phonograph,
had *uncommon* ability as an inventor.

remarkable	political	rare
uninteresting	unusual	unknown

Synonyms and Antonyms

The four words below each phrase are either synonyms or antonyms of the italicized word in the phrase.

Write S beside each synonym, or word with the same or almost the same meaning.   Write A beside each antonym, or word with the opposite meaning.

generous portions

____ scanty

____ ample

____ sizable

____ stingy

ultimate victory

____ primary

____ final

____ initial

____ beginning

relentless foe

____ pitiless

____ unyielding

____ harsh

____ merciful

infuriated man

____ delighted

____ enraged

____ incensed

____ outraged

prodded by indignation

____ restrained

____ urged

____ checked

____ impelled

captivating story

____ enchanting

____ entrancing

____ dull

____ stupid

ungainly stride

____ awkward

____ graceful

____ lumbering

____ clumsy

extraordinary *hullabaloo*

____ commotion

____ uproar

____ racket

____ silence

unusual *obstinacy*

____ stubbornness

____ balkiness

____ compliance

____ willfulness

cordial hostess

____ friendly

____ rude

____ gracious

____ hostile

spacious home

____ large

____ roomy

____ cramped

____ constricted

date of *expiration*

____ completion

____ starting

____ commencement

____ conclusion

lagging steps

____ dawdling

____ energetic

____ alert

____ reluctant

impudent reply

____ modest

____ courteous

____ saucy

____ impertinent

futile tactics

____ useless

____ profitable

____ vain

____ ineffective

petty consequences

____ slight

____ insignificant

____ important

____ trifling

complied promptly

____ obeyed

____ yielded

____ resisted

____ refused

adjacent state

____ adjoining

____ bordering

____ neighboring

____ distant

Which Word Would You Use?

*Any one of the three words could be used in the sentence,
but only two of the words will answer the questions correctly.
Write the correct word on the dotted line after each question.*

looked   stared   glanced

Ben ____ at the examination paper lying there on his desk.

Which word would show Ben looked quickly at the paper? _____ Which word would show that he looked at the paper for a long time? _____

asked   coaxed   implored

Joe ____ his father to buy a football for him as a birthday present.

Which word would show Joe tried to persuade his father to buy him the football for his birthday? _____ Which word would show he spoke earnestly? _____

talked   chattered   raved

When she telephoned Ann today, Sally ____ for fifteen minutes.

Which word would show Sally sounded like a machine? _____ Which word would show Sally spoke with great enthusiasm? _____

said   wailed   roared

"You didn't save any of the fishing tackle that I wanted," ____ Mr. Williams.

Which word would show Mr. Williams spoke in a loud, angry voice? _____ Which word would not show how the man felt? _____

springs   climbs   crawls

Tim turns off the alarm clock, stretches, and ____ out of bed every morning.

Which word would show Tim leaps lightly out of bed? _____ Which word would show Tim gets out of bed slowly every morning? _____

broke   crashed   shattered

The platter slipped and ____ when Hal took it out of the dishwater.

Which word would make you see the pieces flying in all directions? _____ Which word would make you think it hit the floor with a loud noise? _____

said   advised   ordered

"Dick, put my camera down before you drop it again," ____ Jim.

Which word would show Jim warned Dick an accident might happen? _____ Which word would show that Jim commanded Dick to obey? _____

talking   muttering   groaning

After his fall at the ice-skating rink, Bob was ____ to himself.

Which word would show Bob was complaining about his fall? _____ Which word would show Bob hurt himself when he fell? _____

sighed   moaned   sobbed

"I don't feel well enough to go to the show tonight," ____ Anne.

Which word would show Anne let out a deep breath as she spoke? _____ Which word would show she was crying hard? _____

discussion   argument   quarrel

Some of the boys left as the game ended to avoid any ____ about the score.

Which word would show that some of the boys disagreed about the score? _____ Which word would show some of the boys were angry about the game? _____

What Are They?

Each group of words below contains one word that does not belong with the others. Find that word and draw a line through it. Use the dictionary if you wish. Then at the end of each line, write the general term for the remaining words. The first one is done for you.

scrap basket, tankard, ~~compass,~~ pail, bottle, vase, barrel, basin, drawer, dish _ _*containers*_ _ _ _ _ _ _

tunic, cloak, pajamas, frock, pinafore, shawl, butter, jacket, mitten, trousers _ _ _ _ _ _ _ _ _ _ _ _

tupelo, cypress, poplar, tusk, willow, spruce, pine, maple, oak, birch, larch _ _ _ _ _ _ _ _ _ _ _ _

Louisiana, Kentucky, South Carolina, Wyoming, Utah, Chicago, Oregon, Colorado _ _ _ _ _ _ _ _

slingshot, stiletto, barley, arrow, spear, pike, cannon, gun, sword, battering ram _ _ _ _ _ _ _ _ _

Louisville, Lexington, Baltimore, Shreveport, Utica, Africa, Toledo, Dearborn _ _ _ _ _ _ _ _ _

cabbage, potato, squash, pepper, radish, carrot, lettuce, ruby, bean, pea _ _ _ _ _ _ _ _ _ _ _

peach, grape, olive, fig, andiron, banana, lime, strawberry, apple, cherry, orange _ _ _ _ _ _ _ _ _

boar, coon, muddle, elk, jaguar, moose, mink, weasel, camel, jackal, otter _ _ _ _ _ _ _ _ _ _ _

broom, vacuum cleaner, scrubbing brush, carpet sweeper, petition, mop _ _ _ _ _ _ _ _ _ _ _ _ _

park, hash, pudding, toast, mush, stew, syrup, taffy, pork, steak, ham, bread _ _ _ _ _ _ _ _ _ _

hut, wigwam, igloo, barracks, tent, cottage, fuselage, palace, apartment, lodge _ _ _ _ _ _ _ _ _ _

hammock, cupboard, stool, cot, table, bed, chair, bureau, sofa, desk, roof _ _ _ _ _ _ _ _ _ _ _

crowbar, tunnel, sledge hammer, lathe, vise, hatchet, hacksaw, file, shovel _ _ _ _ _ _ _ _ _ _ _

falcon, loon, condor, wren, hawk, robin, salmon, partridge, goose, eagle _ _ _ _ _ _ _ _ _ _ _ _

tulip, buttercup, marigold, violet, rose, lily, lemon, trillium, columbine _ _ _ _ _ _ _ _ _ _ _ _ _

Abe, Nathaniel, Lizzie, Nick, Tuffy, Paddy, Buster, Winnie, Andy, Dave, Sue _ _ _ _ _ _ _ _ _ _ _

ink, wine, coffee, gong, lemonade, tea, gasoline, blood, sap, kerosene, cider _ _ _ _ _ _ _ _ _ _ _

chariot, cart, automobile, bicycle, taxi, stagecoach, tractor, sermon _ _ _ _ _ _ _ _ _ _ _ _ _ _ _

sieve, scoop, kettle, meat grinder, bead, spoon, butcher knife, fork, beater _ _ _ _ _ _ _ _ _ _ _

eaves, window sill, gangplank, loft, weather vane, latch, porch, rafter, knocker _ _ _ _ _ _ _ _ _ _

chambermaid, clerk, historian, teamster, secretary, admiral, detective, thatch _ _ _ _ _ _ _ _ _ _

A Word Game

Below are the definitions of twenty-two pairs of words. In this game, if you double one of the letters in the first word, you will get the second word. For example, in the first pair the definition reads "wager." The answer would be bet. *By doubling the* e *in* bet *you get the answer to the second definition, "a vegetable," which is* beet.

wager _____

a vegetable _____

policeman (informal) _____

small pen or cage _____

sacred _____

Christmas decoration _____

prolonged unconsciousness _____

mark of punctuation _____

dry, sandy area _____

pie or cake _____

marry _____

useless plant _____

part of the face _____

loop of rope _____

energy (slang) _____

sound made by baby chick _____

let fall _____

hang down _____

wild anger _____

covered with fur _____

a color _____

kind of tall grass _____

male child _____

very shortly _____

suffocate _____

more flat or even _____

belonging to him _____

sound a snake makes _____

halt _____

bend forward _____

decay _____

underground part of plant _____

small child _____

sound of a horn _____

spoke with anger _____

worn into rags _____

more impolite _____

steering device _____

abbreviation for *advertisement* _____

put together _____

under or lower than _____

roar _____

wishing _____

jumping _____

Puts Are Fun

A pun is a play on words, or a humorous use of a word so that it suggests two different meanings at once. Benjamin Franklin made a famous pun when he said, "We must all hang together, or we shall all hang separately."

Sometimes a pun is based on a word or phrase that can mean two different things; sometimes a pun makes use of a word that sounds the same or almost the same as another word.

Underline the word or words in each joke below that make the pun.

POLLY: What's the difference between a cat and a comma?
MOLLY: A cat has claws at the end of its paws, but a comma's a pause at the end of a clause.

FATHER: Now, Tommy, remember to be good while I'm gone.
TOMMY: I sure will, Dad—for a quarter.
FATHER: Why, I'm surprised at you. When I was your age, I was good for nothing!

PAT: What day of the year is a command to go forward?
MIKE: I don't know.
PAT: March 4th.

SIR RICHARD: Why so gloomy, old chap?
SIR JAMES: I've just received word that my uncle has cut me out of his will. He's altered it five times in the last two years.
SIR RICHARD: I say, a fresh heir fiend!

MRS. JENKINS TO A BUTCHER: I have a complaint. The sausages I bought here yesterday were meat at one end and bread crumbs at the other.
BUTCHER: I know, but in these hard times it's almost impossible to make both ends meat!

MR. MIX: Waiter! Remove this coffee immediately! It tastes like mud.
WAITER: Yes, sir. But it was ground only this morning.

TEACHER: I asked you to draw a horse and cart, and you've only drawn a horse!
JOHNNY: Sure. I figured the horse would draw the cart.

PROUD MOTHER: My daughter has arranged a little piece for the piano.
NEIGHBOR: Good! It's about time we had a little peace!

JACK: I et six eggs for breakfast this morning.
TEACHER: You mean *ate*, don't you?
JACK: Well, maybe it *was* eight I et.

LILLY: Can't you play tennis without making all that noise?
MILLY: Don't be silly. How can you play tennis without raising a racket?

RON: How do you like your new chimney-sweeping job?
DON: Oh, it soots me fine.

MOTHER: How are your marks this month?
JIM: They're under water.
MOTHER: What do you mean, under water?
JIM: Below C level!

CAPTAIN OF THE FOOTBALL TEAM: Coach, we're going to present you with a victory for your birthday.
COACH: Good! I was expecting the usual tie.

JUNE: What do you do with your nails—file them?
JANE: No, I just throw them away.

CITY MAN: Say, these mosquitoes you've got here are pretty annoying. Don't you ever shoo them?
FARMER: Nope. Too expensive. We just let 'em go barefoot.

MRS. BROWN: Is your new home a warm one?
MRS. BLACK: It should be. The painter gave it two coats last month.

What's the Reason?

A Fish Story

Chuck and I were loafing by a campfire high in the mountains after a day's fishing. As we looked across the shimmering lake, we saw an eighteen-inch rainbow trout leap high into the air.

"How do you suppose they keep the lakes in this wild territory stocked with fish?" Chuck asked. "Most of the lakes are forty or fifty miles from any settlement, and the only way to reach them is over rough, steep trails."

With no sensible answer coming to mind, I said jokingly, "Maybe it rains fish," and then forgot about the matter.

Next morning as we lay in the sun after a hasty dip in the lake, we heard the lazy drone of an airplane. Far up above us the plane came into view, a tiny speck in the sky. In a few minutes it was gone behind a peak.

We had hardly relaxed our craning necks when we heard the roar of the airplane again. Looking up, we saw the plane reappear over the peak, swerve, and then barely skim the tops of the fir trees that encircled the lake.

Surely the plane would crash in the lake! We watched breathlessly, but the plane leveled out close to the water. When it was halfway across, we saw a foglike spray pour from the belly of the plane. Then the aircraft streaked down the canyon and disappeared.

In the falling mist we saw thousands of tiny objects, glinting like bits of silver, that spread in a widening cloud to fall spattering into the lake.

Chuck looked at me and said, "Well! What do you know about that?"

As much surprised as he, I said, "So it *does* rain fish in these lakes," with an I-told-you-so tone in my voice, although I never dreamed that this was the way it was done.

Within an hour we saw hundreds of two- and three-inch fingerlings gathered in schools along the shallows of the lake, as much alive and seemingly at home as if they had not been dropped from the sky. This, then, was the answer to our question.

Because Chuck and I are curious and conservationists at heart, we later paid a visit to the State Fish and Game Department to find out more about this work.

We were told that, when a mountain lake is to be restocked with fish, the two- or three-inch fingerlings are rushed in fish-tank trucks to the airport from the nearest state hatchery. There they are transferred by buckets to a smaller tank in a plane, and the pilot takes off with his ten thousand finny passengers.

Once over the lake the pilot swoops low and pulls a cord. This opens a trap door in the tank, spilling fifty gallons of water and thousands of tiny trout.

To haul fish to these remote lakes on the backs of pack animals would require two full summers. Using the airplane method, the actual planting of a lake can be done in fifteen minutes.

When Chuck and I say that we saw it rain thousands of trout, people look at us in disbelief. But this is one fish story that is true!

1. Why does the Fish and Game Department stock mountain lakes? _____
   _____

2. Why does the plane carry the fish in water? _____
   _____

3. Why does the pilot swoop so close to the lake? _____
   _____

4. Why are airplanes used for this work? _____
   _____

5. Why are such small fish used for restocking? _____
   _____

The Dust Storm

One smothering hot day in fall, Mr. Ray was driving through a part of the Southwest that urgently needed rain. Suddenly dark clouds blanketed the sky. The wind began to blow with terrible force, lashing the car with dust and sand and almost thrusting it off the highway. Unable to see, Mr. Ray parked by the side of the road.

Though he had rolled up the windows, dust invaded the car. Covering his face with a handkerchief, he sat in the car for a long while. After a time the wind died, and though dust still hung thick in the air he was able to proceed.

As Mr. Ray drove through the flat, treeless plain, he passed farm after farm that had been deserted. Broken fences, half-wrecked buildings, and discarded machinery were deep in dust. He passed farmers gazing hopelessly at their ruined crops, and listless cattle and sheep standing by dried-up water holes. Once roots of trees had helped preserve the water in these natural ponds. But the trees had been cut, and the earth was dry.

On the road Mr. Ray passed the laden trucks of farmers who said they were leaving the region to seek new homes elsewhere.

The Flood

All day the rivers rose, fed by heavy spring rains and rapidly melting mountain snows. Over the plowed fields the water poured unhindered; little streams quickly became roaring, muddy torrents. By four o'clock all who lived near the water fronts had been warned to flee.

At the fork where two rivers join to form a mighty third river, a city was caught in the flood. Water rose so fast that merchants were unable to move their wares to safety. There was no electric power, and all normal activities ceased. People swarmed into stores to buy candles, lanterns, and flashlights. They crowded around parked cars listening to newscasts on battery-powered radios.

As the water rose higher and higher, throngs of sightseers gathered on the hillsides to look down on the flood. Through field glasses they could see automobiles and streetcars almost covered with water, guests trapped in the upper floors of a hotel, rescue crews in boats saving people whose homes had been isolated by the rising water. Once they watched a whole house float down the river, with three men clinging to the roof.

Each year people in all parts of the country become concerned over the damage done by floods and dust storms. Experts say reforestation will prevent such disasters.

Each sentence below states a reason for reforestation projects. Check the sentences that a person interested in preventing floods and dust storms might use in support of reforestation.

____ Large groves or forests make windbreaks for freshly plowed fields.

____ The roots of trees soak up large amounts of water.

____ Forestry offers interesting job opportunities for young men.

____ Trees make the country beautiful.

____ Leaves that fade, fall, and become powdered make the soil richer.

____ Water runs off sun-baked soil; shade trees keep the soil moist.

____ Tree roots prevent the soil from being blown away.

____ Trees provide suitable homes for wildlife.

____ The nation needs to constantly renew its supply of lumber.

____ Ruts on tree-covered mountain slopes are not likely to become gullies.

The First Basketball Game

by Raymond P. Kaighn, as told to Bob Brooks

One December day in 1891, we trotted glumly into the gym at the Y.M.C.A. Training School for our daily workout. After a season of football, indoor exercises seemed mighty tame. We were all set for another dull dose—but we hadn't reckoned on the imagination of our instructor, Jim Naismith.

First, Jim pointed out a peach basket at each end of the gym, fastened at the base of the balcony. Some class members groaned. Were we going to play guinea pig for another instructor's crazy ideas on indoor athletics? But when Jim told us about his new game and read the rules, we perked up. He showed us the soccer ball we'd use and then chose nine men for each side.

Jim threw the ball into play, and we all scrambled for it. Dumbbells and Indian clubs tumbled as we chased the ball around the gym. I'm afraid Jim's hopes of teamwork didn't pan out. Every fellow tried to throw the ball into one of those peach baskets, regardless of where he was. "Pass it!" Jim yelled, blowing his whistle to stop the rough play. But for the first time we were having fun with winter indoor athletics.

Jim had tried to devise an exciting, active game, but he wanted to keep us from tackling each other on the hard gym floor. This was the reason for three of the rules: we could not run with the ball, players could not touch each other, and goals were to be made by throwing the ball into a raised box. The janitor couldn't find boxes so put up baskets.

We used thirteen basic rules in that first game, as against more than two hundred used today.

One of our rules was that when the ball hit the wall it belonged to the side that first got hold of it. There was always an uproar as all eighteen men dived after the ball. We'd have to take time out to gather up players and equipment before we could continue.

Today players worry about getting the ball *in* the basket. Our problem was getting it *out*. The ball just sat inside the basket until someone lifted it out. When we made a goal, someone had to climb up a ladder or be hoisted on a teammate's shoulders to get the ball.

Later, when school kids jammed the balcony to watch us play, we let them reach over and throw the ball back to us. They would also help their favorite team by knocking the ball in or out of the basket. We bawled them out, but they wouldn't stop. One day Jim put a square of wood behind the basket. And that's how the present-day backboard was born.

In our first game we had no boundaries except the walls of the gym. In 1894 a definite boundary line was set at three feet from the wall or fence around the playing area. The number of players varied with the size of the court. This meant that when a team was not playing on its home court, it often had to add or subtract players.

The rules for fouls were simple. You couldn't shoulder, hold, push, trip, or strike an opponent. You couldn't bat the ball with a fist (though you could with your hands); and you couldn't run with the ball. The second foul against a man put him out of the game until the next goal was made—or, if the umpire thought the man was trying to injure an opposing player, the offender could be put out for the whole game, with no substitute allowed.

All of us were sold on the game from the start. When we went out to establish Y.M.C.A. centers ourselves, we took the basketball idea with us.

Write the answers on a separate sheet of paper.

Why did Jim plan for the ball to be thrown into a raised basket?

Why did he put a backboard behind the basket?

Why do you think the modern open-bottom basket was developed?

Why do you think the men liked the new game?

Fireboats to the Rescue

by John J. Floherty

Many cities depend on water transportation for a large share of their commerce. Ships laden with valuable cargoes come from the ends of the earth to the great ports of New York, Boston, New Orleans, San Francisco, and a score of others on lakes and rivers. To handle these cargoes, extensive systems of docks, piers, and warehouses have been built along the waterfront.

The nature and location of these structures make them major fire hazards. They are usually built on wooden piles driven into the mud, and are floored with wood resting on heavy wooden beams. The superstructure is sometimes built of steel, but the roof is usually covered with tar or other material that is resistant to the weather but inflammable. In addition, piers and warehouses often are loaded with thousands of tons of inflammable cargo awaiting shipment.

Unlike a blaze in the heart of a city, which may be attacked from all sides, a waterfront fire defies the usual assembly of fire-fighting apparatus. A burning pier causes special problems. Jutting out over the water sometimes as much as a thousand feet, and presenting only its narrow front to the shore side, a pier is inaccessible to land-based fire equipment. Besides, a pier is often flanked by one or more valuable vessels that become a further hazard and a difficult barrier.

To fight a waterfront conflagration successfully firemen must attack it from the water as well as from land. Fireboats are rushed into the battle.

A fireboat is merely a floating fire engine of enormous strength and water capacity. It can throw a dozen powerful streams from its battery of nozzles. It has couplings for numerous hose lines that may be stretched to distant points. The water on which it floats is its unlimited source of supply. One of New York's fleet of fireboats has a pumping capacity equal to that of twelve of the most modern land engines.

Outside the pilot house, every detail of a fireboat's fittings is planned to enable her crew of sailor firemen to battle every known type of fire occurring on or near the water. Below decks she is packed with power for propulsion and pumping. Every square inch of space is devoted to her mighty engines, to pumps and valves, and to a complex system of piping. There is not enough room for even a bunk on which a man may sleep, and for this there is good reason. A fireboat must always be of limited size, since the nature of her work takes her into tight places inaccessible to most vessels.

Her crew, firemen all, live and eat and sleep in a well-appointed firehouse within a few steps of where their vessel is berthed. Day and night they are subject to the call, "Get out!" from the man on the watch desk. If the men are sleeping, they leap from their beds, dress, sprint to the waiting fireboat, and are under way in the unbelievable time of about forty-five seconds. Sometimes the men have cut their shore communication lines and mooring lines in order to save the few seconds it would take to untie them. On the water, as on land, the fire fighter never forgets the vital importance of the first five minutes of a fire.

Why are waterfront structures likely to be fire hazards? _____
_____
_____
_____

Why does a fireboat have an advantage over a fire engine on land? _____
_____
_____
_____
_____

Why does the crew of a fireboat live on land?
_____
_____
_____

Why are fireboats limited in size? _____
_____
_____

This essay by a high-school student received an award in the Junior Division of Scholastic Magazines Writing Awards for 1956.

Thirteen *by William Dodge*

Thirteen is one of the nicest ages I have ever been. I used to think that being young was nice, too. Now, when I look back on things, I know I would never want to be young again.

For instance, once when I was eleven, Mother took me to the movies. She ordered a half-price ticket for me, and the woman at the ticket booth put up an argument. She said I was too tall to be eleven and should pay full price. Mother said I was only a little boy and she wouldn't pay it. She called the manager. He looked up at me and agreed with the ticket lady. He shouldn't have done that. My mother is a woman of "many" words and she used them all. She wanted justice. The ticket lady wanted her money, the manager wanted peace, and I wanted to drop dead.

But this is all in the past. Now, at thirteen, I buy the tickets, and I don't try to get my mother in for half price either.

There are a lot of things that never happen any more, now that I am thirteen. Nobody tells me what kind of haircut to get. I never hear, "Tell the barber this" or "Tell the barber that." My head now belongs to me. Crew cut or down over the ears, it's all mine.

At home these days, I am called Bill or Billy, never "Honey Boy" or "Little Man." Not even "Angel Child."

I spilled a big gob of cement on the rug last week, and Mother got really mad. I didn't get swatted or sent to my room. She just stamped her foot and raved about "sloppy men" and "impossible male creatures," just the same as she does with my father.

At thirteen a boy can walk down the street with a girl without everybody he knows making fun of him. Girls may not be as nice as regular people, but they're fun to be with, except those who talk real loud and try to look sophisticated. The ones who smile a lot and don't show off are really much nicer.

At thirteen, I can watch any TV show or read any book I please. Yes, I like being grown-up. In fact, I finally gave away my cowboy hat and my six-shooters.

Today I am a man!!!

Part 2

Being thirteen has certain problems that only another thirteen-year-old would understand. The biggest, I think, is learning how to get along well with adults. I have found that when dealing with grown-ups, it is wise to remember two things:

1. Always use your head.
2. Never use your head.

For instance, one day just before supper, my mother sent me to the store for a loaf of whole-wheat bread. They didn't have any whole-wheat. When I told my mother, she said, "Well, what kind did you get?" I told her I didn't get any. She looked at me as if I were some kind of imbecile. "For goodness sakes," she said, "if they didn't have whole-wheat, you should have got something else! Why don't you use your head?"

Not long after that, she sent me for some red oilcloth. The store didn't have any, so I bought seven yards of purple. I thought it was pretty. My mother didn't. She said, "Who ever heard of purple oilcloth in a red kitchen?" I told her I was only trying to use my head. But she said, "Well, don't! And in the future, if you can't get what I send you for, don't get anything!"

See what I mean?

There are other things that seem strange, too. If my father goes out for the evening, he tells me to "look after" my mother and sister. But if the family goes out, and I want to stay home, my father won't let me. He doesn't feel comfortable if I'm home alone. That means I am old enough to "look after" my mother and sister but not old enough to "look after" myself! Figure that out.

Another problem is what you should do when you trip over the cat and land with your head in the refrigerator, causing a large lump to appear above the right eyebrow.

In such a case, your father could feel free to explode with a few choice words. Your sister could shed enough tears to dampen the whole room. Your mother could, and probably would, do both. But you? You are thirteen and can't do anything! You are too young to cuss, and "big boys" don't cry. So you just stand there looking more stupid than usual.

But in spite of all this, I still think thirteen is a wonderful age!

Part 3

Usually, my home is the most peaceful spot on earth. I am part of a very average family consisting of a sister, age 14, a father, age 39, and a mother, with brown hair.

We get along very well together and I would like nothing better than to keep it that way.

Occasionally, though, my peace of mind is completely shattered, and I feel like packing up my other shirt and moving to the wilds of Africa, or Siberia, or even Jersey City. The cause of my distress is a visit from my cousin, a five-year-old named Walter.

I hate to admit that I can become so upset by a mere child, but you must remember that Walter is no ordinary child. He is more like an army tank running amuck in the petunias.

Unfortunately, Walter visits often—sometimes for a whole week. Mother loves to have him. She thinks he's cute. I can't agree. What is "cute" about a kid in coonskin cap splashing around in a bathtub full of water and singing at the top of his lungs, "Daveeee, Davy Crockett"? And what is "cute" about a kid that just stares at you all the time? No matter what I do, he gazes at me with those great big cow eyes of his.

Yesterday was the absolute limit. When I got to the breakfast table, Walter was already sitting there, slurping his oatmeal. I tried to eat, but he gazed at me so hard that I felt uncomfortable. I finally yelled for Mother and told her I couldn't stand the brat another minute. Walter looked up at me with a big, toothless grin—as though I had said something clever. I was just about to yell, "Get lost!" when my mother interrupted. "Can't you see he adores you?" she said. "Why, it's almost hero worship."

It was my turn to stare at *her*. I couldn't say a word! What was there to say?

I went upstairs and quite casually looked into my mirror. For the first time I noticed the lines of my strong, determined chin, and my high, masterful forehead. "Hero, huh?" I said to myself, and although I wasn't sure if a hero looked as stupid as I do at times, I *was* sure of one thing. It's really nice to have a child around the house. Especially an intelligent kid like Walter.

Why is "Thirteen" called an essay? (If necessary, consult your dictionary before answering.)

_____

_____

Why did the artist use cartoonlike illustrations?

_____

Why did William want to "drop dead" at the ticket counter? _____

_____

Why did he not mind being called an "impossible male creature"? _____

_____

Why did William feel that even teen-agers have problems? _____

_____

Why did William change his opinion of Walter?

_____

What were his reasons for never wanting to be young again? _____

_____

_____

_____

_____

The Giants of the Galápagos

Which are the oldest living animals in the world? Naturalists believe they are the huge tortoises found on the Seychelles Islands in the Indian Ocean and on the Galápagos Islands.

The Galápagos are a cluster of barren, lava-rock islands jutting out of the Pacific Ocean about six hundred miles west of Ecuador. Green vegetation is sparse on these islands, yet they are the home of many strange animals that exist nowhere else on earth. The most famous of these are the enormous tortoises, called *galápagos* in Spanish, from which the islands get their name.

Some of the turtles are believed to be from two hundred to four hundred years old. The largest specimens weigh about four hundred pounds and are four feet long—big enough to carry a grown man on their backs.

The giant tortoises are a weird sight as they force their way through the brush. They crawl over shrubs and cactuses at a top speed of one fifth of a mile an hour. Their movement is like the mechanical action of a tank forcing its way over rough ground. They pay no attention to sound; even if a gun is fired near them, they do not respond. But their eyesight is keen. The instant they see a man, even at a distance, they retreat into their shells. As they do, air is pushed out of their lungs with an odd hissing sound.

Before men came to the islands, the turtles had no enemies. Their neighbors, the big land and sea iguanas, were vegetarians that ate seaweed or cactus pads. Other animals inhabiting the area—sea lions, seals, pelicans, flamingos, and penguins—got their food from the sea.

Then men arrived. New England whaling ships made a practice of stopping at the islands to make repairs or get provisions of fresh turtle meat. The whalers would capture two or three hundred of the huge tortoises and store them in the ship's hold. The turtles could survive as long as a year without food or water, thus providing the crew with a continual supply of fresh turtle meat. Enormous numbers were carried away for this purpose. It is estimated that between 1811 and 1884, more than sixteen thousand were taken by whalers. No one knows how many more were carried off by other visitors to the islands or were killed on the spot for the valuable oil in their bodies.

An even greater catastrophe for the tortoises was the introduction of creatures that preyed on them. The rats, dogs, and pigs brought to the islands by man increased rapidly and ate the turtle eggs and the soft-shelled young animals. On most of the islands in the group the giant tortoises have vanished. Only on two islands are they still found in fairly large numbers.

Recently efforts have been made by various people in Ecuador and the United States to have some of the islands declared national parks.

Many of the giant tortoises are now on display in zoos. They seem to adjust themselves quite easily to life in captivity. In place of their diet of cactus pads and mangrove leaves, they have learned to eat bananas and watermelons.

Why do you think the tortoises were so easily captured and destroyed by men? _____
_____

Why were the turtles an especially good source of fresh meat on long voyages? _____
_____
_____
_____

Before men came to the islands, why didn't other animals prey upon the tortoises? _____
_____
_____

Would the Galápagos Islands be a good place for many people to live? _____ Why or why not? _____
_____

It's the Ham in Them

"QRRR—QRRR." The amateur radio operator's emergency call flashed over the air. Somewhere an alert "ham" picked up the distress signal and another rescue mission was accomplished through the magic of radio communication.

All over the world ham operators are using their hobby to help others. Following one extremely bad hurricane season along the East Coast, 1245 hams received awards for their heroic work in keeping up emergency communication. They had rerouted traffic to avoid fallen trees and live wires, directed fire patrols in cities where telephone and fire-alarm circuits were out of commission, and assisted in innumerable other ways.

In 1947, when Texas City was destroyed by a series of explosions, it was an amateur operator who made contact with the outside world and brought in help. He stayed on the air for thirty-six hours, sticking to his key right through one of the earth-shaking blasts.

But more frequent than such feats are the little deeds of kindness performed by hams. In Oregon a small girl bedridden with an incurable illness expressed a wish for watermelon out of season. Hams got busy and relayed messages to Florida. Two ripe watermelons were immediately sent to make a sick child happy.

Once an operator at an arctic station mentioned in a broadcast that their cook was tired of using a flattened tin can as a pancake turner. A ham in Pennsylvania picked up the message, and when the next mail arrived at the outpost, the cook was surprised with a brand-new pancake turner.

Message-relaying, by itself, is a sort of hobby within a hobby for some amateurs. Since 1950 a ham in Indiana has been relaying messages to weathermen in the arctic, who receive mail only once or twice a year. The "arctic mailman" relays a thousand messages a month between the lonely men and their families back home.

Civil defense leaders in the United States consider ham radio the most important hobby in the country. The government encourages young people to take up amateur radio work so that there will be a reserve of trained radio operators and technicians in case of local disaster or national emergency.

Besides doing good deeds and serving their country, hams have contributed many important ideas in the field of electronic communication. Many years ago a mere ham first convinced Westinghouse of the possibilities in commercial broadcasting. It was also a ham who pioneered in using short waves, once considered useless.

Ham radio can be a stepping stone to a career. Many a top-notch engineer and executive in radio and TV started out as a ham. Countless former hams now do communications work in the armed forces or operate their own service businesses.

But the thing that probably keeps thousands of hams glued to their radios is just the fun in it. Imagine the thrill of sitting at your own radio station and talking to another amateur across town, in another city, or even halfway around the world! The color of his skin may be different from yours, his way of life wholly strange. But you know each other better than you know your next-door neighbors. That's why ham radio is doing so much for international good will. One ham put it this way: "If hams ran the world, there'd never be another war. Ham radio is the best cementer of friendship ever invented!"

Why might a shut-in enjoy operating a "ham" radio outfit as a hobby? _____
_____
_____

Why would "ham" radio operators be valuable in any community in an emergency? _____
_____

Why might being a "ham" be valuable to you as an individual? _____
_____
_____

Who Is Handicapped?

Out on Long Island, near New York City, is an industrial plant where no able-bodied person can get a job. Every worker at Abilities, Inc. is a person who, because of a disability such as blindness, loss of limbs, or paralysis, had been considered "unemployable." Even the president of the company wears artificial legs.

Abilities, Inc. acts as subcontractor to some of the country's largest corporations. It produces precision parts used in airplanes, radios, phonographs, and dictating machines. The company also conducts a packaging operation and a letter shop. Every employee must be competent in three different kinds of work by the end of his trial period. Then he can be shifted to another job when a particular contract is finished.

Inspectors for big companies are amazed at the excellent performance of these "handicapped" workers. They find that production at Abilities, Inc. is greater and the quality of work higher than in their own huge plants. For example, in the average plant where delicate parts are assembled, inspectors may reject as many as 40 per cent of the units because they do not meet the required standards. At Abilities, Inc. the rejection rate is less than 4 per cent.

Moreover, these supposedly disabled workers have a far better record of attendance on the job than do the nonhandicapped. National statistics show that workers as a whole have 110 times as many absences as do those at Abilities, Inc.

How has all this been accomplished? Says the works manager, "We do not fit people to a job. Our success comes from the fact that we break down the job to fit the people."

Using imagination and ingenuity, mechanics at the plant (all of them, of course, disabled) have developed many labor-saving devices adapted to the workers' needs. For example, one worker, whose hands had been weakened by polio, was not strong enough to twist the ends of fine cable wires that he had to dip into a special solution. Another worker came up with a mechanical answer, a "cable spinner" operated by a motor. This device did the job better and faster than it could be done by hand.

Abilities, Inc. is not providing "made work" in a sheltered environment. As the president puts it, "Pampering isn't what these people need. They thrive on competition. Our purpose is to provide salable skills." He feels that he has really succeeded when his employees leave him for higher-paying jobs in big companies. Furthermore, he has a long waiting list of workers.

In recent years more and more opportunities for handicapped workers have opened up in regular industry, too. The new philosophy is expressed by the motor company executive who said, "Let's quit harping on what a man *can't* do—let's find out what he *can* do and then give him a job he can handle."

Everyone, he pointed out, is handicapped for some kind of work. If you aren't good at mathematics, you'd make a poor bookkeeper. If you are impatient, you'd be unsuited to work at an information desk. Yet almost everyone can do something well. A good personnel director tries to match each person's abilities with a job.

1. Why is the president of Abilities, Inc. pleased when employees leave to accept other jobs?

----

2. Why might employers like to hire workers trained at Abilities, Inc.? -------------------

----

----

3. The average big company tries to place people in the jobs they can do best. Why does Abilities, Inc. follow a different plan and adapt the jobs to fit their people? --------------------

----

----

4. Why is it actually misleading to refer to "handicapped" and "nonhandicapped" people? -----

----

People who are interested in animals sometimes make a hobby of collecting and preserving the animal footprints they find in the fields and forests. For you, too, taking plaster casts from footprints might well become an engrossing and inexpensive hobby.

Collecting Animal Tracks

Wild-animal tracks can often be found along the banks of a creek where the soft mud retains a sharp, well-defined impression. But you can also start your hobby close to home by using the tracks of your pet dog or cat.

Plaster casts of footprints are easily made, and they preserve the imprint for a lifetime. The only equipment you will need is a mixing bowl or a large tin can, a bag of plaster of Paris, a soft toothbrush, and some narrow strips of cardboard or thin metal strips that bend easily.

When you find a clear imprint of an animal's track, clean away any loose material that may spoil the impression. Then put a collar-wall of cardboard or narrow metal strips in the ground around the print. Leave an inch of space be tween the track and the wall. Allow the strips to protrude above the ground enough to retain the poured plaster. Ordinary paper clips, a rubber band, or string will hold the strips in place.

Now it is time to mix the plaster "batter." Use your hands to combine the plaster and water in a basin or can. Add the plaster to the water, not water to the plaster, and remember that you will need to use about four fifths as much water as plaster. Sprinkle dry plaster slowly into the water until tiny islands appear on the surface. Then stir the mixture slowly with your hands until it feels like heavy cream. If it thickens too quickly, add a few drops of vinegar to slow it up. If the plaster tends to thicken too slowly, a little salt will hurry the process. It is important to avoid lumps and bubbles in the mixture.

Carefully pour the plaster batter in from one side of the wall to avoid disturbing the print. Pour and level the batter to a depth of half or three quarters of an inch. Let the plaster dry for about an hour and then remove the collar-wall and lift the cast carefully from the ground. After the cast has dried for at least twenty-four hours, use the toothbrush to clean the loose dirt from it.

Now you have a "negative" cast that shows the actual animal track in reverse, or standing *out* from the surface of the plaster. This can be used to make a "positive" cast that looks like the real footprint. First make a collar-wall that is a bit larger than the negative cast. Place the circular wall on several thicknesses of newspaper. Pour liquid plaster into this mold.

While the plaster is setting, coat the negative cast with mineral oil so that the fresh plaster will not stick to it. When the plaster in the circular mold has set to the firmness of soft putty, press the negative cast firmly into it. Move the cast slightly from side to side to prevent the two from sticking together. Leave the negative cast in position for a few minutes; then pry the casts apart carefully. Clean the positive cast after it is dry. You now have a positive duplication of the track that you first found. To preserve both the negative and positive casts, coat them with shellac, or paint the surface and track depressions in contrasting colors.

Here are some of the steps in making plaster casts of animal tracks.
Number them to match the order in which they should be done.

____ coat negative cast with oil

____ collect the required equipment

____ paint the surface and track depressions

____ pour plaster into positive mold

____ brush clean the dry positive cast

____ pour liquid plaster over impression

____ find a clear animal track

____ arrange circular collar-wall on newspaper

____ press negative into semihardened plaster

____ place collar-wall around track in earth

____ separate negative from positive cast

____ let plaster dry and lift cast from ground

Old Threetoes

by William H. Bunce

It was a crisp, clear day in late fall. Fifteen-year-old Jamie Gordon was on an expedition into the Bear Swamp when he saw a swarm of crows hovering over a clump of scrub pines. Their raucous clamor made him think that they were mobbing some creature, probably a hawk or an owl. He decided to go and investigate. Knowing that in the woods the silent watcher sees the most, he crept cautiously toward the pine thicket.

Whatever was there in the pines had made the crows behave as if they were terribly wrought up. But Jamie noticed that not a single crow ventured into the thicket. Clutching his twenty-two rifle, the boy peered into the dark branches. He could see nothing. But one of the crows caught sight of him and raised the alarm. Up the noisy mob flew and over the treetops, cawing vigorously.

Jamie stepped into the open and approached the pines. He was staring up into the branches when out of the corner of his eye he caught a flash of color moving on the ground. It was a big red fox, and over his shoulder hung a black object that bounced as he ran. Jamie took it to be a crow, but how the fox could have caught it, he had no idea, for the crow is usually too wary to be caught napping.

There was a good tracking snow and it was two hours till chore time, so the boy decided to follow the fox trail. When he looked at the tracks leading from under the pines, he whistled, for he knew that none other than Threetoes himself had made them. For nearly ten years (almost a fox's lifetime) this old fox had outwitted hounds and hunters and had avoided all manner of traps with a cunning that was almost uncanny. In his youth the fox, while finding out about steel traps, had lost part of his left forepaw, and in snowtime his three-toed track was a familiar sight to farmers. As Jamie stared at the tracks, he felt a thrill of excitement. Perhaps the trail would lead to the old marauder's den!

Jamie came to the den sooner than he expected. He found the two entrances and plenty of fresh tracks. Later, as he made his way homeward, he reached a difficult decision. Unlike most farm boys, he enjoyed watching and studying the creatures of the woods rather than catching them. But fox skins were worth money, and money was scarce right now.

The next Saturday the boy came back again to the den. Taking up a position in the pine thicket, Jamie sat down to wait. He held his rifle in readiness, still thinking of the money that the fox pelt would bring.

Jamie watched for some time before he saw a movement at one of the entrances. A fox was creeping out. It was not Threetoes, but a smaller fox that moved stiffly as though injured. Forgetting his plan to shoot on sight, the lad craned his neck to watch what would happen. Then with disconcerting suddenness, Threetoes appeared, a fringe of plump meadow mice dangling from his mouth. The old fox was bringing food to his injured mate. Some sixth sense at that instant warned the foxes of the boy's presence. With a flash of color they disappeared, and Jamie went home, aware that he had done nothing about collecting the fox pelt.

On a cold, still morning not long after Jamie's visit to the den, Old Threetoes began his daily hunt for food for himself and his mate. He drifted across the buckwheat field like a shadow. He paused at a fence corner to sniff in a woodchuck hole, but the occupant was far down inside, sleeping his winter sleep. He swung off down the lane. Within sight of the Gordon farmhouse, Old Threetoes stopped. A smell was wafted to his sensitive nostrils that set his mouth watering. It came from the Gordon chicken coop. Threetoes did not usually make a business of raiding coops. He preferred to catch chickens roosting in the orchard, where he could more easily make his escape. But another whiff of chicken decided the ravenous fox. Swinging through the orchard at a brisk trot, he entered the barnyard.

At that moment Jamie Gordon stepped soundlessly out into the snow to begin his morning chores. As he slipped around the corner of the woodshed, he spied something dart across the snow and disappear through a low opening in the chicken coop.

With a shout to his uncle, who was just coming out the back door, Jamie dashed toward the coop. At the same instant a wild cackling told him that the intruder was busy. That cackling brought Uncle Win on the run.

Jamie had slammed a heavy board against the opening of the coop to prevent escape of the thieving animal. Uncle Win pounded furiously on the door to keep the prisoner from killing more chickens. A glance at tracks leading into the coop disclosed the marauder's identity.

"We've got Old Threetoes!" cried Uncle Win.

Jamie looked at the tracks and nodded, but there was no triumph on his face.

Inside the coop everything had suddenly grown quiet. Unfastening the lock, Uncle Win opened the door a crack and peered in. He gave an exclamation of surprise. A dead chicken lay on the floor, and beside it lay the limp body of the big red fox.

"Well, I swan," exclaimed Uncle Win as he and the boy entered the coop. "Old Threetoes is dead." He studied the fox for a second. "Yes, sir, limp as a rag. Never heard of such a thing in my life! He must have fallen from the roost and broken his neck."

He picked up the body of Threetoes in one hand and the chicken in the other and laid them side by side in the snow. Then he went back inside the coop to see if any further damage had been done to his chickens.

Jamie stared down at the old marauder. The fox looked thin, hungry, and pitiful. Gently the boy stroked the fine soft fur until Uncle Win called him inside the chicken coop.

When the boy came out again a minute later, he blinked his eyes in bewilderment. There were tracks in the snow and a few feathers, but no fox and no chicken! A quick movement suddenly caught Jamie's eye and made him shout with delight. It was Threetoes! In flying jumps the fox crossed the snow-covered meadow and headed for the swamp, taking the chicken with him. Old Threetoes had played possum and escaped again!

Number the events below in the order in which they happened.

____ Jamie becomes so interested in Old Threetoes that he forgets to kill the fox.

____ Jamie takes the first actual step toward getting the fox.

____ Jamie begins to regret that Threetoes might be captured.

____ Jamie decides to trap or kill the red fox.

____ Jamie is sincerely sorry about the old marauder's fate.

____ Jamie completely discards the idea of ever capturing wily Old Threetoes.

Rose of the West

by Trumbull Reed

Tom Austin squirmed into the sleeping bag.

A few paces distant, Rose of the West and her many children were cozily nestled together.

"So now I sleep with the pigs!" Tom thought contentedly.

The events that had led to this odd arrangement made it reasonable enough.

Rose of the West was Tom's 4-H project. She was a handsome, bronze-coated Duroc Jersey sow. Anticipating the arrival of her babies, Tom had shut Rose in a farrowing pen. She was comfortable there, and apparently placid, when he fed her before starting to school.

When the high-school bus dropped him off at home that afternoon, he had hurried to the pig yard. It was a fearful jolt when he found the gate of the pen pushed ajar and Rose gone.

It is instinct for a sow to hide out when she is about to produce her young. Tom therefore had been pretty certain Rose would have headed for a thick growth of shrubs and vines along the creek. This made ideal cover for a sow lucky enough to escape the usual bounds at farrowing time.

Tom had set off for the pasture at a run.

It was dark when, tired and glum, he finally gave up the search and returned home.

"Don't worry, Son," his father said. "Sometimes a litter of pigs does better in the open than in the pen. But, of course," he added, "that's when a coyote doesn't find them."

Tom's face clouded momentarily. Then he grinned at his father. "Anyhow, I don't have to worry that you'll grab my sow and sell her because I let her get out of the pen."

He was referring to the unfortunate behavior of Mr. Young on the next farm. A pen failed to hold the pig his son Frank was raising as a 4-H project, and the pig had invaded the family garden. Mr. Young had confiscated the half-grown animal and sold it.

The 4-H Club members were outraged, but there was nothing they could do about it. Frank had set his heart on a swine-raising project, and in his humiliation he had dropped out of the club.

On the morning following Rose's disappearance, Tom glumly boarded the school bus. At the next stop Frank Young came aboard and sat down by him. This surprised Tom, for Frank had been rather stand-offish since the loss of his pig. But this morning Frank said eagerly to him, "That's a grand bunch of pigs your Rose of the West farrowed."

"What's that?" Tom snapped.

"Didn't you know? She's down in the bottom near our fence line."

"How many pigs?" Tom asked breathlessly.

Frank hesitated. "Twelve anyway. Hard to count them when you're sneaking a look without letting the sow know you're there."

"How did you find them?" Tom asked.

"I happened to be down there this morning. Heard them wrestling for their breakfast. Husky little guys! It's lucky there are only twelve of them. Rose couldn't feed thirteen, and one would have been a runt. Maybe died."

"Why, no!" Tom exclaimed. "Rose is a registered purebred from a line of fine mothers. I chose her because she can feed fourteen pigs."

Frank's eyes widened. "Oh—oh, I didn't know that." He repeated, "I didn't know that." Since it made no difference to Frank how many babies Rose could feed, Tom wondered why he looked so dashed.

Tom explained that a litter should never be counted until it was at least three days old. "Too many things can happen to the babies. I sure hope a coyote doesn't happen to them," he added fervently.

To make certain a coyote didn't "happen," Tom was sleeping with the pigs. Rose was resigned to his familiar presence. He had announced his approach by speaking gently to her, and she had grunted her recognition without getting up. No sly coyote would venture close when it picked up human smell.

Tom was glad to have an excuse for sleeping out. The night was clear, and a full moon rose from behind the trees. An owl hooted softly. A rustle and a tiny squeak told Tom that a little field mouse was going about its business.

All was well. Tom fell asleep.

Three hours later he wakened with a startled sense of something happening.

He raised his head and looked about. The moon shone brightly. Tom was in deep shadow, but the light shone on Rose and her pigs.

He lay down again, though he was not sleepy now. Propping his head on his arms, he stared up into the moonlit trees. His thoughts were not as romantic as the scene deserved. He was mentally figuring how much Rose's twelve pigs would weigh in a hundred eighty days. With pleasurable excitement he decided that they stood a good chance of hitting the ton-litter mark.

At that moment he saw something moving— something vaguely visible in the shadows beyond Rose. He checked his impulse to warn it away with a yell. The worst thing possible would be to awaken Rose suddenly. She would scramble to her feet, scattering the babies cuddled against her, and perhaps trample them in her rush.

Keeping his eyes on the stealthy motion among the shadows, Tom started worming himself out of the bag. It was no coyote. That was sure. It stood too tall. Maybe a cow or a colt. But neither of these would move stealthily.

The something moved into the light. It was a human figure, stealing with elaborate caution toward Rose's nest. From his right hand dangled an object that moved but made no sound.

Suddenly Tom was concentrating hard on the success of this silent approach. *"Please, Rose, don't wake up!"* he thought.

As the visitor bent above the pigs and extended his hand, Tom held his breath. Then the empty hand was withdrawn, and the visitor retreated.

Tom's mind was racing. No one had counted the pigs before Frank found them. Could it be that the thirteenth pig had suggested an opportunity for Frank to have a 4-H project? Had he taken the pig, honestly believing that Rose could not care for more than a dozen babies?

That was the answer! When Frank learned that Rose could feed a thirteenth pig, things had looked different. Frank wasn't a thief!

Next morning Tom beckoned Frank to a seat beside him in the bus. "Say, Frank! What do you know! Rose has thirteen pigs."

"That's fine." Frank's enthusiasm sounded hollow. "Good thing Rose can care for so many."

"Maybe so. Maybe not," Tom said judicially. "Twelve might come nearer hitting the ton-litter mark than thirteen. Tell you what I'll do, Frank. I'll sell you one."

"I haven't any money."

"That's O.K. Most of us club members start out on credit. You can pay when you sell. My dad would let you have feed, too, on the same basis, if the deal interests you."

"You bet it interests me, but——" Frank swallowed hard.

"It's a deal," Tom said briskly. "You'll need a good tight pen. Be glad to help you build it."

"Well—say—well, thanks," Frank said.

"You've sort of earned an interest in the pigs," Tom said, "finding them like you did." He couldn't resist adding, "Funny about the thirteenth pig, wasn't it? An elf must have dropped it in the nest after we'd counted an even dozen there."

Number the events below in the order in which they actually occurred.

___ Tom sleeps in the woods to protect the pigs.

___ Frank realizes he has done something wrong.

___ Tom puts Rose in a farrowing pen.

___ Tom sees Frank bring the baby pig back.

___ Tom offers to sell a pig to Frank.

___ Frank discovers Rose and the pigs.

___ Rose disappears from the pen.

___ Frank tells Tom where Rose is to be found.

___ Frank takes a pig from the nest.

___ Tom realizes why Frank took the pig.

The Sentence Tells You

The two words above each sentence are pronounced alike but they are spelled differently and they have different meanings. Such words are called homonyms. *Read each sentence and write the correct homonym in each blank.*

tide　　tied

After Joe had _____ his boat to the dock, he strolled to the end of the pier to watch the _____ come in.

waste　　waist

"It would certainly be a _____ of material to make this belt go twice around your _____," said Mrs. Jones.

heard　　herd

Tom had often _____ other people tell about the huge _____ of buffalo that lived in the park.

their　　there

"Oh, _____ they are!" shouted the girls when they spied _____ friends in the crowd.

fare　　fair

After Bob paid his bus _____, he did not have enough money left to go to the _____.

cereal　　serial

"You can't read your _____ until after you've finished eating your breakfast _____," said June's mother.

seen　　scene

"I have never _____ such jagged mountains," exclaimed Ann as she gazed at the _____ before her.

mane　　main

The frisky young horse pranced and tossed its _____ as Fred rode down the _____ street of the town.

weigh　　way

"This huge box must _____ a ton," muttered Mr. Reed, "but we have to find a _____ to move it."

fourth　　forth

The day before setting _____ on their camping trip, the three boys decided to take a _____ friend along.

steak　　stake

After Al drove the last _____ into the ground, he was hungry enough to eat the biggest _____ in town.

sale　　sail

After Ed learned to _____ a boat, he tried to buy the trim craft that he had seen advertised for _____.

taught　　taut

The horse had been _____ to hold a rope _____ while the cowhand caught and tied a calf for branding.

not　　knot

The dog gnawed at the _____ in the rope that tied him to the tree, but he could _____ get loose.

Context Determines the Meaning

The three words above each pair of sentences can mean almost the same thing or they can have different meanings. Put a check mark in front of the sentence in which all three words could be used without changing the meaning of the sentence. Use your dictionary if you wish.

arrest   stop   check

When we finished eating, Mr. Williams asked the waitress for the ＿＿.

The dentist filled the tooth to ＿✓＿ the decay.

rare   unusual   uncommon

"I'm about to barbecue the steaks," said Jack. "Is yours to be ＿＿, medium, or well done?"

A total eclipse of the sun is ＿✓＿.

tale   yarn   story

"I need seven skeins of dark blue ＿＿," Emily informed the salesgirl.

The old sea captain told the children a hair-raising ＿✓＿ about his adventures.

vain   futile   unsuccessful

"I made several ＿✓＿ attempts to reach Ann by telephone," complained Jane.

Unfortunately she is ＿＿ about her beauty.

bough   branch   limb

"The road divides at the bottom of the hill," he explained. "The left ＿＿ goes to Lincoln."

Every ＿✓＿ of the magnolia tree seemed to be covered with lovely white blossoms.

severe   stern   harsh

The judge imposed a ＿＿ sentence on the man who violated the speed laws.

Across the ＿✓＿ of the boat was painted the name *Seafarer*.

shake   tremble   quiver

A case used to hold a number of arrows is called a ＿＿.

During the last earthquake that occurred we could feel our house ＿✓＿.

polite   civil   courteous

The guide who escorted us around the factory answered all our questions in a ＿✓＿ manner.

Every citizen has his ＿＿ rights and duties.

fair   honest   just

While visiting his cousin, Henry attended a county ＿＿ for the first time.

We felt the principal's remarks were ＿✓＿.

mend   patch   repair

Mrs. Lee planted several varieties of flowers on the small ＿＿ of ground.

Tim asked his mother to ＿✓＿ the torn sleeve of his jacket.

principal   main   chief

John wrote a newspaper article about Chicago, the ＿＿ city in Illinois.

Mr. Mead is now ＿✓＿ of our high school.

erect   construct   build

The boys volunteered to ＿✓＿ a speaker's platform for the football rally.

In spite of the hot sun, all members of the R.O.T.C. unit stood ＿＿ during the review.

journey   trip   voyage

"Don't ＿＿ over that loose board at the top of the stairs," Sam warned his sister.

Phil promised to show the colored slides of his ＿✓＿ to the entire class on Monday.

new   novel   original

Everyone in the class was asked to make a book report on a ＿＿ of his own choice.

The committee had several ＿✓＿ ideas for decorating the gymnasium.

Getting Word Meaning from Context Clues

Sometimes you can guess what a word means by its use in a sentence. Read each sentence below; then write on the blank after it what you think the italicized word means.

1. A high platform had been *erected* so that the crowd watching the water carnival could get a good view of the diving stunts.

----

2. The temperature on the afternoon of the carnival was so *mild* that none of the spectators wore a coat.

----

3. Even though he was a good diver, Bill felt slightly *timorous* as he poised on the high springboard before taking off for a jackknife.

----

4. The sight of his proud parents among the spectators *whetted* Bill's desire to make a perfect dive.

----

5. The diving was stopped for a time because the lifeguard saw part of a floating tree *protruding* from the water.

----

6. Two lifeguards *demonstrated* the best way to save a drowning person.

----

7. The heads of two of the swimmers in the pyramid formation suddenly *collided* with a painful bump.

----

8. In another formation eight girls swam on their backs and formed a wheel that *pivoted* round and round as they flutter-kicked with their feet.

----

9. The strength and endurance required for the half-mile race proved that the swimmers who took part in it were no *namby-pamby* fellows.

----

10. When the wind died down, the boys who had raced to the island in their sailboats were *marooned* and couldn't get back.

----

11. As Tom struggled hastily into his swimming trunks, he accidentally *jabbed* a hole in them with his finger.

----

12. In one stunt race, potato sacks were tied around the legs of the swimmers to *handicap* their movements.

----

13. When the spectators rushed to the side of the raft to see the finish of the race, the raft *capsized*, spilling them into the lake.

----

14. A man who had fallen into the muddy water with his clothes on looked *bedraggled* after his accident.

----

15. A rowboat that had pulled loose from its *moorings* was drifting down the river.

----

16. One boy added comedy to the carnival by *persisting* in his attempts to make a swan dive, even though he always landed flat in the water.

----

17. The children *capered* on the grass with joy when it was announced that a spectacular display of fireworks would be next on the program.

----

18. When the carnival was over, the spectators *trooped* forward to congratulate the winners of the many contests.

On the previous page the general idea expressed in the sentence suggests what the italicized word means. On this page each sentence contains specific clues to the meaning of the word. Often there is a word or a phrase that means the same thing. In two cases the passage contains a contrasting idea that helps explain the word. Underline any words or phrases in the passages that give you a hint as to the possible meaning of the italicized words.

1. The beacon flashed on and off, on and off, lighting up the room at regular *intervals*.

2. The two boys took turns as *attendant* at the filling station. One said, "I'll wait on people for gas and oil for a couple of hours, and then you can service the cars."

3. The night that lightning struck the power plant, lights were *extinguished* all over town. After the lights went out, I went to bed.

4. Frank found this description of his rock in the library: "Limestone is often *pitted* with holes that were hollowed out by water long ago."

5. Marcia saw clearly that Hal's plan for raising money would not work, and she spoke out against it. Her *discerning* comments persuaded the class to turn to other proposals.

6. In the first two quarters the visiting team blocked all of Central's carefully planned plays. The time between halves was spent in *devising* new ones.

7. Flying above the fields, the pilot mapped the *drainage* system. He traced the flow of water, noting that it ran down to a series of ditches.

8. Ferry boats *ply* New York Harbor, providing frequent service between Staten Island and Manhattan.

9. Mrs. Lee was thankful for her neighbor's kindness when Mr. Lee was ill. She showed her *gratitude* by sending the neighbor a pie.

10. Writing hastily, Rose *scribbled* a note to her sister and put it in their locker.

11. Dick looked at the lawn mower with *distaste*. Next door he could see his friends playing touch football. He longed to join the game and to spend the afternoon doing something he liked.

12. From his place on top of the dam, Mr. Page shifted his glance eastward to the *channel* of the river where the water was swirling angrily through its narrowed passageway.

13. Pete decided that training for the spring meet would *overtax* him. He felt burdened already by his part-time job and his heavy load of courses.

14. Before school opened, a crew of workmen painted the walls and woodwork and repaired the desks. As part of this general *renovation* the library was given new lighting.

15. Our Indian friend worked for us in a *dual* capacity. In the mornings he guided us to spots where the big fish bit. At noon he doubled as cook and fried the morning's catch.

16. When Dad gave me my ice skates he began *reminiscing* about his childhood. "They called me 'Jelly Knees,'" he recalled, "because I wobbled like a pudding while I was learning to skate."

17. Last year the juniors lost money on their class play. This year, however, twice as many tickets have been sold, while expenses have been cut. It appears that this time the undertaking will prove to be a *lucrative* one.

Each paragraph on this page contains an italicized word. This word may be unknown to you, but the paragraph in which it is used will give you clues to its meaning. After you have read each paragraph, write in your own words what you think the italicized word means.

The feathers of the North American grouse blend well with the colors of his natural *habitat.* His brownish wings, speckled back, and greenish-black neck feathers make him practically invisible among trees and bushes that cover the parts of the country where he makes his home.

The word *habitat* means _____

_____

The methods and length of time needed for *incubation* of birds' eggs vary widely. Sometimes the female alone performs the duty; sometimes both birds take turns; and in a few instances, as in the case of the ostrich, the male alone sits on the eggs during the entire time. The period of incubation for most birds is ten to twelve days, though some of the larger species require a month or more to hatch their eggs.

The word *incubation* means _____

_____

Many tales of horror have been told about the octopus, or devilfish. Actually, most of these creatures are harmless, but they are so ugly that people automatically feel they must be very vicious. The eight snakelike *tentacles* around its mouth give the octopus a weird appearance. It uses these tentacles to seize and carry its prey into the horny jaws of its mouth. The underside of each tentacle is lined with two rows of powerful cuplike disks. These prevent the victim from wriggling out of the octopus' arms. The octopus swims by drawing water into its body through a funnellike opening beneath its head and then forcing it out. The sudden force shoots its body backward like a jet-propelled rocket, with the eight tentacles streaming out behind it.

The word *tentacles* means _____

_____

Coyotes, leopards, and cougars belong to the large group of *carnivorous* mammals. The members of this group are well equipped for capturing and devouring the smaller animals that are their chief source of food. All have toes with sharp claws that are helpful in combat. All these meat eaters also possess strong, sharp teeth especially adapted for seizing and eating their prey.

The word *carnivorous* means _____

_____

It is a well-known fact that many animals spend the cold months of the year in an inactive condition. Bears and woodchucks, for instance, crawl into their dens and hibernate until warm weather comes. But there are also animals that are able to escape the hot, dry seasons by becoming almost completely inactive. Certain types of snails conceal themselves in a sheltered place and withdraw into their shells. After sealing up the openings with a liquid substance that hardens, they *estivate* until the weather is more to their liking.

The word *estivate* means _____

_____

The furry, winged creatures known as bats are found in many different parts of the world. Most of them, like the owls, are *nocturnal* in their habits. They fly about at night searching for food, feeding chiefly on insects that they catch and eat while in flight. Although bats have small eyes, they can see quite well in the dark. Nature has further equipped them for nighttime activity by endowing them with a special sense that enables them to avoid objects in their paths. During the day, bats find a dark place where they can hang, head downward, suspended by their claws.

The word *nocturnal* means _____

_____

Two-Legged Fish

If you don't mind tangling with the *denizens* of the deep in their underwater back yards, you have the first *requisite* for becoming a skin diver.

A skin diver's equipment consists of his swim trunks, fins for his feet, and a mask for his nose and eyes. After putting these on, he takes an easy breath and noses down into the ocean looking for beauty and excitement.

Most fish are just as curious about you as you are about them. Some will swim up close and stare inquiringly at the strange monster that has suddenly invaded their realm.

Not many fish will make an unprovoked attack. Two exceptions are the *pugnacious* six-foot Maori eel, a mean-tempered fighter with long needlelike teeth, and the barracuda, the tiger of the sea. Neither makes a *congenial* playmate.

In the blue-green underwater world everything seems to move in slow motion. Tall grasses wave gracefully in the current. Silver clouds of tiny minnows drift by. Giant rocks shelter the myriad varieties of sea life. Fairyland forests of brown *kelp* rise from the bottom and serve both as hunting ground and sanctuary for the less aggressive of the finny tribe.

All this is seen about twenty feet down in some waters, although dives of more than forty feet can be made by skillful swimmers. You peer through a four-inch glass window set in a soft rubber waterproof mounting that fits snugly over your eyes and nose.

Your hands are quite free for action, since the sixteen-inch rubber swim fins that extend your feet to froglike proportions enable you to travel up to a hundred feet underwater in half a minute, which is the average underwater time for a dive.

The wise skin diver keeps swimming with his head lower than his feet. As long as he does that, he is, to all appearances, just another fish. Only the experienced diver walks around on the floor of the ocean. Too many well-camouflaged hazards, such as the sting ray, lie in wait there defying disturbance.

Contrary to common belief, you don't take a whopping big breath just before going under. You take an ordinary breath, dive down, and conserve your breath by swimming calmly and unhurriedly with an easy, continuous flutter of the swim fins on your feet. When you have used up that batch of air, you shoot back to the surface for a few fresh breaths.

Despite the *potential* dangers of skin diving, the actual dangers are few. Serious underwater accidents among experienced skin divers are practically unheard of. By exercising ordinary *precautions*, the average skin diver is safer underwater in some secluded cove than he is crossing the street. There are rules for underwater safety just as there are rules for any sport.

Skin diving is most popular in coastal waters. However, it is also becoming extremely popular inland, in the fresh-water lakes. Today, many a swimmer is donning swim fins and diving mask to nose far down into the watery deep searching for new, undreamed-of beauties and adventure.

The italicized words in the article are listed at the left below. From the definitions following each word, underline the one you think is correct.

denizens: emblems hardships denseness inhabitants

requisite: opportunity requirement advantage equipment

pugnacious: quarrelsome strenuous sluggish large-sized

congenial: casual usual agreeable constant

kelp: fish shells lumber seaweed

potential: plentiful possible powerful numberless

precautions: preparations safety swimming ability care

Which Word Completes the Meaning?

As you read each paragraph, think carefully about what it tells you.   Underline the word below that you think best completes the meaning of the paragraph.

Tim's Spanish teacher wanted her pupils to speak Spanish with the correct accent. Therefore, she always took pains to pronounce each word ____.

    precisely   easily

    pleasantly   impressively

Although he was a busy man, the owner of the factory spent the morning ____ conducting his friends around the plant. He wanted to be sure they saw its operations in the correct order.

    briefly   independently

    personally   absent-mindedly

The champion, bruised and bleeding, was in the ring defending his world title. Time after time he staggered up from the ropes to fight on ____.

    vigorously   impulsively

    patriotically   doggedly

Instinct made the fox move stealthily across the trail of the hunters so that he would not be seen or heard. Always hugging the shadows, he went ____ along the banks of the stream.

    sliding   slinking

    bouncing   floundering

Dreaming of the past, the old sea captain sat quietly in the sun, looking off into space. "As I think back," he ____, "I realize that the old days were best."

    exclaimed   bellowed

    scoffed   mused

As Jack watched the artist carve animals from wood, he admired the sure movements of the man's ____ hands.

    careless   skillful

    cautious   fumbling

Turning gracefully, the dancer pivoted on one toe. Then, as the music increased in speed, she whirled faster and faster while the fascinated audience watched ____.

    dreamily   wearily

    grudgingly   breathlessly

Clyde's family watched ____ as he sat silently at the table, hungry but unable to eat. Each one wanted to help Clyde, yet no one could think of the right thing to say.

    joyously   sympathetically

    proudly   bravely

George measured and marked the board before sawing it. It did not fit the space exactly, so he carefully measured again. He was ____ in his efforts.

    persistent   timid

    hesitant   casual

Going downstairs proudly in the dress she had made, Sue decided it was finished ____. She could wear her leather belt with it to the picnic and make a white belt and scarf later.

    partially   completely

    sufficiently   imperfectly

The assignment on movie-making was not an easy one, but it sounded so interesting that more than a dozen students ____ volunteered to do the work.

    sluggishly   eagerly

    desperately   reluctantly

Ed finally found the small mouth of the cave. He ____ into the entrance, wondering if anyone had ever gone through a narrower opening.

    leaped   stepped

    squeezed   rushed

Who Said It?

On January 12, 1951, a huge warehouse in Chicago caught fire and TV history was made. Television cameras from a nearby studio were trained on the frightening scene and millions of televiewers saw a "live" telecast showing firemen battling the blaze, rescue squads in operation, and police handling the crowds of spectators. For the first time pictures of such an event were sent out over TV while it was actually happening.

While the fire and the telecast were going on, various comments must have been made and various orders given. Match each imaginary remark below with the person who might have made it.

a television commentator	a newspaperman	a spectator at the fire
an engineer in the studio	a policeman	a doctor in a rescue squad
a television viewer	a fire chief	the owner of the warehouse

"Haul out all emergency equipment immediately! We'll make a forcible entry to rescue that hose crew! Put on smoke masks, men! Now stretch those lines and cover the men moving into the building!"

- -

"And now a special report. We were made especially proud today by an event that spotlighted the enormous potential of this medium. No longer will a station limit its horizons to the four walls of the studio. From this day forward our viewers have a front seat at an event occurring anywhere in our nation!"

- -

"Stand back! Everybody! Move along! Give those men room to work! Look out, there! The roof may fall in any minute now. Back, everyone! Move back, please!"

- -

"Did you ever in your whole life see so much smoke? That place is really blazing. I spotted the flames from my office; so I thought I'd take a coffee break and see what's going on. But, ugh! This smoke is suffocating me. I'm heading back!"

- -

"Look at those poor men. They were carried out of the building. I suppose they'll be rushed to a hospital. What a terrible sight! I can almost smell the smoke and feel blisters from the heat of the flames!"

- -

"Everything's ruined! All the records and equipment and stock! Everything! All gone up in smoke! Luckily, everybody who was working in the place got out. It would be horrible if anyone were trapped in that furnace! It will take months—maybe even years—to straighten out the mess."

- -

"Careful now. Move him gently. There now. Cover him with that blanket. His pulse is too fast. Get the inhalator. Administer oxygen. Hurry!"

- -

"Is there a rewrite man on? OK! Here goes. Warehouse fire along the Chicago River gets full on-the-spot TV coverage. Three cameras relay pictures of blaze to New York, Washington, Pittsburgh, Philadelphia, Cleveland, and Detroit."

- -

Selecting the Correct Meaning

In each of the sentences below, the italicized word has a different meaning. Put the number of the definition that gives this meaning in front of the sentence. (For example, the first one is number 4.)

board, 1. a broad, thin piece of wood ready for use in building, etc. 2. cover with boards: *Father boards up the windows of our summer cottage in the fall.* 3. food served on a table. 4. group of persons managing something; council: *a board of health.*

_4_ The school *board* approved the plans for the new high school and gymnasium.

____ John thought he could use the pine *board* to make a shelf for the closet.

____ Mr. Wilson thought someone should *board* up the entrance to the old mine shaft before an accident occurred.

op·er·a·tion, 1. working: *The operation of a railroad requires many men.* 2. the way a thing works: *the operation of a machine.* 3. something done to the body, usually with instruments, to improve health: *Taking out the tonsils is a common operation.* 4. movements of soldiers, ships, supplies, etc.: *naval operations.*

____ The company sent Bill to the factory to learn about the *operation* of the new vacuum cleaners that he was to demonstrate.

____ Three days after her *operation*, Betty was allowed to leave the hospital.

____ Details of the military *operation* had been worked out carefully months in advance.

ex·am·ple, 1. one taken to show what others are like; case that shows something; sample: *New York is an example of a busy city.* 2. person or thing to be imitated; model; pattern: *Washington is a good example for boys to follow.* 3. problem in arithmetic, etc. 4. warning to others: *The captain made an example of the soldiers who shirked by making them clean up the camp.*

____ The teacher's explanation of the algebra *example* answered the questions that had arisen in Tom's mind.

____ The man's severe sentence should serve as an *example* to other careless drivers.

____ Modern air travel is an *example* of the progress that has been made in transportation.

____ The boy tried to act as a good *example* to his four younger brothers.

hand, 1. the end part of an arm; part that a person grasps and holds things with. 2. a hired worker who uses his hands: *a factory hand.* 3. give with the hand; pass; pass along: *Please hand me the butter.* 4. part or share in doing something: *He had no hand in the matter.*

____ Anne walked across the room to *hand* her father the magazine.

____ Jack decided that he would like to spend the summer working as a farm *hand*.

____ The principal believed Frank when he said that he had not had a *hand* in preparing or in circulating the petition.

draft, 1. current of air. 2. device for regulating a current of air: *Opening the draft of a furnace makes the fire burn faster.* 3. a rough copy: *He made three different drafts of his speech before he had it in final form.* 4. selection of persons for some special purpose: *In time of war men are often supplied to the army and navy by draft.*

____ Jim and several of his friends have already received their *draft* notices.

____ The members of the student council prepared several *drafts* of the "Code of Behavior" before presenting it to the student body.

____ The door was blown shut by a *draft* from the open window.

cop·y, 1. thing made to be just like another; thing made on the pattern or model of another. A written page, a picture, a dress, or a piece of furniture can be an exact copy of another. 2. make a copy; make a copy of. 3. be like; imitate. 4. one of a number of books, newspapers, magazines, pictures, etc., made at the same printing: *Get six copies of today's newspaper.*

____ The landscape hanging above the fireplace was an excellent *copy* of a famous painting.

____ Mrs. Miller looked everywhere for the March *copy* of the fashion magazine in which she had seen the dress advertised.

____ Joe decided to *copy* the diagram in his notebook so that he could refer to it later.

____ Jane did not realize that she was trying to *copy* everything that her older sister did.

The Language of Sports

The paragraphs below were adapted from articles in the sports section of a weekly news magazine. After each paragraph, write the name of the sport that is being described. Then underline the words and phrases that gave you your clues.

Last week State attacked with a vengeance. Halfback Barry slammed through the opposing line for the first touchdown soon after the kick-off, then sprinted 82 yards to score a second time. State added two more touchdowns in the fourth quarter. Butterfingered Central lost eight of its nine fumbles, completed only one pass, while State romped to a 26–0 triumph.

On her second self-propelled crossing of the channel, Joan Bauman set a new speed record, splashing ashore 15 hr. 55 min. after leaving the other side. Her time was eleven minutes faster than the record.

In the semifinals of the regatta Monroe's unbeaten 150-lb. eight loafed to the finish line far ahead of Reed's crew. In the finals Monroe didn't dally, and pulled rapidly through the choppy waters of the Thames to beat Britain's oarsmen and win the silver cup by an impressive length.

On the final green Laird needed a birdie three to tie Edwards. An 11-ft. downhill putt would have done it. The ball rimmed the edge of the cup, but it refused to drop.

Head Man trailed Easy Ace the entire mile and a furlong at Jamaica, finished 2½ lengths back, but was awarded first place after films showed Easy Ace bore out and cut off Head Man in the stretch.

Kay glided into the "school figures," the required set of tight patterns that each contestant had to trace and retrace with geometric certainty. She was careful to lean so that she rode on only one edge of her hollow-ground blades, giving the appearance of complete control. The five judges watched her intricate gyrations, listened to the whisper of steel on ice, inspected the size of the circles, the accuracy of her retracings, the telltale scrapings that signified "flats."

Pro teams have plenty of men who match Smith's colossal height, and they would chop him to size if he stuck to playing off the boards. This center will have to develop a variety of offensive skills: hook and jump shots from close in, set shots from outside, driving lay-ups from the give-and-go.

In the Jamestown net tourney, Norman Wilson served the first ball. His powerful forehand and backhand drives kept his opponent on the base line. Then he dropped a short shot over the net to take that set. Trouncing John Park, 6-3, 6-2, Wilson won the final match and applause from the enthusiastic gallery.

Wringing a few more figures out of their record books, score-keeping fans found that five of the best nine pitchers in the American League were left-handers. Best of all was the Chicago White Sox player with an earned run average of 1.97.

Consonant Sounds

Pronounce the word above each group of three pictures and think of the sound that the boldface consonant letter or letters stand for.

Then say the name of each picture in the group and decide whether you hear this consonant sound at the beginning, *in the* middle, *or at the* end *of the word. Show where you hear it in each word by writing the letter in the first, middle, or last blank under the picture.*

The first group is marked for you. Complete this and the next page.

t e n

t __ __ __ t t __ t __

m i l k

__ __ __ __ __ __ __ __ __

j a m

__ __ __ __ __ __ __ __ __

d i s h

__ __ __ __ __ __ __ __ __

n a i l

__ __ __ __ __ __ __ __ __

r a i n

__ __ __ __ __ __ __ __ __

g i f t

__ __ __ __ __ __ __ __ __

p a n

  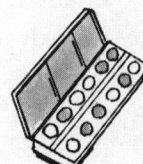

__ __ __ __ __ __ __ __ __

l a k e

__ __ __ __ __ __ __ __ __

y e l l o w

 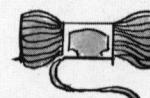 

__ __ __ __ __ __ __ __ __

head

 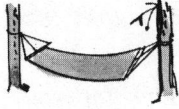 

_ _ _ _ _ _ _ _ _

keep

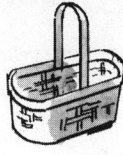  

_ _ _ _ _ _ _ _ _

wind

 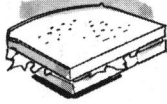 

_ _ _ _ _ _ _ _ _

back

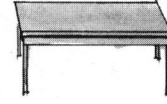 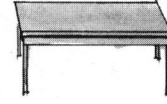 

_ _ _ _ _ _ _ _ _

zoo

_ _ _ _ _ _ _ _ _

vine

  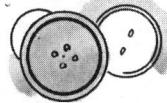

_ _ _ _ _ _ _ _ _

top

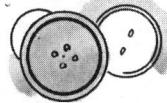  

_ _ _ _ _ _ _ _ _

fun

_ _ _ _ _ _ _ _ _

salt

_ _ _ _ _ _ _ _ _

bang

_ _ _ _ _ _ _ _ _

child

  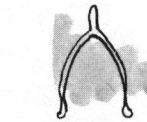

_ _ _ _ _ _ _ _ _

shop

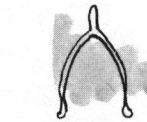  

_ _ _ _ _ _ _ _ _

thick

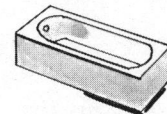  

_ _ _ _ _ _ _ _ _

when

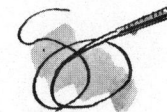 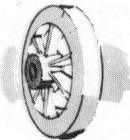

_ _ _ _ _ _ _ _ _

Consonant Blends

Pronounce the words below, and think of the consonant sounds that you blend together at the beginning of each one. Underline the letters that make up this consonant blend. The first one is done for you.

b̲l̲ a s t	f r a m e	s k i l l	s p r a w l
g l a n c e	b r a n c h	s p e e d	s t r a i g h t
c l i f f	p r i c e	s t a r v e	s p l a s h
p l a n e	t r a p	s n e e z e	t h r e a t
f l a s h	d r i n k	s w i f t	s c r a p e d

Think of the name of each pictured object. Then write the missing consonant blend in each blank to complete the name of the object.

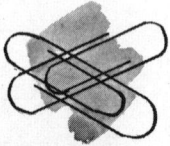 ------ ips

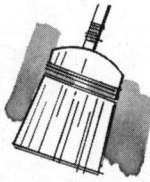 ------ oom

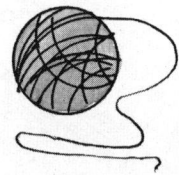 ------ ing

 ------ ower

 ------ ail

 ------ ate

 ------ apes

 ------ ade

 ------ uck

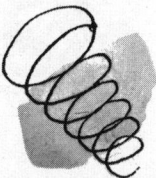 ------ ing

 ------ ead

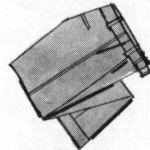 ------ acks

Pronounce each of these words and think of the consonant blend or blends you hear in each one. Underline the consonant blends.

a f r a i d	i n c l u d e	f l a v o r	t e l e s c o p e
e m b l e m	p e r s p i r e	d e g r e e s	s l e n d e r
c r i m s o n	c o m p l e t e	s m o l d e r	c e l e b r a t e
c o n s t r a i n	s p l e n d i d	d e s c r i b e	s k e l e t o n
f o r e s t	s w e a t e r	g l i m m e r	t h r o t t l e
p r o t r u d e	s n o w d r o p	s p r i n k l e	e y e b r o w

The sounds of the consonants ____, ____, or ____ blend easily with almost all other consonant sounds to form consonant blends.

Which Sound Is It?

The letter c *may stand for the* k *sound as in* cat *or for the* s *sound as in* city. *Write the letter* k *or* s *below each* c *in these words to show what sound the letter* c *stands for.*

The letter s *may stand for the* s *sound as in* sad *or for the* z *sound as in* runs. *Write the letter* s *or* z *under each* s *in these words to show what sound the letter* s *stands for.*

a n n o u n c e --	c o r r i d o r --
c a r e e r --	c o n c e a l -- --

m e r c y
    --
	b r a c e l e t
	      --

c i r c u l a t e -- --	p e c u l i a r --
e d u c a t i o n --	c i r c u s -- --
b r o a d c a s t --	c o m i c a l -- --
c i r c u m s t a n c e -- -- --	c y l i n d e r --

a n s w e r
  --
	m i s t a k e n
	    --

s a t i s f y -- --	w e a s e l --

m u s e u m
    --
	p e r s u a d e s
	    -- --

s e a s o n -- --	d r o w s y --
p r e s e r v e --	s a l u t e s -- --

w h i s p e r
    --
	n o i s i l y
	    --

n o n s e n s e -- --	s u r p r i s e -- --

The letter g *may stand for the* g *sound as in* gun *or for the* j *sound as in* gentle. *Write the letter* g *or* j *under each* g *in these words to show what sound the letter* g *stands for.*

The letters ch *may stand for the* ch *sound as in* child, *the* k *sound as in* chorus, *or the* sh *sound as in* chute. *Write* ch, k, *or* sh *under each* ch *in these words to show what sound* ch *stands for.*

c o u r a g e --	g a r b a g e -- --
g a d g e t -- --	r e g u l a r --

a p o l o g i z e
    --
	e n g a g e
	  -- --

d r a g o n
    --
	g u i l t y
	  --

g i g a n t i c -- --	g o r g e o u s -- --

e n g i n e e r
  --
	a r g u e d
	    --

g o r i l l a --	i m a g i n e --

b u t c h e r
    ---- 	
	m e r c h a n t
	    ---- 	

c h e m i s t ----	t e a c h e r ----
C h i c a g o ----	h e a d a c h e ----
s t o m a c h ----	c h e e s e ----
c h a m p i o n ----	c h a r a c t e r ----

o r c h e s t r a
    ---- 	
	m a t c h e s
	    ---- 	

m e c h a n i c ----	c h i v a l r y ----

When the letter *c* is followed by *e*, *i*, or *y* in a word, the *c* usually stands for the ____ sound. When *c* is followed by *a*, *o*, or *u*, it usually stands for the ____ sound.
When the letter *g* is followed by *e* or *i* in a word, it often stands for the ____ sound. When *g* is followed by *a*, *o*, or *u*, it usually stands for the ____ sound.

Vowel Sounds

On each part of the page, say the numbered words to yourself and think of the vowel sound you hear in each one. Then show which vowel sound you hear in the name of each picture below by putting the number of the key word in front of the picture.

1. it   2. ice

----   ----   ----   ----   ----

1. let   2. be   3. her

----   ----   ----   ----   ----

1. hot   2. go   3. or

----   ----   ----   ----   ----

1. hat   2. ate   3. care   4. far

  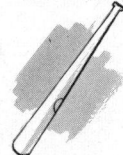 

----   ----   ----   ----   ----

1. up   2. suit   3. put   4. use

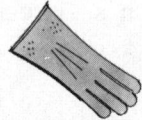 

----   ----   ----   ----   ----

1. boil   2. out

   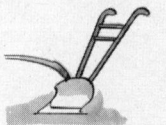

----   ----   ----   ----   ----

*In each group underline the words in which you hear the same
vowel sound as you hear in the italicized word at the top.*

a as in *ate*

display	mane
tackle	
lard	sale

a as in *hat*

faint	cracker
pantry	
clasp	explain

a as in *far*

garden	date
department	
advice	articles

a as in *saw*

naughty	sprawl
crate	
yawn	hall

a as in *care*

pair	tame
compare	
square	squash

e as in *be*

sleeve	elm
deed	
neat	elbow

e as in *let*

professor	peaceful
health	
tempt	clenched

e as in *her*

message	person
mercy	
perched	reverse

i as in *ice*

bicycle	flight
lizard	
polite	require

i as in *it*

whisk	giant
litter	
lighter	whisper

i as in *bird*

committee	whirl
thirsty	
third	swish

o as in *go*

oatmeal	crock
telephone	
bowl	wrote

o as in *for*

produce	morning
impossible	
perform	greenhorn

o as in *hot*

mob	border
stroke	
confident	copper

u as in *put*

lump	pudding
bushel	
sputter	push

u as in *burn*

tube	stuff
church	
turn	hurt

u as in *cup*

tub	July
puzzle	
fuel	hush

u as in *use*

butter	cute
uniform	
chum	argue

Do You Hear the Same Vowel Sound?

In the spellings of words, different vowel letters may stand for the same vowel sound.

Read the phrase at the left of each group of words, and think of the vowel sound you hear in the italicized word. Underline the words in the line that contain the same vowel sound as the italicized word.

a silk *tie*—eye .... aisle .... string .... tile .... pie .... dye .... cry .... night .... buy

easy *chair*—there .... chains .... bear .... their .... pearl .... fair .... stairs .... dare

fish pond—thirst .... sieve .... hymns .... find .... since .... shine .... built .... which

ear of *corn*—horn .... caught .... hawk .... work .... all .... fold .... storm .... ought

foreign *stamp*—stage .... patch .... ate .... drag .... laugh .... park .... walk .... plaid

fishing *boat*—road .... though .... toes .... drops .... sew .... rope .... bold .... snow

brown *leaf*—head .... team .... brief .... bee .... ski .... lie .... key .... piece .... eat

bright *star*—stand .... carve .... scarce .... heart .... fact .... mean .... parch .... farm

ice *cubes*—use .... view .... feud .... dust .... plunge .... few .... cue .... luck .... mule

red apples—shell .... meat .... friends .... said .... feed .... went .... says .... bread

strange *noise*—boy .... point .... cloud .... joint .... joy .... moist .... bray .... voices

science *book*—took .... good .... push .... tooth .... full .... could .... south .... should

green *ferns*—shirt .... learn .... burn .... term .... wires .... fort .... word .... first

small *house*—plow .... show .... bough .... proud .... four .... howl .... sound .... tow

clothes *brush*—burst .... come .... lunch .... stunt .... tough .... flood .... pool .... does

spice *cake*—weigh .... raced .... steak .... bank .... they .... train .... vein .... tray

alarm *clock*—bolt .... odd .... mock .... cord .... cone .... dodge .... watch .... loud

silver *spoon*—shoe .... bruise .... rule .... move .... blue .... grew .... soup .... moon

Clues to Vowel Sounds

Here are five clues that will help in determining which vowel sound you would expect to hear in a one-syllable word:

1. As in *hat*, *let*, *it*, *hot*, and *cup*, a single vowel letter at the beginning or in the middle is a clue to a short vowel sound.

2. As in *we*, *by*, and *go*, a single vowel letter at the end is a clue to a long vowel sound.

3. As in *rain*, *day*, *dream*, *feel*, and *boat*, two vowel letters together are a clue to a long vowel sound.

4. As in *age*, *these*, *ice*, *bone*, and *cube*, two vowel letters, one of which is final *e*, are a clue to a long vowel sound.

5. As in *far*, *bird*, *her*, *horn*, *care*, *hair*, and *there*, a vowel letter followed by *r* is a clue to a vowel sound that is neither long nor short.

In the blank before each word, write the number of the statement above that would help you determine the vowel sound in the word.

____ sky	____ sort	____ match	____ germ
____ grab	____ brick	____ note	____ least
____ claim	____ slack	____ where	____ knock
____ bench	____ steam	____ toad	____ glide
____ pride	____ raid	____ ink	____ up
____ sharp	____ perch	____ me	____ flare
____ bleak	____ mule	____ goal	____ stone
____ no	____ blush	____ melt	____ add
____ jeep	____ gray	____ daze	____ seem
____ lair	____ air	____ curb	____ fuse
____ cane	____ cede	____ odd	____ cork
____ dirt	____ mail	____ crate	____ stop
____ blunt	____ ebb	____ firm	____ hurl
____ code	____ stare	____ crisp	____ try
____ toast	____ she	____ chart	____ coach
____ prompt	____ stay	____ heel	____ scar

Bill climbed up into the huge oak tree to get a better look at the surrounding country. Then for at least five minutes he just sat on a limb and enjoyed the scene that stretched out before his eyes. Suddenly he became aware that he was not entirely alone. He could hear the cheep of a thrush, the croak of a frog, and the buzz of a bee. Several jays began to screech and some crickets started to chirp. A flock of ducks flew by over the treetops.

On the ground beneath him Bill saw a skunk with a white stripe down his back. He saw a beaver sink its sharp teeth into the tender bark of a beech sapling. A shy doe peeked from a clump of elms and then stepped daintily into the open. A fox squirrel scampered toward the trunk of a nearby pine tree.

In many of the words in the above paragraphs you hear only one vowel sound. In the spelling of some of these words you will find clues to a short vowel sound, a long vowel sound, or a vowel sound controlled by r. *List as many of these words as you can find under the correct headings below.*

Two vowel letters together in a word as in *train, day, beat, feed, coat:* ------------------------------
----

A single vowel letter at the end of a word as in *no, fly, she:* ------------------------------
----

Two vowel letters, one of which is final *e*, in a word as in *cane, kite, cone, cube:* ------------
----

A vowel letter followed by *r* in a word as in *car, bird, her, corn, chair:* ------------------------
----

A single vowel letter at the beginning or in the middle of a word as in *ant, bent, in, hot, cup:* ------
----

Consonant and Vowel Sounds—Dictionary Symbols

In the pronunciations on this page, each consonant letter stands for its most common sound, and each vowel letter stands for its short sound.

Look at each picture and the four pronunciations below it. Check the pronunciation that is the name of the picture.

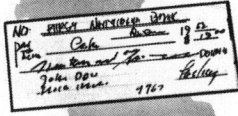

____ (klas)	____ (dek)	____ (dim)	____ (not)	____ (kud)
____ (gras)	____ (flek)	____ (brij)	____ (rok)	____ (buk)
____ (bras)	____ (rek)	____ (lim)	____ (nob)	____ (duk)
____ (glas)	____ (chek)	____ (brig)	____ (sok)	____ (kub)

In each part below are the pronunciations of four words and the meanings of these words. Pronounce each word and then write the number of the pronunciation beside the correct definition.

1. (laf)   ____ a young sheep
2. (lam)   ____ show amusement
3. (stak)   ____ a large bag
4. (sak)   ____ a pile of anything

1. (nek)   ____ hit; strike a blow
2. (nik)   ____ special skill
3. (nak)   ____ part of the body
4. (nok)   ____ notch; groove

1. (ej)   ____ a large deer
2. (egz)   ____ other; different; instead
3. (els)   ____ side
4. (elk)   ____ what a hen lays

1. (pil)   ____ write the letters of a word
2. (spil)   ____ medicine
3. (spel)   ____ exchange for money
4. (sel)   ____ let run or fall

1. (klok)   ____ a door fastening
2. (lok)   ____ a narrow bed
3. (klog)   ____ fill up; choke up
4. (kot)   ____ instrument for showing time

1. (fiks)   ____ mend or repair
2. (fuj)   ____ an enclosure or barrier
3. (foks)   ____ kind of soft candy
4. (fens)   ____ a wild animal

1. (luv)   ____ a young dog
2. (kup)   ____ covering for the hand
3. (pup)   ____ dish to drink from
4. (gluv)   ____ strong affection

1. (chans)   ____ a game
2. (ches)   ____ unpleasant coldness
3. (chil)   ____ narrow opening; crack
4. (chingk)   ____ opportunity

1. (kwit)   ____ stop; leave
2. (kwiz)   ____ bed cover
3. (kwik)   ____ test the knowledge of
4. (kwilt)   ____ fast and sudden; swift

1. (krush)   ____ roughly built hut
2. (shak)   ____ wash or clean by rubbing
3. (sik)   ____ having some disease
4. (skrub)   ____ squeeze together violently

Vowel Sounds and Dictionary Symbols

In dictionary pronunciations a mark over a vowel letter indicates a certain vowel sound. These marks are called diacritical marks.

Look at the pictures and decide which key word at the bottom of the page has the same vowel sound as the object pictured. Write the key word under each picture.

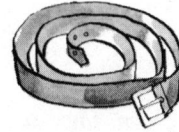

--------- --------- --------- --------- ---------

--------- --------- --------- --------- ---------

--------- --------- --------- ---------

One of the three pronunciations below each sentence is right for the missing word. Use the key at the bottom of the page to help you say the pronunciations to yourself. Then draw a line under the right one.

In places where moonlight did not penetrate the forest, the trail was ____ too clear.

    (nōn)   (nun)   (nün)

In the springtime the scent of blossoms fills the warm, ____ air with fragrance.

    (mōst)   (mist)   (moist)

When Henry weighed the letter, he found it was an ____ over the air-mail limit.

    (ōnz)   (on)   (ouns)

Dorothy's grandfather maintained that sunshine was the best ____ for a cold.

    (kôr)   (kūr)   (kär)

The letter Ben Hall received from his sister in June, 1673, was written with a ____ pen.

    (kwil)   (kwāl)   (kwel)

Thunder and lightning are ____ on some of the South Pacific Islands, even in rainy seasons.

    (rãr)   (rēr)   (rôr)

As the river flows toward the south, it follows a path that is one ____ after another.

    (kärv)   (kėrv)   (krāv)

The farmer made a special trip to the city to buy ____ for the spring planting.

    (sed)   (sēd)   (sīd)

hat, āge, cãre, fär; let, ēqual, tėrm; it, īce; hot, ōpen, ôrder; oil, out; cut, pů̇t, rüle, ūse

What Does a Sentence Tell You?

*Read each sentence carefully. Then answer the questions below it
by underlining or checking the correct answer for each question.*

Jim's brother swept the sidewalk in front of George Day's hot-dog stand.

Who swept the walk?

Jim   George Day   Jim's brother

What did George Day sell?

animals   sandwiches   groceries

The changing light of the sinking sun bathed the huge cactus plants and the great stretches of sand in rainbow colors.

What time of day was it?

noon   dawn   evening

Where did this take place?

in the mountains   by a waterfall   in the desert

The applause, continuing long after the final curtain, brought tears to the soloist's eyes.

How did the soloist feel?

worried   elated   bored

When did tears fill the soloist's eyes?

---- near the end of the performance

---- at the beginning of the performance

---- after the performance was over

Before her neighbors arrived with a welcome picnic lunch, Mrs. Dix arranged all the furniture that the movers had delivered that morning.

What did Mrs. Dix do first?

---- ate a picnic lunch

---- put chairs, tables, and other things in place

---- helped load the moving van

When did the neighbors arrive?

at noon   after dark   before breakfast

While he waited for gasoline, Mr. Smith asked which would be the shortest route to Chicago.

Where was Mr. Smith?

on a highway   in a filling station   in Chicago

Whom did he ask about the routes?

Mrs. Smith   a Chicago friend   the attendant

How was he traveling?

in an automobile   in an airplane   in a train

Smiling passengers thanked the pilot, who had flown them through the thick gray mist to a safe landing on the icy runway.

What kind of weather was it?

sunny and cold   warm and dry   foggy and cold

How did the pilot probably look?

amazed   scornful   pleased

Unless Al improved his grades, all his efforts to make the freshman team would be lost.

Why did Al have to improve his grades?

---- to stay on the team

---- to get on the team

---- to travel with the team

What would keep Al off the team?

indifference   lack of practice   low grades

Moonlight bleached the trail as the boys began their ascent to Red Rock Cabin, a halfway house far above the shadowy canyon.

How did the trail look to the boys?

dark   white   bluish

Where did they plan to sleep?

on the mountaintop   in the cabin   in the valley

Pronouns, such as her, it, them, *and* that, *often cause trouble for the reader unless he keeps in mind the person or thing that each pronoun stands for. Read the sentences below. Then write on the blank line the word or words for which the italicized pronoun stands.*

1. Kathy Johnson had often dreamed of having a mechanical maid in *her* kitchen—*one* that would scrub the floor, dispose of garbage, scrape the dishes and then wash and dry *them*.

her _____

one _____

them _____

2. Then at a Miracle Kitchen exhibit, Kathy thought *her* dreams had come true. She saw a mechanical maid *whose* "brain" was located in a planning desk from *which* electronic messages were beamed to put appliances to work.

her _____

whose _____

which _____

3. A fashion model was demonstrating the exhibit, in *which she* represented Mrs. Homemaker. With a touch of *her* finger on the control board, she sent a serving cart-dishwasher unit to the dining room with dishes for setting the table.

which _____

she _____

her _____

4. After the meal, Mrs. Homemaker's dishes were placed in the unit, and *it* went scooting back to *its* nest in the wall to wash *them* and dispose of the waste.

it _____

its _____

them _____

5. Also on display was a mobile floor cleaner *that* was operated by push button. *It* automatically scrubbed Mrs. Homemaker's kitchen floor, then returned to its cabinet and instantly recharged *itself* with a washing agent and water, in preparation for the next scrubbing job.

that _____

It _____

itself _____

6. Seated at *her* control center, Mrs. Homemaker could operate an automatic meal maker that plucked prepared foods out of storage and sent *them* on to compartments for cooling, warming, or cooking.

her _____

them _____

7. Kathy discovered to her amazement that the Miracle Kitchen also had a device called an electronic memory *that* automatically informed the grocer when canned goods were used so that *he* could send replacements for *them*.

that _____

he _____

them _____

8. Food-storage shelves lowered *themselves* from *their* wall cabinets; the refrigerator moved down from *its* wall cabinet; vegetable storage bins glided out at a wave of the model's hand.

themselves _____

their _____

its _____

9. Kathy was fascinated by another mechanism— a dispenser *that* automatically opened a can of food and emptied it. *This* done, *it* destroyed the container.

that _____

This _____

it _____

10. Kathy Johnson wanted to order these electronic wonders immediately, but *she* discovered that they are still in the research stage and that the reaction of the general public will determine whether *they* are to be available for *her* home of the future.

she _____

they _____

her _____

When Did It Happen?

In each sentence below, two things happen. The word before *or* after *in a sentence is a clue that the two actions take place at different times. The words* while, as, *or* when *are clues that both things happen at the same time.*

Read each sentence and then decide when the two actions listed below each sentence took place. If they happened at different times, write 1 in front of the first action and 2 in front of the last. If the two things took place at the same time, write the letter S before both.

Before Sue unlocked the door, she saw her sister running toward the house.

____ Sue unlocked the door

____ Sue saw her sister

As he watched the movie, Ed wished that he could sail across the Pacific Ocean on a raft.

____ wished he could cross the ocean on a raft

____ watched a movie

Willie squeezed through the line at the curb when he heard the band coming up the street.

____ heard the band coming

____ squeezed through the crowd

Caroline typed all the information she needed for her science notebook before she returned the books to the library.

____ typed all the needed information

____ returned the books to the library

When he drove around the block in search of a parking place, Philip saw several people that he knew.

____ saw some friends

____ drove around the block

The driver went home after he transferred the load of machinery parts to the truck that was scheduled to leave for Texas the next morning.

____ went home

____ transferred the load

As she joined the party, Ann saw a birthday cake on the table in the dining room.

____ joined the party

____ saw a cake on the table

Don had to get a clean bath towel from the linen closet before he took his shower.

____ took his shower

____ found a clean bath towel

After the Wright brothers tried out their first flying machine on the dunes at Kitty Hawk, they rebuilt the engine.

____ tried out the machine

____ rebuilt the engine

While he mowed the lawn, George sang all the songs he could remember.

____ mowed the lawn

____ sang the songs he remembered

After studying the record of his earnings, Sam figured out how much he could put in his savings account each month.

____ decided how much money he could save

____ studied the record of his earnings

Gordon painted all the porch chairs bright green while his sister Nora made the new white pillow covers.

____ Gordon painted the chairs

____ Nora made the pillow covers

How Are the Ideas in a Sentence Related?

Each sentence below expresses two ideas. The ideas are related, but one can stand alone as a complete sentence and the other cannot. The idea that cannot stand alone is introduced by such words as when, if, *or* because; *these words show the relationship between the two ideas.*

Draw a line under the idea that is complete and therefore can stand alone. Then, on the line below, write the word that introduces the incomplete idea. Beside it, write either time, reason, *or* condition *to show the relationship between the two parts of the sentence. The first three are done for you.*

As the huge structure burned, <u>sooty clouds of smoke billowed skyward.</u>

......*as   time*..........................

<u>The butcher was despondent</u> because he had so few customers.

......*because   reason*..........................

<u>Sally agreed to pay her brother's admission to the neighborhood movie</u> if he would help her dig clams on the beach.

......*if   condition*..........................

As the storm grew worse, the ship strained at its moorings.

While Ben was in San Francisco, he took a picture of the Golden Gate Bridge.

James would not buy one of the red caps because he realized that they were just a fad.

When he saw the destruction caused by water, the governor decided to take some action about flood control.

William could not fasten the new vise to his workbench in the basement because he had lost the clamp.

As Dan was taking his morning walk, he saw three reapers working together in one of the largest fields.

Mrs. Ellis was angry with the painter because he had splashed enamel on her new green and white tiled floor.

While the father was fishing on the rocks, the children stayed on the bridge.

If the lumber arrives today, the carpenter will be able to make our new picnic table.

The hunter could not see the alligator because it was submerged in the water.

The wrecked car will obstruct traffic if it is not removed.

After he had heard the treasurer's report, the president insisted that all expenses be listed in the final report.

If Anita had broken the dish deliberately, her mother would have scolded her.

Saying Things in Different Ways

In each group of three sentences below, two sentences express about the same general idea, although not in just the same words. The other sentence has a slightly different meaning. Check the two sentences in each group that say about the same thing. Pay special attention to the words that point up the relationship of ideas within the sentence.

Cora knew the light would change eventually if she would just be patient.

As she waited for the traffic light to change, Cora was hardly able to restrain her eagerness to get across the street.

Cora stood at the intersection impatiently waiting for the light to turn green.

As he listened to Walt's angry outburst, Mack considered giving him a punch in the jaw.

While the blistering tirade continued, Mack clenched his fists in readiness for a fight.

After Walt's tantrum had finally come to an end, Mack realized that he must not be too quick with his fists.

Although the classes were assembled to commemorate a solemn occasion, there was an air of gaiety in the auditorium.

Whenever the group gathered, its members had to be warned frequently about engaging in tomfoolery.

Despite the importance of the occasion, there was a great deal of light-hearted chattering among the students.

After Dick was made a member of the team, his time was almost completely taken up with football practice.

Dick had trouble finding time in which to keep up with other activities once he made the football team.

When Dick accepted the position of fullback, he planned his time so that he could continue with his former interests.

After relining the brakes, the mechanic tested the speedometer on the car.

The mechanic tested the speedometer of the car and then relined the brakes.

Before he tested the speedometer of the automobile, the garage mechanic finished the job of relining the brakes.

Karen stamped angrily out of the gallery because her poster had not won a prize.

As she stalked out of the art gallery, Karen kept insisting that her poster had been judged unfairly.

Karen's poster did not even receive an honorable mention, and she continued to dispute the judge's decision as she left the gallery.

Mary was delighted at the prospect of going to Washington until she realized that if she went she would miss the class party.

Mary was not so happy over the prospect of going to Washington when she discovered the class party was scheduled for the same weekend.

Although Mary knew about the class party, she planned to go to Washington that weekend.

Announcement of the annual fancy-dress ball set Betty to mulling over the problem of a costume for weeks before the event occurred.

Before Betty finally chose a Cinderella costume, she browsed through several books that showed pictures of other fairy-tale characters.

After searching through the pictorial sections of costume books, Betty decided to wear a hoop-skirted dress and glass slippers.

Similes

A simile is a comparison introduced by the words like *or* as. *It compares two things that differ in most ways, but are strikingly alike in some way, such as:* Tom's face was as red as a beet.

Read each unfinished sentence. Then read the numbered parts of sentences at the right. Write in the blank space the number of the part that best completes each simile.

Leaves drifted down from the maple tree like ____.	1. a great waterfall
The frisky puppy was as hard to catch as ____.	2. children at recess
Yesterday's quiet brook now roars like ____.	3. a slippery eel
The chattering starlings were as noisy as ____.	4. a field of hay
The king's men cut down the enemy like ____.	5. tiny parachutes

He approached silently, picking his way like ____.	1. shoe leather
From the plane the cars on the road looked like ____.	2. a buzz saw
Raindrops on the grass sparkled like ____.	3. a wary cat
His voice was as monotonous as ____.	4. diamonds
The steak was as tough as ____.	5. crawling bugs

Steady rain beating on the roof sounded like ____.	1. a drifting canoe
The March wind swept the street as briskly as ____.	2. a withered apple
Grandfather's snore buzzed now and then like ____.	3. a broom
In the porch swing, Claude swayed as lazily as ____.	4. tap dancers
The old man's face had as many wrinkles as ____.	5. a motorboat

Complete each of these sentences with as many similes as you can.

Flames crawled across the roof like _____

_____

Frontiersman Daniel Boone was as brave as _____

_____

Cold and damp, the room was as uncomfortable as _____

_____

Three soldiers crept forward like _____

_____

Metaphors

A metaphor suggests or implies a comparison, without using the words like or as. For example, in the sentence Palm trees bombarded us with coconuts, *the palm trees are described as if they were cannons.*

In each sentence below, a word or phrase describes one thing as if it were something else. Complete the line under each sentence by writing in the thing the comparison suggests.

The swirling wind shuffled the leaves and then dealt them all again.

The leaves are described as if they were --

The carpenter zipped up the summer cottage for the winter.

The cottage is described as if it were --

The waves were leapfrogging toward the shore of the bay.

The waves are described as if they were --

Up ahead were huge brick chimneys contentedly smoking their morning pipes.

The chimneys are described as if they were --

The wind put its shoulder to the door and tried to force it off the hinges.

The wind is described as if it were --

At dawn the grass looked as if it had been starched with frost.

The grass is described as if it were --

On their shining tracks the waiting Diesel engines purred softly.

The engines are described as if they were --

Gliding and skimming over the road, a dust cloud traced loops and figure eights.

The dust cloud is described as if it were --

In the pitch-dark room the cat turned her glowing headlights in my direction.

The cat is described as if it were --

The soaking rain gave the earth an injection of life-giving serum.

The rain is described as if it were --

Swallows were stunt flying at low altitude over the red barn.

The swallows are described as if they were --

A flash of lightning danced across the sky, and thunder applauded in the distance.

The thunder is described as if it were --

Martin Campbell scoffingly said, "My sister talks in high gear and thinks in low."

The girl is described as if she were --

Irony

Sometimes people say one thing when they really mean just the opposite. After reading each part of this page, write on the dotted lines what you think each person meant by his last remark.

Suspense gripped the crowd of anxious and excited spectators on shore as the speedboat race neared its close. All of the boats pushed hard at the last turn but two were surging ahead of the others.

Jill and Barney Whittle could scarcely breathe as they watched their brother's boat, the *Seattle Queen*, slice through the crests of the waves. Neck and neck, speeding along with the *Queen*, was her old rival, the *Liberty*. The two boats seemed to fly across the surface of the water toward the finish line. Jill grasped the railing in front of her to keep her hands from quivering. Barney seemed frozen to the spot. Could the *Queen* win?

Almost at the finish line, the *Queen's* engine coughed and died. The *Liberty* won by a length. "Isn't that great luck!" Barney said.

What Barney really meant was ----------

For a long time, husky Gregory Wills stood and stared dejectedly out through the blurred window. Rain was pelting down steadily from the gloomy lead-colored sky. Today should have been an important day in Gregory's life. It was the morning of the final day in the annual city-wide baseball series—and it was raining! Gregory, a senior and the pitcher for his team, had been eagerly looking forward to this special morning. With shoulders hunched up, he leaned against the window and gazed dismally at the torrents of rain that poured out of the angry gray sky.

Finally he sat down in a nearby chair.

"Gosh," he said out loud, "what a perfect day for baseball!"

What Gregory really meant was ----------

"Any local bus that comes along will take you to the subway station," Bill said. "Then just ask someone there what train to take."

"Thanks," Dave said. "It must be easier than I thought to get around in the city."

Bill nodded. "Well, so long." And he walked away, leaving Dave standing on the street corner. In a few minutes a bus came along, and Dave boarded it without a second thought. After he had been riding for a time he decided to ask the driver how far it was to the subway station.

"Subway station!" the driver exclaimed. "This is an express bus. It doesn't make any more stops until Fifty-third Street. You'll have to get off there, and catch a bus going back north."

"Fine," Dave thought as he sat down again. "That's just what I want to do—ride back and forth on the bus lines for the rest of the day."

What Dave really meant was ----------

"Where did you and Sue go last night?" Bud asked Howard.

"It's a long story," Howard replied. "At the last minute Dad had to use the car, so I had no transportation. I persuaded my uncle to loan me his car, and it had a flat tire before I had gone a couple of miles. When I started to fix it, there was no jack. I had to walk back to my uncle's garage to get it. Finally I got the tire changed.

"But that's not all," he added. "When I got to Sue's house more than an hour late, she was so mad that she wouldn't even let me explain what had happened.

"You can see," Howard ended his story, "that it was really my night."

What Howard really meant was ----------

What Do the Sentences Mean?

1. It is disappointing to be unable to get tickets for a show you want to see.

Does this sentence mean that you would be glad if you were able to get the tickets? _ _ _ _ _ _ _ _ _ _ _ _

2. No one has the right to injure another person if he can help it.

Does this sentence mean that a person does not have the right to injure another person if he can help it? _ _ _ _ _ _ _ _ _ _ _ _

3. Henry's mother said, "I don't like it when you don't get my permission before taking the car."

Does this sentence mean that Henry's mother did not want him to drive the car? _ _ _ _ _ _ _ _ _ _ _ _

4. Even though you do not feel too unwell, you should rest for several days after an attack of the flu.

Does this sentence mean that you should rest if you do not feel well? _ _ _ _ _ _ _ _ _ _ _ _

5. Bob decided that no matter how much his sister laughed at him, he would not give up his plan to organize a jazz orchestra.

Does this sentence mean that Bob decided to continue with his plan? _ _ _ _ _ _ _ _ _ _ _ _

6. Not realizing that he had barely escaped being hit by a speeding car, the old man continued down the street as calmly as though he had never been in any danger.

Does this sentence mean that the old man was almost hit by the speeding car? _ _ _ _ _ _ _ _ _ _ _ _

7. Sally sighed with relief as she said, "Dad wasn't the least bit angry when I told him that the pup had chewed up his old slippers."

Does this sentence mean that Sally's father was somewhat angry? _ _ _ _ _ _ _ _ _ _ _ _

8. "It should be illegal to go slower than forty miles an hour on the superhighway," said Mr. Hall.

Does this sentence mean that Mr. Hall thought the speed limit on the superhighway should be forty miles an hour? _ _ _ _ _ _ _ _ _ _ _ _

9. The day on which Joseph decided to paint the garage was a bright Saturday, not unlike many other fall Saturdays.

Does this sentence mean that the weather was much better than usual on the day when Joseph decided to paint the garage? _ _ _ _ _ _ _ _ _ _ _ _

10. One should never go out in deep water in a flimsy homemade boat unless he wears a life preserver.

Does this sentence mean that one should wear a life preserver in a homemade boat? _ _ _ _ _ _ _ _ _ _ _ _

11. It was not that the members of the team did not like Chuck, but simply that they thought Phil would make a better captain.

Does this sentence mean that the boys did not like Chuck? _ _ _ _ _ _ _ _ _ _ _ _

12. The farmer warned his hired man not to neglect to latch the barnyard gate.

Does this sentence mean that the farmer wanted the gate latched? _ _ _ _ _ _ _ _ _ _ _ _

13. Miss Hill had forbidden the class to leave the room unless the fire bell rang.

Does this sentence mean that Miss Hill permitted the class to leave the room when the fire bell rang? _ _ _ _ _ _ _ _ _ _ _ _

14. The dog's owner disliked people who disliked dogs and he didn't mind telling them so.

Does this sentence mean that the owner of the dog disliked telling dog-haters that he did not like them? _ _ _ _ _ _ _ _ _ _ _ _

15. No matter how convinced you are that you are a skillful driver, don't get careless, for you aren't driving the other fellow's car.

Does this sentence mean that even a skillful driver should be careful not to drive another person's car? _ _ _ _ _ _ _ _ _ _ _ _

16. Never seek praise without being willing to give it.

Does this sentence mean that you should not seek praise if unwilling to give it? _ _ _ _ _ _ _ _ _ _ _ _

Root Words

*The italicized word in each sentence is a root word to which an ending
(-ing, -ed, -er, -est, -en, or -es) has been added.   Before the ending was
added, one of these changes was made in the root word:*

1.   the final consonant was doubled
2.   the final e was dropped
3.   the final y was changed to i

*Below each sentence write the root word from which the italicized word
was formed, the change made in the root, and the ending added.*

Lawrence spent most of Saturday afternoon *scrubbing* the basement floor.

Root word _____

Change in root _____

Ending added _____

New York and Chicago are the two largest *cities* in the United States.

Root word _____

Change in root _____

Ending added _____

Tests proved that the inventor's first machine was *safer* than the second one.

Root word _____

Change in root _____

Ending added _____

The *heaviest* snowfall of the year occurred unexpectedly in November.

Root word _____

Change in root _____

Ending added _____

Someone *estimated* that two thousand people would attend the concert.

Root word _____

Change in root _____

Ending added _____

People are *forbidden* to swim in areas that are not protected by lifeguards.

Root word _____

Change in root _____

Ending added _____

Robert gave every detail of the crash without *blaming* any one person for the accident.

Root word _____

Change in root _____

Ending added _____

Wires much *thinner* than hairs are used in some machines.

Root word _____

Change in root _____

Ending added _____

The *opposing* team managed to score in the last few minutes of play.

Root word _____

Change in root _____

Ending added _____

George *applied* for a summer job in one of Pittsburgh's largest steel mills.

Root word _____

Change in root _____

Ending added _____

The newspaper article *omitted* any mention of Mr. Brown's contribution to the project.

Root word _____

Change in root _____

Ending added _____

The president of the student council spoke in a *convincing* manner.

Root word _____

Change in root _____

Ending added _____

Prefixes Have Meaning

The prefixes un-, dis-, *and* non- *when added to words often mean* not *or* the opposite of. *One of these prefixes is missing from a word in the second sentence of each pair below. Put the proper prefix in the blank.*

Tom and Bill had not agreed on the picnic date.
Tom explained why he ____agreed with Bill.

Martha was not aware of the tap at the door.
She was ____aware, too, that the door opened.

The plane did not stop until it reached Chicago.
Sixty passengers were on the ____stop flight.

"I don't approve of that," said Susan.
"I think I've always ____approved of it."

The article Harold read failed to convince him.
He was still ____convinced by my explanation.

The cocker spaniel had not touched his food.
He left it ____touched all day.

The boy realized he had not obeyed the rules.
He readily admitted he had ____obeyed them.

No one had expected hot weather in October.
The ____expected weather surprised everyone.

Not all the club members paid dues.
The ____paying members were honorary ones.

Frank was not certain what the question meant.
He was ____certain about how to answer it.

The prefix in- *may also mean* not *or* the opposite of. *The spelling of the prefix* in-, *however, is usually changed to* im- *before words beginning with the letters* m *or* p; *to* ir- *before words beginning with* r; *and to* il- *before words beginning with* l. *Read each pair of sentences below and write the prefix* in-, im-, ir-, *or* il- *in the blank.*

Ed did not complete part of his science notebook.
Since it was ____complete, he got a poor grade.

Joe's handwriting was not legible.
Even he admitted it was too ____legible to read.

When Sue smiled, no one could resist her charm.
Her smile was ____resistible.

The new helicopter did not seem practical.
Tests soon proved it was ____practical.

The audience was not at all attentive.
The ____attentive audience disturbed the pianist.

The bus was not on a regular schedule.
Its ____regular schedule confused passengers.

The old kitchen was not convenient to work in.
Even though it was ____convenient, we liked it.

"The plants that were not mature died.
____mature plants can't survive frost," said Al.

The glee club had not had sufficient practice.
The practice had been ____sufficient.

It is not legal to hunt some animals at any time.
It is ____legal to hunt others out of season.

Prefixes Are Dictionary Entries

The italicized word in each sentence is made up of a familiar word and one of the prefixes defined below. Read each sentence. Next, decide which meaning of the prefix is used in the italicized word. Then write the meaning of the italicized word on the line below the sentence.

fore-, prefix meaning:
1. front; in front; at or near the front, as in *foredeck*.
2. before; beforehand, as in *foreknow, foresee*.

mis-, prefix meaning: bad or badly; wrong or wrongly, as in *misconduct, misprint*, and *misrule*.

pre-, prefix meaning: before in place, time, order, or rank, as in *prepay, prewar*.

re-, prefix meaning:
1. again; anew; once more, as in *reappear, rebuild, reheat, reopen*.
2. back, as in *recall, replace*.

semi-, prefix meaning:
1. half: *Semicircle=half circle*.
2. partly; incompletely: *Semicivilized=partly civilized*.
3. twice: *Semiannually=every half year, or twice a year*.

sub-, prefix meaning:
1. under; below, as in *subway, submarine*.
2. near, as in *subconscious*.
3. slightly; somewhat, as in *subacid*.
4. of less importance, as in *subhead*.

trans-, prefix meaning: across; over; through; beyond; on the other side of, as in *transcontinental*.

The *semimonthly* meeting of the Music Appreciation Club was held in the auditorium.

The word *semimonthly* means _____

The studio received many requests for the hour-long TV program to be *rebroadcast*.

The word *rebroadcast* means _____

No one could definitely *foretell* whether or not the experiment would be successful.

The word *foretell* means _____

The garage for the apartment was in the basement and the furnace room was in the *subbasement*.

The word *subbasement* means _____

Mr. Ferris rented a *semifurnished* room on the third floor of the building.

The word *semifurnished* means _____

Miss Chase carefully explained the test directions so that no one would *misinterpret* them.

The word *misinterpret* means _____

The *transatlantic* flight broke all existing speed records.

The word *transatlantic* means _____

The directions said to *preheat* the oven while mixing the ingredients for the cake.

The word *preheat* means _____

Within three months Henry *repaid* the money he had borrowed from his father.

The word *repaid* means _____

Phil looked at the main title of the article and then glanced at each *subtitle*.

The word *subtitle* means _____

Suffixes Have Meaning

-y, -ly, -er, -ish, -ful, -ness, -less

The word above each sentence is a root word to which some of these suffixes may be added. Read each sentence carefully. Then rewrite the italicized part of the sentence, using the root word with the appropriate suffix added to it. The first one is done for you.

use

"That old tire is *of no use* to me," Mr. Page told the garageman.

useless

polite

Everyone was impressed by the *polite behavior* of the students who attended the conference.

----

tune

Mr. Evans, the *man who tunes pianos*, had his name listed in the telephone book.

----

pain

Although the injury to Dave's knee was not serious, it was *causing him pain*.

----

harsh

Mr. James spoke *in a harsh manner* to the two boys who were loitering near the car.

----

point

"That really is a *story without a point*," Tony whispered to his friend Ben.

----

child

"Don't act *like a child*," Frannie warned her younger sister.

----

dry

The man was demonstrating the *machine that is used to dry clothes*.

----

hope

We were all *full of hope* that the sailors would be rescued from the sinking ship.

----

noise

"That boy is certainly *making a lot of noise*," complained Mrs. Mills.

----

alert

"Many accidents are prevented by *being alert*," commented Mr. Stoner.

----

expert

Mr. Williams complimented his daughter on handling the car *in an expert manner*.

----

brown

Immediately after the violent storm the water in the lake was *somewhat brown* in color rather than the usual blue-green.

----

cloud

For a long time, Margaret stood at the kitchen window and stared at the *sky, which was covered with clouds*.

Prefixes and Suffixes

Which word could you use instead of the italicized word or words in the sentences below?

unlabeled   relabeled   mislabeled

The boxes of handkerchiefs in the department store were *not labeled correctly*.

forefathers   fatherless   fatherly

One of Patrick O'Hare's *ancestors* was a store-keeper in an Irish village.

audible   semiaudible   inaudible

The violinist announced his encore, but the applause caused his words to be *only half heard*.

irregular   regularity   regularly

The western boundary of Tennessee along the Mississippi River is *not straight*.

projectionist   projection   projector

The movie was postponed because the *machine for projecting the picture on a screen* was out of order.

employee   employment   employer

The young engineer found *a job* at the University of South Dakota.

irresistible   resistance   unresisting

Because the urge to laugh was *too great to resist*, Bernice guffawed in class, even though she knew that she was liable to be scolded.

occupation   occupants   unoccupied

The new home was ready for the *people who were to live in it*, but the grounds had not yet been cleared of pieces of brick and stone.

displace   replace   placement

Mrs. Cory bought new plants to *take the place of* the geraniums that had been frozen.

mispronounce   pronounceable   pronunciation

After the English teacher put a list of unusual words on the blackboard, the students tried to give the right *sounds* for each word.

modesty   immodest   modestly

"You must have seemed *vain* to the rest of the class when you boasted about your prize in front of them," Cal's mother chided him.

friendly   friendship   friendless

During the American Revolution, there was little *friendly feeling* between the Tories and the patriots who supported the revolt.

plantation   planter   transplant

Mrs. Maynard decided that her garden would look prettier if she would *dig up and move* the iris to the bed south of the oak tree.

payable   repay   overpaid

Mrs. Pringle wondered whether she had *paid too much money to* the Mexican woman for the hand-woven shawl.

healthiness   unhealthy   healthful

Dave's Airedale was all right, but his Scottie was listless and looked *sick*.

undervalued   invaluable   valueless

Ross decided not to sell his album of stamps because the dealer *put too low a value on* it.

Root Words and Words Formed from Them

A root word retains one of its meanings when a prefix, suffix, or ending is added to it. In each part of this page you will find a root word and some of its meanings. The italicized words in the sentences below are formed from this root word. Decide which meaning of the root is used in each sentence. Then write the number of the meaning in front of the sentence. The first one is done for you.

> **stead y,** **1.** changing little; uniform; regular: *steady progress.* **2.** firmly fixed; firm; not swaying or shaking: *hold a ladder steady.* **3.** having good habits; reliable: *a steady young man.*

_ 3 _ The workers were chosen for their *steadiness* as well as for their ability.

_ _ _ _ Rain fell *steadily* all day Wednesday, flooding every street in town.

_ _ _ _ Henry noticed that the hook supporting the large, plate-glass mirror was *unsteady.*

_ _ _ _ After testing the two ladders, Tom decided the first one was much *steadier* than the second.

> **at tend,** **1.** be present at: *Children must attend school.* **2.** give care and thought; pay attention: *Attend to the laboratory instructions.* **3.** go with; accompany: *Noble ladies attend the queen.*

_ _ _ _ The engineer gave all his *attention* to the difficult job of modernizing the old building.

_ _ _ _ While *attending* the conference, Don met a friend he had not seen for years.

_ _ _ _ The bride's *attendants* wore pink dresses and carried bouquets of pink and white rosebuds.

_ _ _ _ Those in charge of the meeting were quite pleased by the large *attendance.*

> **di rect,** **1.** manage; control; guide: *The teacher directs the work of the pupils.* **2.** tell or show the way; give information about where to go, what to do, etc.: *Can you direct me to the railroad station?* **3.** proceeding in a straight line; straight: *a direct route. Overwork and great strain were the direct cause of his death.*

_ _ _ _ After reading the *directions* three times, John started to mark the test.

_ _ _ _ The doctor thought that worry was an *indirect* cause of the man's illness.

_ _ _ _ Mr. Williams was chosen as the *director* of the boys' club, which is located on Oak Street.

_ _ _ _ The policeman *directed* the motorist to the south gate of the county fairgrounds.

_ _ _ _ When the homing pigeon was released, it flew *directly* to its loft.

> **ob serve,** **1.** see and note; notice: *I observed nothing unusual about the package.* **2.** examine for some special purpose; study: *An astronomer observes the stars.* **3.** remark: *"Bad weather," the captain observed.* **4.** show regard for; celebrate: *observe the Sabbath.*

_ _ _ _ The weather *observers* studied the instruments carefully before making a report.

_ _ _ _ All stores were closed for the *observance* of Thanksgiving Day.

_ _ _ _ The scientists were especially interested in any *observable* changes in the polar icecaps.

_ _ _ _ Ray resented the stranger's *observation* that everyone who lived in Central City was a "hick."

_ _ _ _ Although astronomers saw the comet, it was *unobserved* by most people.

Which Words Are Related in Meaning?

In each group of phrases, three of the italicized words are related in meaning. They are formed from the same English root word. Even though you see some of the same letters in the fourth word, it comes from a different root word and has an entirely different meaning. Check the three phrases that contain words formed from the same root.

---- on a *rainy* day in March

---- *rainiest* day this month

---- snowing and *raining* all day

---- haunting *refrain* of a song

---- *countless* stars in the sky

---- largest *country* in the world

---- *recounted* the money in his pocket

---- *miscounted* the people present

---- hard-working *colonies* of ants

---- wooden pegs in *colonial* furniture

---- orders from an air-force *colonel*

---- last *colonist* to leave the fort

---- first *explosion* of an atom bomb

---- early French and English *explorers*

---- *explosives* used in fireworks

---- two *unexploded* shotgun shells

---- *decided* after numerous conferences

---- called a *decisive* American victory

---- two *decimal* points to the right

---- final *decision* of the judge

---- *overpass* on the superhighway

---- cars streaming through the *underpass*

---- warning about *impassable* roads

---- her great *passion* for music

---- airfield closed because of low *visibility*

---- *division* of opinion within the group

---- even numbers *divisible* by eleven

---- on the *dividing* line between two counties

---- crumbling *relic* of the Revolutionary War

---- *relies* upon his own efforts

---- listening to a *reliable* news commentator

---- more *reliant* members of the group

---- large city *amusement* park

---- most *amusing* remark of all

---- *unamused* by the whole affair

---- going to the art *museum*

---- determining the *purity* of the water

---- heard the cat *purring*

---- breathing *impure* air in the city

---- *purest* water in the town

---- *addition* of flour to the gravy

---- money for *additional* expenses

---- North Oak Street *address*

---- *adding* some rocks to the pile

---- beautiful *entrance* to the park

---- *reëntered* the building

---- *entertain* the audience in the auditorium

---- anyone *entering* by that door

---- many *inventive* people

---- several unwise *investments*

---- *invention* of gunpowder

---- *inventor* of the electric light

---- modern methods of *refrigeration*

---- *refrigerate* meat and fruit

---- locks removed from discarded *refrigerators*

---- three-masted *frigate* used in 1755

What Made the Sound?

A high-school class presented a play on the local radio station. The setting of the play was a lonely lighthouse on a stormy night. To make the atmosphere seem realistic, they used many varied sound effects.

The following paragraphs describe the sounds that occurred in the play. The sentences under the paragraphs describe things the sound-effects man did to make the radio listeners actually hear what happened. In each (   ) put the number of the thing you think the sound-effects man did to make that sound.

The steady beating of rain against the lighthouse windows (   ) is broken by a long, loud roll of thunder (   ). A terrific gale (   ) dashes huge waves against the stone foundation of the lighthouse (   ). The monotonous hissing of a beacon light (   ) high on the tower can be heard above the sounds of the storm.

Suddenly the hissing arc light sputters, gives one gasp (   ), and is silent. Through the howling gale (   ) sounds the foghorn (   ) of a distant freighter. The sound of the foghorn comes closer and closer. From the ship's wireless comes one frantic S O S (   ).

Just one call, and then at the very base of the lighthouse there is a mighty crash (   ) as the freighter hits the rocks. Men shout in wild confusion (   ). The boiler of the freighter suddenly explodes with a boom (   ), and steam rushes out (   ).

Then only the wind (   ), the beating rain (   ), and the dashing waves (   ) can be heard. The wrecked freighter sinks into the stormy sea.

1. He placed a record labeled "Fright (Male Voices Only)" on a turntable.

2. He sprinkled sand on tightly drawn cellophane.

3. He opened the valve of a compressed-air tank just enough to release a small, steady stream of air.

4. He worked a wind machine.

5. He vigorously rocked back and forth a container filled with water.

6. With one hand he grasped the handle on a big square sheet of metal and shook it vigorously; with the other hand he beat on a small drum.

7. He closed and opened the valve of the compressed-air tank and then shut the air off completely.

8. He quickly clicked out the code call for help on a telegraph key.

9. He struck one heavy blow on a bass drum.

10. He opened wide the valve of the compressed-air tank.

11. He placed a record labeled "Crash" on a turntable and crushed wooden strawberry boxes in his hands.

12. He placed a record labeled "Loud, Deep Horns" on the turntable.

Words That Make You See and Hear

A sentence like "The elephant made a noise" states a fact, but does not tell you what kind of sound the animal made. But when a writer says that the elephant "schlooped up a schloop of mud," or that someone fell into the water with a plop, you actually hear a particular kind of sound. In the lists below, number the words that describe a sound to match the thing that might make that kind of sound.

1. distant thunder	_ _ _ _ clackety-clack	1. an electric light switch	_ _ _ _ whoosh
2. soft tires rounding a curve	_ _ _ _ squish	2. a dog drinking	_ _ _ _ click
3. water-soaked shoes	_ _ _ _ crackle	3. eating peanut brittle	_ _ _ _ rustle
4. escaping steam	_ _ _ _ gurgle	4. an electric fan	_ _ _ _ crunch
5. a pebble dropping into a pond	_ _ _ _ screech	5. taffeta petticoats	_ _ _ _ clank
6. liquid poured from a full bottle	_ _ _ _ plunk	6. frying bacon	_ _ _ _ slup
7. dry twigs burning	_ _ _ _ rumble	7. waves on a rocky shore	_ _ _ _ sizzle
8. train wheels	_ _ _ _ hiss	8. links of an iron chain	_ _ _ _ whir

There are also many words to describe special ways of moving that can be used in place of such overworked words as "went." For example, a writer might say that an animal "scuffled down the bank and floundered into the water." Number the words below to match the thing that would move in that particular way.

1. a fat duck	_ _ _ _ cavort	1. a woman in high heels	_ _ _ _ scamper
2. idle people in a park	_ _ _ _ sprint	2. a car on a slippery street	_ _ _ _ meander
3. waves on a quiet day	_ _ _ _ saunter	3. mice after seeing a cat	_ _ _ _ bustle
4. an ailing old man	_ _ _ _ glide	4. a camel caravan in the desert	_ _ _ _ twirl
5. happy lambs	_ _ _ _ waddle	5. a busy housewife	_ _ _ _ stride
6. a scattered group of people	_ _ _ _ straggle	6. a shallow river in flat country	_ _ _ _ plod
7. an escaping robber	_ _ _ _ totter	7. sea gulls going after fish	_ _ _ _ mince
8. an expert skater	_ _ _ _ stampede	8. a top	_ _ _ _ skid
9. frightened cattle	_ _ _ _ ripple	9. an energetic, long-legged man	_ _ _ _ swoop

"Said" is a useful word, but it tells you nothing about the speaker's feelings or tone of voice. After each sentence below, write the number of the word that would tell more vividly or exactly how the speaker felt and how he sounded as he spoke.

1. begged

2. gushed

3. warned

4. bellowed

5. whined

6. boasted

7. mumbled

"Coach, if something isn't done to correct the grievances of the team, there'll be trouble," *said* Norman. _ _ _ _

"Please hurry, Doctor," *said* Mrs. Grey. "I'm afraid my little girl has diphtheria!" _ _ _ _

"Why do I have to eat these smelly old oysters, Mom?" Alfred *said*. _ _ _ _

"Oh, I do think your ruffled dress is simply gorgeous!" Ethel *said*. _ _ _ _

Ken *said* that he could win the match blindfolded. _ _ _ _

Agnes *said* something that the teacher couldn't understand. _ _ _ _

"Hey, don't you fellers know how to use a lariat?" *said* the foreman when he saw the mustang get away. _ _ _ _

What Is It?

A device authors sometimes use to make a story amusing is to describe something in terms that might lead you to picture one thing while they are really referring to something else. A good example of this little trick is found in the first paragraph of a story about a pony named Hatty:

We all went down to meet Hatty at the station. She was coming on the 2:15 from a farm about forty miles away, and this was going to be our first meeting. We had no idea what Hatty looked like. Edward said that he hoped she would be a blonde. . . .

If this were all that you knew about Hatty, what picture of her would you have in mind? _ _ _ _

_ _

_ _

. . . But Robert, although three years younger than Edward, corrected him scornfully. Blonde was the wrong word, Robert told him. One should say either bay or dun.

Underline the words that give you a clue as to Hatty's real identity. Why are they clues? _ _ _ _

_ _

_ _

Now see what impression you get from reading the paragraphs that follow.

Anita thought, "How can the flow continue to gush out at such a rate? One would think that even an ocean would dry up after such an outpouring." Still the apparently ceaseless stream rushed on and on and on.

What picture do you have in mind? _ _ _ _ _ _ _ _

_ _

_ _

Underline the words that gave this impression.

For a few minutes more Anita continued to listen in silence. Finally she could stand it no longer. "For heaven's sake, Lucy," she interrupted, "at least stop to catch your breath."

What is really being described? _ _ _ _ _ _ _

_ _

_ _

Jill's face was taut as she sat down at the keyboard. Her fingers felt numb, and her stomach seemed to be turning somersaults. Would she never conquer her fear at having to face a critical audience? She took a deep breath, sat up straight, and wiped her perspiring hands. It was now or never. Her career depended on her performance today.

What picture do you have in mind? _ _ _ _ _ _ _ _

_ _

_ _

Underline the words that gave this impression.

Determinedly, Jill began to strike the keys. Miraculously, letters registered on the sheet of paper, first in accurately spelled words, then in sentences.

"That's fine," Jill heard the supervisor say. "I think you'll do."

What is really being described? _ _ _ _ _ _ _

_ _

_ _

A sudden feeling of panic swept over Ron. All about him were swaying, rushing hordes. The intense heat seemed to be choking him. The roaring noise was deafening. Suddenly Ron felt a sharp pain in his foot as something heavy came down on his instep.

What do you picture happening here? _ _ _ _ _ _

_ _

_ _

Underline the words that gave this impression.

Shuddering, Ron stared about for some means of escape before he collapsed. At the moment he located an exit, he felt a powerful hand clasp his shoulder.

"Hi, Ron!" he heard his uncle's voice saying. "How do you like it? I understand that this is the first time you've been here during the Christmas rush season."

What is really being described? _ _ _ _ _ _ _

_ _

_ _

Using Sensory Imagery

Authors sometimes write descriptive details in such a way as to cause their readers to mentally see, hear, smell, taste, or feel the things being described. After each paragraph, indicate the sense to which you think the author meant chiefly to appeal—sight, sound, smell, taste, or touch.

As Kenneth started eating, his beaming face expressed his enjoyment. Thick, tender slices from the breast of roast turkey, great mounds of whipped potatoes, pools of well-seasoned gravy, a generous helping of sage dressing, tart cranberries, a peppery sauce, nippy apples in a salad, crusty biscuits dripping with honey—and then the spiciness of Grandmother's pumpkin pie.

Even at night the old barn was filled with life. The little mice scampered with swift, pattering feet across the floor of the loft and scurried down the walls. The horses in the stalls below shifted their feet about with muffled thuds, snorting now and then as the restless wind banged the creaking barn door. And through it all, subdued as a background of muted violins, came the ceaseless chirping of the crickets telling the moon of the harvest.

Flaming banners of bright crimson, interlaced with long ribbons of delicate lavender, streamed across the western sky. The sun, a blazing globe of flame, was just disappearing behind the snowy mountain peak. The tranquil waters of the mountain lake on which our canoe drifted reflected the beauty of the day's farewell.

Stinging needles of icy sleet cut into my face as I struggled onward against the fierce gale. It seemed as if I had been walking for an eternity. My feet were so cold that each step made me wince with anguish. The scarf that I had tied over my mouth for protection was hoary and brittle with frost and chafed my face. The heavy snow caught at my feet like grasping arms. How I longed for the genial warmth of my fireside!

Against the somber background of pines, the maples stood like dancers with outspread scarlet skirts, ready to swirl into the swift movement of a dance. Among them, at intervals, the silvery gleam of white birches could be seen. A little fleecy cloud floated slowly overhead as if unwilling to leave such a spot of beauty. But the wind pitilessly urged it onward.

Marvin awoke at daybreak. He could hear the cows addressing a chorus of complaining moos toward the back door, while the calves in a pen nearby added their plaintive voices to the din. The hens clucked noisily as their busy feet uncovered worms for breakfast. The ducks took off for the pond with loud quacks, and Rover interrupted a yawn to bark excitedly as he chased a squirrel away from the woodpile. Another day on the farm had begun.

As Don swung along the country road, his fishing rod pressed lightly against his shoulder, he thought happily of the pleasant day before him. The sun's rays beat warmly on his back, and the soft dust in the road felt good to his bare feet. Suddenly he uttered a cry. He had stubbed his toe on a sharp stone buried in the dust.

It was a great day to be alive. The air was crystal clear, and the morning breeze carried the salty freshness of the sea. As Mrs. Simpson stood in the doorway of the long-unused cabin, she forgot its stuffiness, the stifling smoke from the faulty chimney that wouldn't draw, and the telltale odor of woolen blankets long laid away in moth balls. She breathed deeply. She just couldn't get enough of the fresh sea air.

Mark Twain drew on memories of his own childhood when he wrote such books as Tom Sawyer *and* Huckleberry Finn. *This selection from his* Autobiography *describes some of his boyhood impressions of a farm where he used to visit.*

A Boy's Heaven

by Mark Twain

My uncle's farm was a heavenly place for a boy. I can call back still the solemn twilight and mystery of the deep woods, the earthy smells, the faint odors of the wild flowers, the sheen of rain-washed foliage, the rattling clatter of drops when the wind shook the trees, the far-off hammering of woodpeckers and the muffled drumming of wood pheasants in the remoteness of the forest, the snapshot glimpses of disturbed wild creatures scurrying through the grass—I can call it all back and make it as real as it ever was, and as blessed.

I can see the woods in their autumn dress, the oaks purple, the hickories washed with gold, the maples and the sumachs luminous with crimson fires, and I can hear the rustle made by the fallen leaves as we plowed through them. I can see the blue clusters of wild grapes hanging among the foliage of the saplings, and I remember the taste of them and the smell. I know how the wild blackberries looked, and how they tasted. And I can feel the thumping rain, upon my head, of hickory nuts and walnuts when we were out in the frosty dawn to scramble for them with the pigs, and the gusts of wind loosed them and sent them down.

I know how a prize watermelon looks when it is sunning its fat rotundity among pumpkin vines and squash; I know how to tell when it is ripe without "plugging" it; I know how inviting it looks when it is cooling itself in a tub of water under the bed, waiting; I know how it looks when it lies on the table, and the children gathered for the sacrifice and their mouths watering; I know the crackling sound it makes when the carving knife enters its end. I can see its halves fall apart and display the rich red meat and the black seeds, and the heart standing up, a luxury fit for the elect. I know how a boy looks behind a yard-long slice of that melon, and I know how he feels, for I have been there.

I know the look of green apples and peaches and pears on the trees. I know how pretty the ripe ones look when they are piled in pyramids under the trees. I know how a frozen apple looks, in a barrel down cellar in the wintertime, and how hard it is to bite, and how the frost makes the teeth ache, and yet how good it is notwithstanding. I know the look of an apple that is roasting and sizzling on a hearth of a winter's evening, and I know the comfort of eating it hot, along with some sugar and a drench of cream.

I can remember the bare wooden stairway in my uncle's house, and the rafters and the slanting roof over my bed, and the squares of moonlight on the floor, and the white cold world of snow outside. I can remember the howling of the wind and the quaking of the house on stormy nights, and how snug and cozy one felt, under the blankets listening; and how the powdery snow used to sift in and lie in little ridges on the floor and make the place look chilly in the morning and curb the wild desire to get up—in case there was any. I can remember how dismal was the hoo-hooing of the owl and the wailing of the wolf.

I remember the raging of the rain on that roof, summer nights, and how pleasant it was to lie and listen to it, and enjoy the white splendor of the lightning and the majestic booming and crashing of the thunder.

This selection contains many words and phrases calling up images of sight, sound, touch, smell, and taste. Underline the phrases that make you think of sounds.

What do the following phrases mean?

"sunning its fat rotundity" _____

"snapshot glimpses" _____

"children gathered for the sacrifice" _____

"a luxury fit for the elect" _____

Here are paragraphs from a story about a college boy who took a job in a steel mill for the summer. Read them and answer the questions.

Win Bennett followed a brisk staff assistant across the mill property. Even before they were near the shabby armory-like building that housed the open hearth, the noise of the wheels, whistles, and escaping steam was deafening. Win shrugged his shoulders. It hadn't been his idea to come in the first place.

Was Win ambling along? _____ Did the building look old and worn? _____ Was Win enthusiastic about working in a steel mill? _____

Inside, Win stared at the great, gloomy cavern where he was to begin work. One side was open to the air; the other walls were black and sooty. Win and the assistant walked across the cindery floor to a spot where they could look up at the dark backs of the furnaces.

Did Win get an impression of light and airiness? _____ Did his shoes make a crunching noise as he walked? _____

The night in the boarding house didn't add to Win's peace of mind. The bed was lumpy, and the night was punctuated by blasts of sound from the plant. An especially loud whistle at six found Win already up and climbing into work clothes that were stiff with newness.

Did Win sleep soundly all night? _____ Did he drowsily open his eyes as the six o'clock whistle blew? _____ Did the clothes feel a little scratchy as he put them on? _____

Win couldn't speak. He could only see and hear. The noises he had heard yesterday were doubled. Across the black, cindery floor loomed the round domes of the open hearths with great, red eyes of fire staring toward him. A steam whistle went off at his elbow, and he jumped.

Had Win's voice been permanently injured? _____ Did the furnaces seem dwarfed by the size of the room? _____ Was Win perturbed? _____

"Now we'll test," Polowski said, and indicated that Win was to help him manage the long steel dipper. "You grab the end of the spoon," he said, and Win grabbed. They came so close to the furnace that Win's skin tightened and his eyes were in agony. What were they going to do? They couldn't go close enough to dip out some of the boiling metal in that spoon!

Were Win's arms relaxed? _____ Did Win instinctively cringe from the heat? _____ Did he gasp with apprehension? _____

The place was already hotter than anything Win had dreamed a man could stand—hotter and noisier. Win walked forward, slowly, heavily, holding onto the handle behind Polowski. Then he half tripped on the rough dirt of the floor. "Pick up your feet, clumsy!" Polowski yelled.

Was the air scorching? _____ Was Win's shirt wet with perspiration? _____ Did Polowski's face wear a patient expression? _____

Polowski raked the coals as fast as he could. Then came a blinding belch of smoke, a crackling roar of fire! The red, choking fury of steel began to run into the ladle. "We've got to move!" Win shrieked. "I'm—I'm frying!"

Was Win's heart pounding? _____ Was there an acrid smell in the air? _____ Did the smoke sift out in wisps? _____ Did melted steel flow in an incandescent stream? _____

Win crouched back, but he could not escape. Below him was the ladle filling with the writhing, whirling liquid fire. Behind him was the furnace and the chute to the ladle. The only way out was blocked by Polowski, his body big and threatening in the gruesome light.

Did Win see weird shadows? _____ Did he feel panicky? _____ Was Polowski's presence reassuring to Win? _____

By the end of two weeks, life was a little more bearable. Win knew enough now not to jump at shrieking valves and whistles. He could duck the overhead crane without looking up. He found order in what had seemed to be chaos two weeks before. When the furnace was tapped and the steel came rushing forth, there was a crude sort of glory he learned to admire.

Do you think that Win stuck to his job in the mill for the rest of the summer? _____

Adapted from *Adventures in Steel* by Lavinia R. Davis; copyright, 1938, by Lavinia R. Davis. Published by Modern Age Books, Inc.

The sea with its many moods is a favorite sub-ject for writers. "The face of the sea is always changing," says Rachel Carson, who has written several fine books about the sea. "Crossed by colors, lights, and moving shadows, sparkling in the sun, mysterious in the twilight, its aspects and its moods vary hour by hour."

As you read each passage below, note how it makes you feel.

1. "The morning was one peculiar to that coast. Everything was mute and calm; everything grey. . . . Flights of troubled grey fowl, kith and kin with flights of troubled grey vapours among which they were mixed, skimmed low and fitfully over the waters, as swallows over meadows before storms. Shadows present, foreshadowing deeper shadows to come."

Herman Melville

2. "The sea! the sea! the open sea!
The blue, the fresh, the ever free!
Without a mark, without a bound,
It runneth the earth's wide regions round;
It plays with the clouds; it mocks the skies;
Or like a cradled creature lies."

Bryan Waller Procter

3. ". . . The sky was clear and silvery; during the night the haze had melted, and the morning was brilliant. . . . A late star twinkled palely close to the horizon. There was a shimmer on the sea as though a loitering breeze passed playful fin-gers over its surface."[1]

W. Somerset Maugham

4. "The storm increased with the night. The sea was lashed into tremendous confusion. There was a fearful, sullen sound of rushing waves and broken surges. Deep called unto deep. At times the black volume of clouds overhead seemed rent asunder by flashes of lightning that quivered along the foaming billows, and made the succeeding darkness doubly terrible. The thunders bellowed over the wild waste of waters, and were echoed and prolonged by the mountain waves. . . ."

Washington Irving

5. "During the long voyage, the sea lay quietly, calmly, as if sleeping. Days passed in a golden haze of sunlight. Nights slipped by in the silver glow of the moon. And all this the sea reflected like a dark mirror."

Anonymous

6. ". . . Half a mile out, where is the reef, the white-headed combers thrust suddenly skyward out of the placid turquoise-blue and come rolling in to shore. One after another they come, a mile long, with smoking crests, the white battal-ions of the infinite army of the sea. And one sits and listens to the perpetual roar, and watches the unending procession, and feels tiny and fragile before this tremendous force expressing itself in fury and foam and sound. . . ."

Jack London

7. "The sky was no longer blue, but a dead, level white; its surface was too even to give the effect of cloud; it was as though in the upper air the heat hung like a pall. There was no breeze and the sea, as colourless as the sky, was smooth and shining like the dye in a dyer's vat."[1]

W. Somerset Maugham

8. "The sea was as still as an inland lake; the light trade-wind was gently and steadily breath-ing from astern; the dark blue sky was studded with the tropical stars; there was no sound but the rippling of the water under the stem; and the sails were spread out, wide and high. . . . So quiet . . . was the sea, and so steady the breeze that if these sails had been sculptured marble, they could not have been more motionless. Not a ripple upon the surface of the canvas; not even a quivering of the extreme edges of the sail."

Richard Henry Dana, Jr.

Which selection or selections create an im-pression of:

power and majesty? -

light-heartedness? -

ominous quiet? -

terror? -

peace and tranquillity? - - - - - - - - - - - - - - - -

[1] From "P. & O." in *The Casuarina Tree* by W. Somerset Maugham; copyright, 1926, by W. Somerset Maugham; reprinted by permission of the author and Doubleday & Co., Inc., and Messrs. Heinemann, Ltd.

Vowel Sounds and Syllables

The number of vowel sounds you hear in a word tells you how many syllables there are in that word.

Say the name of each picture below and think of the number of the vowel sounds you hear in the word. Write the number of syllables on the dotted line under the picture.

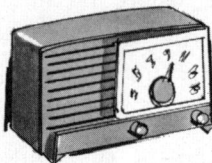   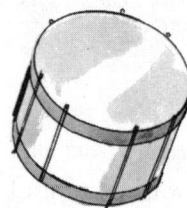

_ _ _ _   _ _ _ _   _ _ _ _   _ _ _ _

Say each of the words below to yourself. After each word write the number of syllables you hear. Remember that it is the number of vowel sounds you hear, not the number of vowel letters you see, that tells you how many syllables there are in a word.

sting _ _ _ _	destroy _ _ _ _	picnic _ _ _ _
mercury _ _ _ _	Halloween _ _ _ _	interpret _ _ _ _
repair _ _ _ _	inquire _ _ _ _	accent _ _ _ _
choice _ _ _ _	advantage _ _ _ _	sauce _ _ _ _
refugee _ _ _ _	obey _ _ _ _	bamboo _ _ _ _
bridge _ _ _ _	wheelbarrow _ _ _ _	imperfectly _ _ _ _
electronic _ _ _ _	sieve _ _ _ _	tuberculosis _ _ _ _
nonsense _ _ _ _	extinguish _ _ _ _	escape _ _ _ _
encourage _ _ _ _	terrace _ _ _ _	beforehand _ _ _ _
index _ _ _ _	barbaric _ _ _ _	juice _ _ _ _
satisfy _ _ _ _	trustworthy _ _ _ _	whirlpool _ _ _ _
impressively _ _ _ _	immense _ _ _ _	chemistry _ _ _ _
bandage _ _ _ _	humiliate _ _ _ _	checkbook _ _ _ _
porcupine _ _ _ _	calculate _ _ _ _	unhappiness _ _ _ _
dishonesty _ _ _ _	belfry _ _ _ _	occupy _ _ _ _
exclaim _ _ _ _	executive _ _ _ _	modest _ _ _ _
demerit _ _ _ _	thoroughbred _ _ _ _	library _ _ _ _
patriotic _ _ _ _	inaccurately _ _ _ _	wherewithal _ _ _ _

Dividing Words into Syllables

Here are three clues that will help you divide words into syllables:

1. As in *can dy* and *mit ten*, the first of the two consonants following the first vowel element usually ends the first syllable.

2. As in *o pen*, *bea con*, and *no tice*, the single consonant following the first vowel element usually begins the second syllable.

3. As in *bu gle*, *rum ble*, and *strug gle*, the consonant preceding final *le* usually begins the last syllable.

Look at each word below and decide where the first syllable ends. Rewrite the word, leaving a space between the first and second syllable. Then write the number of the clue to show how you know where the first syllable ends. The first one is done for you.

harness	*har ness* 1	ample
startle		pupil
license		borrow
cotton		feeble
feature		purpose
stubborn		scramble
daisy		reason
wobble		cargo
witness		pebble
needle		elbow
acorn		pilot
absence		idle
glimmer		bacon
eagle		pepper
season		candle
grumble		sentence
vacant		eager
hobby		lazy
tailor		thimble
handle		pronounce

Special Clues to Syllables in Words

When you see a consonant blend or the letters ch, sh, th, *or* ck *together in a word, be careful! Here are some clues that will help you divide such words into syllables.*

1. As in *re ply, a fraid, chil dren,* and *de stroy,* the syllables in a word do not often break between consonant blends.

2. As in *oth er, ei ther, bush el,* and *a shamed,* the syllables in a word do not often break between the letters *ch, th, sh;* these letters may go with either the first or last syllable.

3. As in *jack et* and *buck le,* the syllables in a word do not break between the letters *ck,* and *ck* goes with the preceding vowel.

Read each sentence, and decide where the first syllable ends in the italicized word. On the line below the sentence write this word, leaving a space between the first and last syllable. Then write the number of the above clue that helped you.

When Harry threw the log on the campfire, the wood began to *crackle.*

- -

George *explored* his family's new home from the basement to the attic.

- -

Joan's mother told her to put the carnations in water before they began to *wither.*

- -

John and his brother found a *secret* drawer in the old walnut desk they were refinishing.

- -

The doctor prescribed a new medicine that gave the suffering man *instant* relief from pain.

- -

On Tuesday Mrs. Stevens picked two *buckets* of apples; on Wednesday she and her daughter made and canned applesauce.

- -

The *usher* who showed us to our seats forgot to return our ticket stubs, so we called him back.

- -

The customer became extremely impatient when his *package* could not be found.

- -

Mr. James *instructs* the evening swimming classes at the downtown Y.M.C.A.

- -

Every member of Tom's public-speaking class participated in the assembly *program.*

- -

"If you're hungry, why don't you fix a *chicken* sandwich?" Mrs. Stoner asked her daughter, who had just come home from play practice.

- -

Mike and Dave decided that *neither* of their ideas for fixing the motor would work.

- -

What Is the First Syllable?

Read each sentence and notice the italicized word. Next,
write that word on the dotted line below the sentence, leaving
a space between the first and last syllable.

Telegraph messages are sent under the ocean or under the ground by means of a *cable*.

"We must get a yard of *canvas* and patch the tear in our tent before we leave next week," Al reminded his brother Thursday morning.

"I do not know *whether* he will come," said Tim, "but I will try to find out and arrange the time to satisfy all of us."

Mrs. Stoner gave her *baggage* to a redcap at the station and asked him to put it on the two o'clock train to Indianapolis.

The heavy trucks and buses that traveled the street shook the house so much that one could feel the walls and floors *vibrate*.

The company presented Mr. Williams with a handsome watch as a *token* of appreciation for his twenty-five years of service.

At the first meeting of the high school's newly organized swimming club, the members decided to adopt the dolphin as their *emblem*.

Freighters from foreign countries entered the *harbor*, bringing various kinds of cargo to be unloaded at the docks.

We drove to Grand Island last Saturday to hear a concert given by the *Minstrel* Singers.

Since complete concentration was necessary, the hypnotist requested that the audience keep *silent* while he performed his act.

Ed was so absorbed in his own thoughts that he did not notice the electric cord until he tripped over it and jerked it out of the *socket*.

When Elizabeth took her riding lesson last Friday, the instructor showed her two different kinds of *saddles* used today.

The farmer's wife made sweet *pickles* from the cucumbers she had picked in her own garden and the ones a neighbor had given her.

The *author* of the controversial book of essays felt honored that the university had asked him to speak at the graduation ceremonies.

"Trying to cross the street against the traffic light can be a *fatal* mistake," the police officer warned the pedestrian.

In some of the African *jungles* that are near the equator, the average yearly rainfall exceeds eighty inches.

Can You Hear the Accented Syllable in a Word?

In a welcoming cheer for a visiting team, the cheerleaders are emphasizing the last syllable of hello and the first syllable of Parker.

When you emphasize a syllable in a word, you stress the vowel sound in that syllable. And when you stress the vowel sound in a syllable of a word, you accent that syllable.

One syllable of each word below is accented more than the other syllable. Sometimes it is the first syllable, as in foolish. Sometimes it is the last syllable, as in asleep. Put an accent mark after the accented syllable in each word below. Two are marked for you.

fool'ish	ex plain	to night	twen ty
a sleep'	hol ly	for get	a go
er rand	cer tain	rib bon	East er
Tues day	far ther	bea ver	ar range
a lone	sup per	con tain	jin gle
kitch en	be have	cir cle	wel come
ar rive	lis ten	be came	a gainst
be tween	rob in	de light	les son
mo ment	at tend	a pron	fid dle
in vite	per haps	a shamed	fol low
sprin kle	pro vide	birth day	re ply
sup pose	din ner	a muse	hun dred

Clues to Vowel Sounds in Accented Syllables

1. A single vowel letter at the beginning or in the middle of an accented syllable is a clue to the vowel sounds shown by these key words: hat, let, it, hot, cup.

2. A single vowel letter at the end of an accented syllable is a clue to the vowel sounds shown by these key words: āge, ēqual, īce, ōpen, ūse.

3. Two vowel letters together in an accented syllable are a clue to the vowel sounds shown by these key words: āge, ēqual, īce, ōpen, ūse.

4. Two vowel letters in an accented syllable, one of which is final *e*, are a clue to the vowel sounds shown by these key words: āge, ēqual, īce, ōpen, ūse.

5. A vowel letter followed by *r* in an accented syllable is a clue to the vowel sounds shown by these key words: cãre, cär, tẽrm, ôrder.

Look at the accented syllable in each word below. After the word, put the number of the clue that tells you the vowel sound in that syllable. Then write the key word for that sound. The first one is done for you.

bri′dle _____2____ *īce* _____

writ′ten _____

de par′ture _____

ca′per _____

a ware′ _____

af fec′tion _____

ac quaint′ed _____

for sake′ _____

com ple′tion _____

en clo′sure _____

a muse′ment _____

har′vest ing _____

re duce′ _____

arc′tic _____

bot′tle _____

por′trait _____

vi′o lent _____

pur′pose _____

weav′er _____

lone′ly _____

re late′ _____

sub due′ _____

gar′bage _____

val′u a ble _____

pre serve′ _____

al le′giance _____

ap proach′ _____

sum′mer _____

a stride′ _____

com pare′ _____

fu′ture _____

in quire′ _____

ex treme′ _____

tur′key _____

cab′bage _____

dis play′ _____

Unaccented Syllables

The first syllable in each of the following words is accented, and the last syllable is unaccented. You will notice that the vowel sound in each of the unaccented syllables is the same, even though the vowel letters representing it are different. This is a soft, reduced vowel sound called a schwa.

can'vas	tak'en	squir'rel
cac'tus	com'mon	care'ful
fa'mous	mo'tion	roy'al
ther'mos	cap'tain	A'pril

Pronounce each word below to yourself and listen for the schwa sound in the unaccented syllable. Be careful! The unaccented syllable may be either the first or the last syllable. Underline the vowel letter or letters that stand for the schwa sound. The first three are done for you.

a bout'	sum'mon	per'il	de'mon
com plain'	ma rine'	com pose'	break'fast
va'cant	serv'ant	fo'cus	gi'ant
blos'som	suf'fer	a lack'	bal loon'
si'lent	mil'lion	king'dom	beck'on
bal'lot	pa'tient	o'cean	se rene'
ob tain'	weap'on	pa rade'	fire'man
sup pose'	can'yon	bliz'zard	stom'ach
trac'tor	jeal'ous	mad'am	a bide'
prob'lem	as sure'	a broad'	cau'tious
sup port'	cho'rus	na'tion	po lite'
at tract'	a mount'	can'non	stir'rup
re'gion	sol'emn	par'rot	ov'en

The Schwa Sound and Symbol

In dictionary pronunciations the schwa symbol (ə) may stand for the vowel sound in unaccented syllables.

What is the vowel letter in the unaccented syllable of these words?
What is the vowel sound in the unaccented syllable?

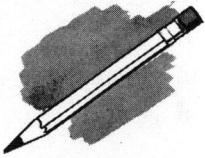

pen′cil   (pen′səl)

vowel letter _ _ _ _ _ _ _ _ _

vowel sound _ _ _ _ _ _ _ _ _

po lice′   (pə lēs′)

vowel letter _ _ _ _ _ _ _ _ _

vowel sound _ _ _ _ _ _ _ _ _

tas′sel   (tas′əl)

vowel letter _ _ _ _ _ _ _ _ _

vowel sound _ _ _ _ _ _ _ _ _

pa trol′   (pə trōl′)

vowel letter _ _ _ _ _ _ _ _ _

vowel sound _ _ _ _ _ _ _ _ _

car′cass   (kär′kəs)

vowel letter _ _ _ _ _ _ _ _ _

vowel sound _ _ _ _ _ _ _ _ _

maid′en   (mād′ən)

vowel letter _ _ _ _ _ _ _ _ _

vowel sound _ _ _ _ _ _ _ _ _

cir′cus   (sėr′kəs)

vowel letter _ _ _ _ _ _ _ _ _

vowel sound _ _ _ _ _ _ _ _ _

mel′on   (mel′ən)

vowel letter _ _ _ _ _ _ _ _ _

vowel sound _ _ _ _ _ _ _ _ _

Below you will find the spelling of one word and the pronunciation for two. Use the key at the bottom of the page to help you with the pronunciations. Then underline the pronunciation of the word for which the spelling is given.

apple	(ə pēl′) (ap′əl)	conceal	(kən sēl′) (koun′səl)	machine	(mā′sən) (mə shēn′)
carton	(kär′tən) (kär tün′)	ravine	(rā′vən) (rə vēn′)	severe	(sə vēr′) (sev′ər)
corral	(kôr′əl) (kə ral′)	comet	(kə mit′) (kom′it)	camera	(kə mēr′ə) (kam′ər ə)

hat, āge, cāre, fär; let, ēqual, tèrm; it, īce; hot, ōpen, ôrder; oil, out; cup, pùt, rüle, ūse; ch, child;
ng, long; th, thin; ᴛʜ, then; zh, measure; ə represents *a* in about, *e* in taken, *i* in pencil, *o* in lemon, *u* in circus.

Word Quiz

Check the correct statement below each word.

safety

This word has three syllables.
This word has two syllables.

dispute

The first syllable of *dispute* is accented.
The last syllable of *dispute* is accented.

scoundrel

The first syllable rhymes with *frown*.
The first syllable rhymes with the first syllable of *country*.

juice

The word rhymes with *spice*.
The word rhymes with *truce*.

residence

The *c* is pronounced like the *c* in *placid*.
The *c* is pronounced like the *c* in *canary*.

blown

The *ow* is pronounced like the *ow* in *known*.
The *ow* is pronounced like the *ow* in *crown*.

sardine

The last syllable rhymes with *whine*.
The last syllable rhymes with the last syllable of *marine*.

melancholy

The *ch* is pronounced like the *ch* in *chauffeur*.
The *ch* is pronounced like the *ch* in *chalk*.
The *ch* is pronounced like the *ch* in *chorus*.

conspicuous

This word has three syllables.
This word has four syllables.

fragrant

The first syllable of *fragrant* is *frag*.
The first syllable of *fragrant* is *fra*.

wreath

The *th* is pronounced like the *th* in *oath*.
The *th* is pronounced like the *th* in *thy*.

beetle

The first syllable in *beetle* is *bee*.
The first syllable in *beetle* is *beet*.

gossip

The *g* is pronounced like the *g* in *gypsies*.
The *g* is pronounced like the *g* in *galley*.

mountain

The first syllable of *mountain* is accented.
The last syllable of *mountain* is accented.

knoll

The *k* is pronounced like the *k*'s in *kink*.
The *k* is silent like the *k* in *knelt*.

dominoes

The last syllable rhymes with the last syllable of *broncos*.
The last syllable rhymes with the last syllable of *canoes*.

smear

This word rhymes with *swear*.
This word rhymes with *veer*.

zenith

The first syllable of *zenith* is *zen*.
The first syllable of *zenith* is *ze*.

rove

This word rhymes with *shove*.
This word rhymes with *clove*.

volunteer

This word has three syllables.
This word has two syllables.

weasel

The *s* is pronounced like the *s* in *raise*.
The *s* is pronounced like the *s* in *false*.

An Attempted Robbery

John Anderson, a jewelry salesman, was the victim of an attempted robbery. The incident took place in his room at the Atlas Hotel at exactly six o'clock.

Mr. Anderson was unable to identify the robber, but a room-service waiter confessed that he had attempted the robbery. When the police examined his statements, they became disgusted and told him to stop wasting their time. They knew that he was not guilty because he said so many things that could not possibly have been true.

The picture below shows the scene just at the time of the attempted robbery. Study the picture; then read the waiter's story and underline anything he said that was incorrect or could not have happened.

The Waiter's Story

On the afternoon of the attempted robbery I stood on the corner of Central Street and Moore Avenue, looking at the clock on the top of the post office. Then I went into the drugstore at Baron Street and Moore Avenue. It was just five o'clock as I came out. I was supposed to report for duty at five-thirty.

I immediately went to the thirteenth floor of the hotel and changed into my uniform. Then I hid in the hall. In a few minutes a boy came past with a telegram. I shoved him into a linen room, took the telegram, and locked the door. Then I knocked on Mr. Anderson's door, entered with the telegram, and snatched the display case full of jewelry.

When he yelled, I dropped the case and rushed to the roof of the hotel. There I climbed down the ladder on the north side of the building to the roof of the Miller Building. I entered the top floor through a trap door, rode down in the elevator, and came out at 58 Baron Street. I hid in the basement of the empty store around the corner until I saw the police begin to search the people in the hotel drugstore. Then I came to the police station and confessed.

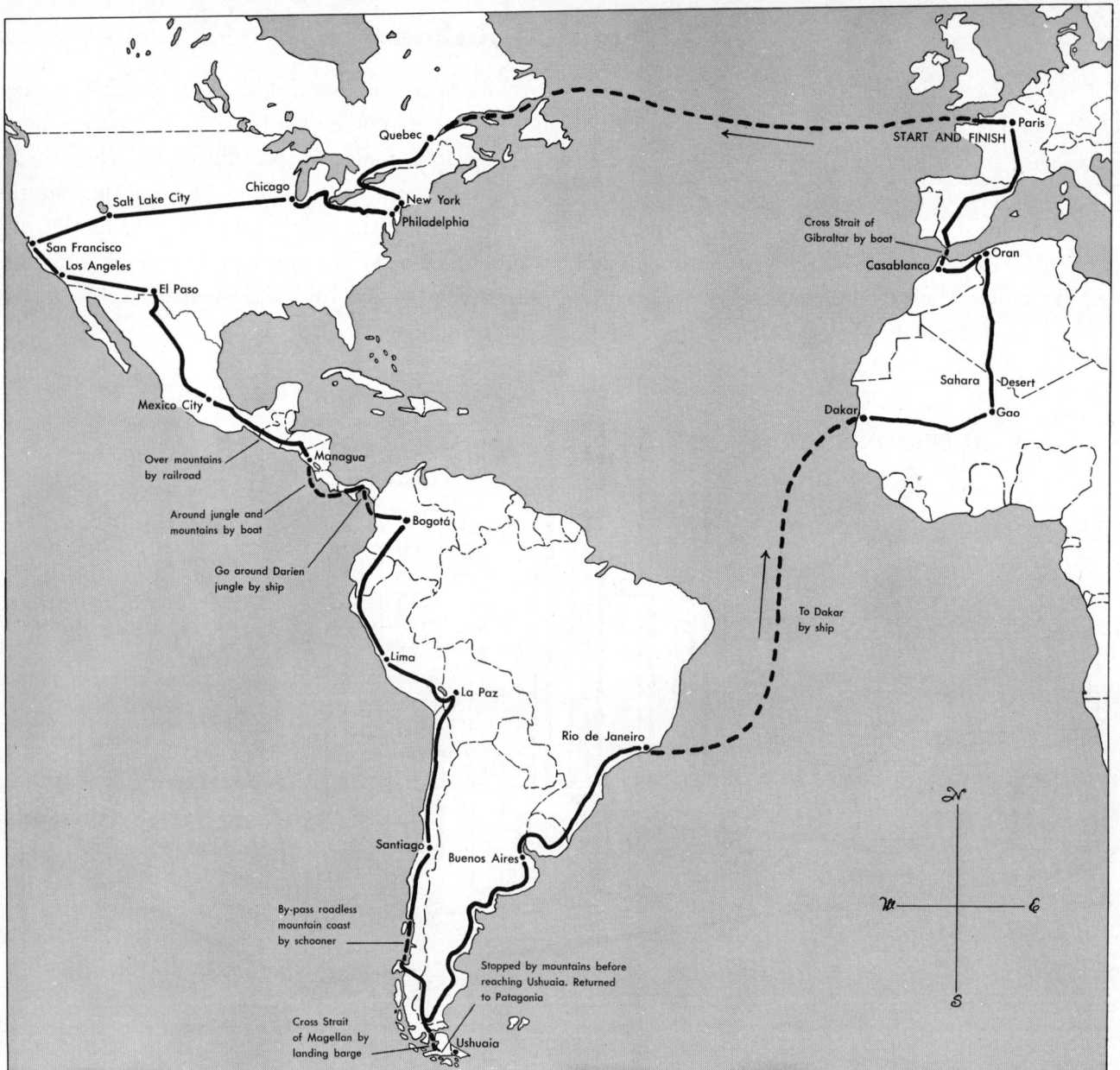

The map shows a route with the following labels:

Paris — START AND FINISH

Quebec, New York, Philadelphia, Chicago, Salt Lake City, San Francisco, Los Angeles, El Paso, Mexico City

Over mountains by railroad

Around jungle and mountains by boat

Go around Darien jungle by ship

Managua, Bogotá, Lima, La Paz, Santiago, Buenos Aires, Rio de Janeiro

By-pass roadless mountain coast by schooner

Stopped by mountains before reaching Ushuaia. Returned to Patagonia

Cross Strait of Magellan by landing barge

Ushuaia

To Dakar by ship

Cross Strait of Gibraltar by boat

Casablanca, Oran, Dakar, Gao

Sahara Desert

Across Four Continents, *by Jacques Cornet, as told to Richard F. Dempewolff*

My friend Henri Lochon and I had often talked of touring America. Henri yearned to drive a car down the Pan-American Highway, and I wanted to tour North America.

"Why not do both?" Henri said one day. And that is what we did. The trip lasted 367 days and parts of it would have put a bulldozer to the supreme test.

Because of its small size, light weight, and the fact that it can be easily dismantled, we chose a Citroën for our journey. We stocked the car with light-weight equipment and on May 8, 1953, we left Paris. We traveled to North America by boat and began our great adventure on wheels at Quebec.

The first leg, on good Canadian and United States roads, whizzed by. We headed west via Chicago and Salt Lake City, reaching San Francisco and Los Angeles as planned, and swerved southeast toward El Paso. On the blacktop highways of Mexico we spun southward past mountains and fields and Indians trudging to market. As we neared the lower border we ran out of hard-surface highway and never saw any again until Oran, in Africa, 20,000 miles later.

Now the fun began. The road dwindled to a foot trail through towering forests, and the mountains of Guatemala loomed ahead. We forded the first river we came to, pushed the car across the second, and bogged in the third. After hours of labor with rope and tackle, we inched the car to the shore. Steaming heat descended like fog upon us. "To the Mexican Railway," Henri announced. So we stripped the car and pulled it by hand line some ten miles to the tracks. We skirted the mountains on the first freight that came along. Then back to the road.

For hundreds of miles through Central America everything was great, but in Nicaragua the mountains, the jungle, and the rainy season forced us to take to the sea. We bypassed Costa Rica, and though the roads in Panama were good, we gave up all thought of tackling the Darien jungle beyond Panama City when we learned we could go by ship to Colombia in South America.

The road to Bogotá was passable, but the bridges gave us many a qualm. We crashed through one at night, and the next morning the car limped into the city on flat tires, with wheels bent and axle broken. After a two-day wait for parts to be flown from Paris, we had the Citro repaired. We bounded over the rocky roads of Ecuador, drowned by tropical rains one moment and baked dry by the white-hot sun the next.

At Lima we put the battered car into such fine shape that we decided to alter course and try for an altitude record in the Bolivian Andes. We made the record when we chugged up the roadless slopes of a 17,777-foot peak—an all-time high for a Citroën.

From there it was all downhill and mostly around hairpin curves. South of Santiago the roads gave way to mountains that plunged vertically into the sea. The only way to continue was by boarding a schooner for Patagonia.

In roadless Patagonia the winds come from the south polar seas. Gales of sixty to ninety miles an hour lashed and blinded us and tossed pebbles the size of marbles at our faces and hands. We drove by compass.

Hoping to reach Ushuaia, bottom-most town of South America, we took a landing barge across the Strait of Magellan. Our attempt ended on a mountain trail so narrow that one of the back wheels spun out over sheer space. There was nothing to do but return to Patagonia.

After that, the trip to Buenos Aires was an anticlimax, though we drove the last 2000 miles on the rims and sounded like a rolling garbage can full of loose rivets.

In Rio we foolishly decided to add another continent to our score, and sailed for Dakar and the Sahara. The Sahara is cruel. It's a wonder we made it. Tires overheated and blew, the battery died, wheels stuck in the sand. For a thousand miles beyond Gao we had only the compass as guide. On a day that we felt would spell our end, we were rescued by a caravan and towed ingloriously to an oasis by camel.

Then came Oran, and hard-top roads again, and at a tourist's amble we made it back to Paris. Would we do it again? Speaking for myself, I think I shall be content to settle down.

1. On what four continents did the car travel?

----

2. Which continent did the car cross completely?

---------------------------- in what direction? ----------------------------

3. On which continent did the route of the car follow roughly the shoreline? ----------------

4. On which continent did the car travel the least number of miles? ----------------

5. Seven sections of the journey were made by boat. Where were they? ----------------

----

----

6. In what general direction was the car traveling the first time the men had to rely on the compass? --

7. In what direction were they traveling the second time they were guided by compass? ------

8. At what point in South America was it necessary to retrace their route? ----------------

9. Approximately how many times farther did the car travel to reach Bogotá than the plane from Paris did? ----------------

10. In what two portions of the journey did the travelers probably have ready access to service stations? ----------------------------------

Four Views of Pike's Peak

*Each of the incidents described below took place on one of the
following dates: 1806, 1858, 1895, or 1955. Read each incident
and write on the line above it the date that you think fits.*

- - - - - - - - - - -

The peak rose majestically before the weary little group of men on horseback. For days the party had journeyed farther and farther into the wilderness, seeing no other white men, eating the flesh of wild animals for food, and sleeping under the stars at night, wrapped in blankets.

And now at last, their hardships forgotten for the moment, the explorers stood at the foot of the towering peak—the first white men to behold its imposing height.

They removed their coonskin caps and stood spellbound with bared heads. Then one of them pulled a folded paper from his saddlebag and sketched some lines on a map.

"We have seen the peak and mapped its surroundings," he said. "But alas, friends! no man will ever conquer this glorious peak and stand upon its summit."

- - - - - - - - - - -

Piloting a plane over the Rockies was a challenge to Eliot Jones, who knew the nature of every mountain in the area. Some peaks were bare, with an occasional flat surface big enough to accommodate an emergency landing. Others were covered with forests, and a plane landing on one of them would have its wings sheared off by the tall pines.

The king of the peaks, however, was snow-covered. Day after day Jones flew past this mountain, knowing that even with the latest make of airplane he dared not come too close to the jagged monster. He had felt sudden gales sweep down its slopes, and he had seen how the clouds could spread out without warning and bar his vision. But he knew too that his plane was safe from crashing so long as he flew on the beam that would keep him miles from the peak.

- - - - - - - - - - -

Carriages deposited groups of sightseers at the station, where a cogwheel railway waited to take them up the mountain. Women in long, tight-waisted dresses and huge feathered hats clutched the hands of little boys in tight suits and girls in ruffled dresses and buttoned boots. There was much confusion as the excited crowd pushed into the little car and found seats on the hard wooden benches.

At last the train started, and beautiful views of the mountain began to slip past the windows. The track crossed valleys, passed over high bridges, and wound around curves that had been cut through solid rock. The engine poured out clouds of black smoke, and ashes peppered the passengers. But no discomfort could spoil the pleasure of the sightseers, who did not dream that in a few years tourists would scale the peak in comfortable automobiles over a broad highway.

- - - - - - - - - - -

To the miner, weary from his long westward journey by covered wagon, the majestic peak meant only one thing—gold! He never so much as lifted his eyes to the stern, overhanging cliffs or turned his head at the cry of an eagle circling the clouds, for his mind was centered on one thing only—where the precious vein was hidden. He had burrowed into every cave, studied the cracks and seams in countless rocks. To him the wrinkles in each towering cliff were like faces beckoning him as he searched hopefully in this direction and that for the always elusive vein of gold.

Evenings found him with pan still in hand, washing sand and gravel from his findings. And while his eyes sought the gleam of gold in the dull pan, the sunset turned the fields of snow overhead into the color of the gold for which he constantly searched.

When Did It Happen?

One of the most interesting wild beasts found in British East Africa is the elephant. Ordinarily elephants do not attack humans, but if one of them does become a "rogue," or dangerous killer, it is necessary to send hunters out into the depths of the jungle after him.

In this story of an elephant hunt, as told by a famous hunter, the different parts below are not given in the right order. Number the parts in the order in which they should appear. The underlined phrases will help you. The first part is numbered for you.

____ On the fourth day we again took up Shukra's tracks. Long before noon we were getting very close to our powerful, vicious enemy, and the killer must have been aware that he was being pursued. With hearts pounding, we faced an area of dense bush. Had the rogue gone on, or was he waiting for us in the jungle?

_1_ Of all man-killing rogue elephants I have encountered, none was more dangerous than "Shukra the Killer." In less than a week this elephant had killed three natives.

On Monday morning, Ohalla the woodcarver brought us the news of the three killings. By early afternoon the young assistant to the district officer had gone in search of the killer, taking only two native boys as guides. Though he had never hunted big game, the young man succeeded in twice wounding the rogue and followed him farther and farther into the depths of the jungle.

____ The instant I saw him charge, I aimed at the mighty head and fired. The kick of the heavy double-barreled rifle threw me off balance and it was a few seconds before I could fire again. In the meantime, my other gun-bearer got in a shot from my spare rifle. His bullet must have hit a vital spot, for the elephant's body shuddered. As the rogue screamed and threshed about in rage, he was the most fearful sight I had ever seen. With feverish haste I reloaded, snapped the action together, aimed just below the ear, and fired.

____ For the next three days, my two gun-bearers and I combed the slopes of the mountain where Shukra was hiding. Twice the elephant lay in waiting for us, and only luck saved us from a horrible fate.

____ That last shot paid for the lives of the young official and the three natives. Small trees and bushes were smashed as Shukra crashed to the ground. With perspiration streaming from my body, I thanked God that we were still alive.

____ Later that same afternoon, the murderous beast unexpectedly charged out of thick bush and killed the inexperienced young assistant.

Night had fallen when the two native boys, their eyes wide with terror, ran up to my veranda and blurted out the story of how Shukra had claimed his fourth victim. I immediately volunteered to go after the man-killing rogue.

____ Before I could decide what to do, one of my gun-bearers settled the question in his own way. He removed his clothing and shoes, and as stealthily and silently as a cat, wriggled into the bush. At last—it seemed like hours later—he crept back and nodded his head. Shukra was waiting! Quietly we began to cut away the thickly twined branches and vines to make a better opening.

Suddenly the forest rang with piercing elephant screams. With upraised trunk and ears outspread, tons of animal fury slashed through the thicket. Shukra was charging directly toward us!

From "Fifteen Years in the Wilds of Tanganyika" by A. R. Siedentopf in *Travel;* copyright, 1946, by Robert M. McBride & Company, Inc.; adapted by permission of the publishers.

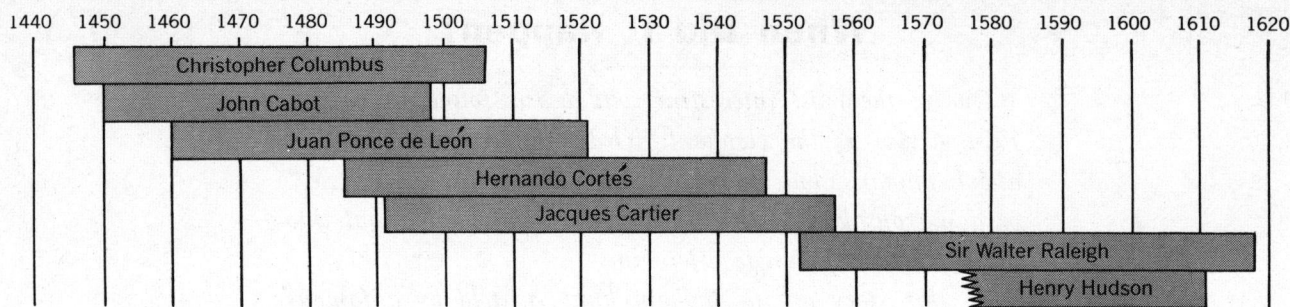

| 1440 | 1450 | 1460 | 1470 | 1480 | 1490 | 1500 | 1510 | 1520 | 1530 | 1540 | 1550 | 1560 | 1570 | 1580 | 1590 | 1600 | 1610 | 1620 |

Christopher Columbus
John Cabot
Juan Ponce de León
Hernando Cortés
Jacques Cartier
Sir Walter Raleigh
Henry Hudson

The men whose life spans are charted above all played a part in the discovery and settlement of the New World.

After his famous voyage to the "Indies" in 1492, Columbus returned to the New World three times. In 1493 he went to Haiti and established the first permanent settlement of Europeans in the Western Hemisphere. In 1498 and 1502–1504, he explored parts of the coasts of Central and South America.

John Cabot was an Italian navigator employed by the English. When he heard about Columbus' supposed discovery of Asia, Cabot decided to head an expedition himself. In 1497 he landed at Nova Scotia, in Canada, and sailed along the coast of Newfoundland. On a second voyage in 1498 he explored the coast of North America as far south as Chesapeake Bay.

Juan Ponce de León was one of the first Spaniards who came to the New World to stay. He accompanied Columbus on his second voyage, in 1493, when Puerto Rico was discovered. Later Ponce de León sailed from this island toward the unknown north. In 1513 he landed and took possession of a region that he called Florida.

In the spring of 1519, Hernando Cortés and a group of Spanish soldiers sailed westward from Cuba and invaded the land of the Aztecs in the Valley of Mexico. They found gold, a beautiful city of tall buildings, and an ancient culture.

Between 1534 and 1541, Jacques Cartier, a French navigator, made three voyages to North America. On the first voyage he skirted the coast of Newfoundland and sailed into the Gulf of St. Lawrence. On subsequent trips he went up the St. Lawrence River and spent a winter near the present site of Quebec.

Sir Walter Raleigh, in 1584, sent out ships from England with a patent to establish a colony in the New World. The settlers landed on Roanoke Island and named the country Virginia. But when additional supply ships were sent out in 1586, the colony was found to be deserted. Twenty-one years passed before a permanent colony was established, at Jamestown.

In 1609, Henry Hudson sailed under the flag of Holland in a vessel called the *Half Moon*. He and his crew sailed down the North American coast from Newfoundland to a point south of Jamestown, Virginia. On this same trip he discovered the Hudson River and sailed up it as far as the present city of Albany.

Could Christopher Columbus have visited the Aztec cities in the Valley of Mexico as the guest of Hernando Cortés? _____

When Henry Hudson sailed down the coast of Virginia, might he have seen Europeans on Roanoke Island? _____ at Jamestown? _____

Was the area now called Canada discovered before the invasion of Mexico? _____

In 1610, the Jamestown colonists feared that the Spanish in Florida might claim their territory. If this had happened, could Ponce de León have been among the invaders? _____

If you were shown a letter from Columbus to Raleigh, containing a description of Haiti, would you judge it to be a fake? _____

Could Henry Hudson and John Cabot have traveled together to the New World? _____

Could Jacques Cartier have met Indians in eastern Canada who previously had seen white men? _____

The Time Zones

"In fifteen seconds it will be exactly six o'clock." These words are familiar to anyone who has ever listened to radio or watched television.

However, not all the clocks in the United States would show six o'clock at that moment. Because our country is so large, the sunlight reaches the eastern coast hours before it reaches the western coast. The United States is therefore divided into the four time zones shown on the map above.

Standard time varies by an hour from one zone to the next. Going east, you must set your watch an hour ahead every time you pass into another time zone. Going west, you must set your watch back an hour when you pass into another zone.

If a man in Reno, Nevada, telephoned a friend in Columbus, Ohio, at 9:00 P.M. Nevada time, when would the friend get the call? _____

When it is 11:00 A.M. in Washington, D.C., what time is it in the state of Washington? _____

If a singer broadcasts from California at 7:00 P.M., when would people in Illinois tune in for this broadcast? _____

Why must certain early morning programs televised in New York be repeated later in the day? _____

_____

Suppose that you traveled by plane from Denver, Colorado, to Pittsburgh, Pennsylvania, and arrived there in time for a six-o'clock dinner. Would you be eating your dinner sooner or later than people back in Denver who also ate at six? _____

Answer the questions on this page by referring to the dictionary entries below.

Bach (bäн), **Johann Sebastian,** 1685-1750, German composer and organist. *n.*

Bee tho ven (bā′tō vən), **Ludwig van,** 1770-1827, German composer. *n.*

Bull (búl), **Ole,** 1810-1880, Norwegian violinist. *n.*

Cho pin (shō′pan), **Frédéric,** 1809-1849, Polish composer and pianist. *n.*

Grieg (grēg), **Edvard,** 1843-1907, Norwegian composer. *n.*

Haupt mann (houpt′män), **Moritz,** 1792-1868, German violinist and teacher of music theory. *n.*

Ib sen (ib′sən), **Henrik,** 1828-1906, Norwegian dramatist and poet. *n.*

Liszt (list), **Franz,** 1811-1886, Hungarian composer, pianist, and conductor. *n.*

Mac Dow ell (mək dou′əl), **Edward,** 1861-1908, American composer and pianist. *n.*

Mo zart (mō′tsärt), **Wolfgang,** 1756-1791, Austrian composer and pianist. *n.*

Nor draak (nôr′drôk), **Rikard,** 1842-1866, Norwegian composer. *n.*

Schu bert (shü′bərt), **Franz,** 1797-1828, Austrian composer. *n.*

Schu mann (shü′män), **Robert (Alexander),** 1810-1856, German composer. *n.*

Strauss (strous), **Richard,** 1864-1949, German composer and conductor. *n.*

Wag ner (väg′nər), **Richard,** 1813-1883, German composer and conductor, famous for his operas. *n.*

When Edvard Grieg was about fifteen years old, the famous violinist Ole Bull paid a visit to the Grieg home in Bergen, Norway. Was Ole Bull also an immature youth at this time? _____

Not long after this, Grieg went to Leipzig, in Germany, to study. One of his teachers, Moritz Hauptmann, lived in a house that had been the home of Johann Sebastian Bach. Could Hauptmann have met Bach? _____

Grieg married the singer Nina Hagerup in 1867. About how old was he then? _____

One of Grieg's most beautiful compositions is his piano concerto, which he wrote a short time after his marriage. Could the composer Robert Schumann have heard it? _____

An important period in Grieg's life was the time he spent in Copenhagen, Denmark. This is when he met Rikard Nordraak, who stimulated him to re-create the spirit of Norway in his music. Did Grieg go to Copenhagen before or after 1866? _____

Ibsen wrote his poetic drama *Peer Gynt* in 1867. Seven years later he asked Grieg to write background music for the play. Was Grieg married when he heard from Ibsen? _____

The famous opera *Elektra* by Richard Strauss was performed for the first time in 1909. There is a story that Grieg was present at the performance, but disliked the jangling harmonies so much that he walked out of the theater. Could this story be true? _____

In 1879 Grieg performed his famous piano concerto in Leipzig. Could his teacher, Hauptmann, have heard the performance? _____

Edward MacDowell, the first important American composer, was in France and Germany between 1876 and 1888. Many people think there are resemblances between his music and that of Grieg, Liszt, and Wagner. Do you think that the latter three composers probably got their musical ideas from MacDowell? _____

Chopin and Franz Liszt were lifelong friends. Which one was the older? _____

Like Grieg, Richard Wagner for a time studied music in Leipzig. He enrolled in the University of Leipzig in 1830. Could he have met Grieg there? _____

Ole Bull made his first concert tour of North America in the year of Grieg's birth. What year was this? _____ Bull's last tour of North America was in 1879. About how long was this before Bull's death? _____

In 1787 Beethoven took a few violin lessons from Mozart. Was Mozart an old man then? _____

Franz Schubert ardently admired Beethoven, from whose music he felt he had learned a great deal. Though both men lived in Vienna, they were not personally acquainted. During the last years of his life, Schubert once passed Beethoven on the street but was too shy to speak to him. Must this have happened a fairly short time before Beethoven's death? _____

*Each sentence on this page, if completed correctly, states an analogy; that is, a
likeness in some respect between things that are otherwise unlike. For example,
"Cup is to dishes as chair is to furniture" is an analogy.*

Underline the word following each sentence that correctly completes the analogy.

Salmon is to fish as oatmeal is to................cooky   cereal   breakfast

Rocket is to spaceship as gasoline is to...........oil well   hinge   car

Coach is to team as teacher is to................book   class   study hall

Reporter is to newspaper as actor is to...........play   box office   program

Lace is to shoe as button is to..................campaign   fastening   coat

Cowboy is to rodeo as skater is to...............skates   ice show   costume

Cold is to ice as hot is to......................summer   soup   fire

Peacock is to bird as Cadillac is to..............travel   automobile   sedan

Franc is to France as dollar is to................price   inflation   United States

Ax is to lumberjack as skillet is to...............cook   eggs   metal

Milk is to cow as egg is to.....................ham   Easter   hen

Jazz is to music as stadium is to................college   football   building

Popcorn is to popper as pancake is to...........syrup   stack   griddle

President is to White House as king is to.........country   palace   ruler

Spider is to web as beaver is to.................fur coat   busyness   dam

Fuzz is to peach as scales are to................weight   fish   mountains

Narrow is to alley as wide is to.................tall   spread   avenue

Wool is to blanket as paper is to................envelope   write   pencil

Jewel is to ruby as weapon is to.................steel   hunting   rifle

Wrist is to bracelet as finger is to...............nail   ring   thumb

Toboggan is to slide as parachute is to...........load   float   pilot

Deer is to doe as sheep is to....................ewe   shepherd   bleat

Twitch is to movement as twang is to...........sound   taste   touch

Cyclone is to breeze as downpour is to...........draggle   drizzle   scuttle

Peal is to peel as bald is to.....................bog   scald   bawled

Library is to books as art museum is to..........exhibits   paintings   gallery

Fast is to slow as sweet is to...................candy   pickles   sour

Americans Yesterday and Today

1. It is a far cry from covered-wagon days to our modern way of life. Yet many of our habits, tastes, and ways of thinking have been passed down to us from the pioneering days of our great-great-grandparents.

2. An Englishman who visited this country in 1818 said, "All America seems to be on the move." Everywhere he went, he saw Americans with the urge to keep moving. He saw long lines of covered wagons. Each wagon held a pioneer family going westward.

3. Many of our pioneering great-great-grandparents wanted more elbow room. They wanted the freedom of the wilderness. Always drawn to the West, off they went, on foot or horseback, by cart or covered wagon, by canoe or flatboat. More often than not when they departed, they did not have in mind any particular place to go. They just wanted to keep moving. It is no wonder that we still have the urge to move on. Long ago, we reached the West Coast. Now we even cast a longing eye toward the moon.

4. The western settler's work was rough and hard. He thought fine clothes unimportant because he had few opportunities to dress up. Many of us today are happiest when we are wearing jeans, either at home or roughing it out in the wide-open spaces.

5. Pioneers learned to recognize a man's worth by his friendliness, helpfulness, honesty, and bravery. They had little regard for the man with fancy manners and smooth talk. The man whom they admired was natural and plain like themselves. To this day there is so much of the pioneer in us that we judge people's worth by what they do rather than what they say.

6. Even some of our simple tastes in food come to us from pioneers. On the covered-wagon trail there was rarely time for fancy cooking or oven-baked food. The frying pan was the most commonly used implement on the trail. Today nearly every American likes fried food—eggs, potatoes, chicken, and pancakes. Because fresh meat spoiled quickly, pioneers learned to like salted meats. Ham, bacon, and salt pork were used freely for seasonings. And what American doesn't like pork and beans?

7. Pioneer life was often a lonely life. So when strangers met, they did not wait to be introduced but struck up a conversation at once. Travelers were gladly fed and sheltered for the night. On many occasions pioneers rode for miles merely to help a newcomer. Today Americans take great pride in their friendliness.

8. The days of the covered wagon are over, but traces of the lives lived by our sturdy forefathers still show in our everyday lives.

The author uses a phrase in paragraph three that states a way in which Americans today are like those of yesterday. Underline it. He has stated four other ways in which we are like our pioneer forefathers. Underline them. Complete the sentences below with phrases from the article which state these similarities.

We have ---

We think --

We judge --

We have ---

We take pride in --

Almost everyone has heard of Lafayette, but he is only one of many who have gone to a country not their own to work for a cause they believed in. Here are the stories of three such men.

Fighters for Progress

Count Casimir Pulaski, son of a wealthy Polish nobleman, was a brilliant cavalry officer. He was a leader in the fight to free Poland from Russian domination. He fled to France in 1774 after the revolt failed. There he met Benjamin Franklin and offered to serve as a cavalry leader in the American Revolution, for he felt the cause of the colonists was much like that of the Polish patriots. In 1777 he joined Washington's forces. He distinguished himself in battle and was made a brigadier general. He showed the troops how to carry on guerrilla warfare, which proved very effective against the formal military operations used by the British. Pulaski was fatally wounded during the battle of Savannah two years before the war ended. Even his enemies mourned him. The king of Poland, against whom Pulaski had led revolutionary troops, said, "He died as he lived, a hero, but an enemy of kings."

Simon Bolivar is known as the Liberator of South America. He was born in Venezuela in 1783. As a boy he was constantly aware of the injustices that resulted from Spain's rule of its South American colonies. Though his father was of Spanish descent and had considerable wealth, Simon Bolivar was denied many rights and privileges because he had been born in South America rather than in Spain. He was sent to Europe for his education. As he learned more of other countries, and particularly of the freedom that the United States had recently gained, he resolved to devote his life to freeing his native land from Spain. Though the first two revolts he organized were crushed and Bolivar was sent into exile, he did not give up. He began making plans for uniting all the countries of South America and expelling the Spanish completely. He organized an army and led it through the northern part of the continent, bringing freedom to the countries that are now Panama, Colombia, Peru, Ecuador, Venezuela, and Bolivia. This last country was named for him during his lifetime.

In Valparaiso, Chile, there is a bronze statue of William Wheelwright, a United States citizen to whom South Americans pay tribute. Wheelwright began his South American ventures when he was shipwrecked on the coast of Argentina in 1823. He made his way to the west coast of South America and established a thriving shipping business. In 1828 he took a trip back to the United States. While he was away, his partner lost all their property, and Wheelwright was forced to start over again. He moved to Valparaiso and began to study the natural resources of Chile. He decided the country could make no real gains without better ship service for passengers and freight. At that time steamships were just beginning to replace sailing vessels on the established routes of the Atlantic Ocean, but were almost unknown along the undeveloped Pacific coast. However, Wheelwright formed a company that bought two large steamers which were successfully used along the west coast of South America. He also realized that a method of transportation across the Isthmus of Panama would make trading with Europe and the east coast of North America faster and less expensive. His explorations of Panama started a chain of events that led to the building of the Panama Canal. Wheelwright's final achievement was to begin a system of railroads that would connect all parts of the interior, and someday bring about fulfillment of his dream for uniting the great South American "family of nations."

The statements below refer to one or more of the men on this page. Basing your answers on the material on this page, write P to indicate Pulaski, B for Bolivar, and W for Wheelwright.

_____ He had a strong belief in liberty.

_____ He was born to wealth but fought for the freedom of all.

_____ His interests and efforts extended beyond the bounds of his native country.

_____ He was not easily discouraged.

_____ He died before he knew whether any of his goals would become reality.

_____ He wanted to unite an entire continent.

Put X after the statement above that best expresses the idea of the introductory paragraph.

Locating Dictionary Entries

a b c d e f g h i j k l m n o p q r s t u v w x y z

Alphabetize each group of words below by numbering them to show the order in which they would appear in a dictionary.

.... nonsense	.... diamond	.... wife	.... leaven
.... quack	.... dug	.... wink	.... league
.... beard	.... dock	.... wicked	.... leader
.... house	.... deal	.... wiggle	.... leaden
.... pearl	.... dare	.... witch	.... learn
.... table	.... drank	.... wire	.... leach

When looking up an entry, you will save time if you are aware of the general alphabetical position of letters.   Then you can turn quickly to the right part of the dictionary.

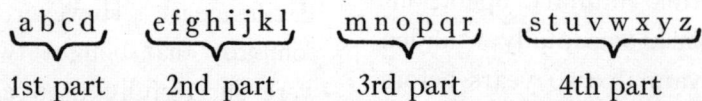

a b c d	e f g h i j k l	m n o p q r	s t u v w x y z
1st part	2nd part	3rd part	4th part

Write 1st, 2nd, 3rd, or 4th on the blank before each word below to show which part of the dictionary you would turn to when looking up the word.

.... throng	.... fringe	.... yonder	.... navigate
.... gravity	.... rescue	.... humidity	.... wrath
.... muscle	.... sheriff	.... currant	.... lagoon
.... boycott	.... vibrate	.... zither	.... disguise
.... ultrasonic	.... profit	.... kindling	.... quaint
.... oxygen	.... jitney	.... egotist	.... intrude

Guide words are the words printed at the top of each page in the main section of the dictionary. The word at the top of the left-hand column is the same as the first word you find on that page; the one at the top of the right-hand column io the same as the last word on the page.

Put a check mark in front of the words below that would be found on a dictionary page where the guide words are fourteen and frangible. If a word comes before that page, write b in the blank. If a word comes after that page, write a.

.... fresh	.... foyer	.... fragment	.... forage
.... frame	.... franc	.... founder	.... fragile
.... foster	.... friction	.... fragrant	.... France
.... foxglove	.... frailty	.... fraction	.... frantic
.... fowl	.... fray	.... fresco	.... fortune
.... fourth	.... fossil	.... foursquare	.... fractious

Select the Right Definition

bran dish (bran′dish), **1.** wave or shake threateningly; flourish: *The knight drew his sword and brandished it.* **2.** a threatening shake; flourish. 1 *v.*, 2 *n.*

bra zen (brā′zən), **1.** made of brass. **2.** like brass in color or strength. **3.** loud and harsh: *the brazen bellow of a horn.* **4.** shameless; impudent: *He was ashamed of his brazen behavior.* **5.** make shameless or impudent. 1-4 *adj.*, 5 *v.* —**bra′zen ly**, *adv.* —**bra′zen ness**, *n.*

con clude (kən klüd′), **1.** end; finish: *The book concluded happily.* **2.** arrange; settle: *The two countries concluded an agreement on trade.* **3.** find out by thinking; reach (certain facts or opinions) as a result of reasoning; infer: *From the tracks we saw we concluded that the animal must have been a deer.* **4.** decide; resolve: *I concluded not to go.* *v.*, **con clud ed, con clud ing.**

con dense (kən dens′), **1.** make or become denser or more compact: *Milk is condensed by evaporating most of the water from it.* **2.** make stronger; concentrate: *Light is condensed by means of lenses.* **3.** change from a gas or vapor to a liquid. If steam comes in contact with cold surfaces, it condenses or is condensed into water. **4.** put into fewer words; express briefly: *He condensed the paragraph into one line.* *v.*, **con densed, con dens ing.**

dis tin guish (dis ting′gwish), **1.** tell apart; see or show the difference in: *Can you distinguish cotton cloth from linen?* **2.** see or show the difference. **3.** see or hear clearly; make out plainly: *It is much too dark for me to distinguish anything.* **4.** make different; be a special quality or feature of: *Ability to talk distinguishes human beings from animals.* **5.** make famous or well-known: *He distinguished himself by winning three prizes.* **6.** separate into different groups. *v.*

ex pire (ek spīr′), **1.** come to an end: *You must obtain a new automobile license when your old one expires.* **2.** die. **3.** breathe out: *expire used air from the lungs.* *v.*, **ex pired, ex pir ing.**

men ace (men′is), **1.** threat: *In dry weather forest fires are a great menace.* **2.** threaten: *Floods menaced the valley with destruction.* 1 *n.*, 2 *v.*, **men aced, men ac ing.** —**men′ac ing ly**, *adv.*

peak (pēk), **1.** the pointed top of a mountain or hill: *snowy peaks.* **2.** mountain that stands alone: *Pike's Peak.* **3.** the highest point: *reach the peak of one's profession.* **4.** any pointed end or top: *the peak of a beard, the peak of a roof.* **5.** the front part or the brim of a cap, which stands out. **6.** the narrow part of a ship's hold at the bow or the stern. **7.** the upper rear corner of a sail. **8.** raise straight up; tilt up. 1-7 *n.*, 8 *v.*

pet ty (pet′i), **1.** having little importance or value; small: *She insisted on telling me all her petty troubles.* **2.** mean; narrow-minded. **3.** lower; subordinate. *adj.*, **pet ti er, pet ti est.**

re spond (ri spond′), **1.** answer; reply. **2.** act in answer; react: *A dog responds to kind treatment by loving its master.* *v.*

rich (rich), **1.** having much money or property: *a rich man.* **2.** well supplied; abounding: *The United States is rich in oil and coal.* **3.** producing or yielding abundantly; fertile: *rich soil, a rich mine.* **4.** valuable: *a rich harvest.* **5.** costly; elegant: *rich dress.* **6.** containing plenty of butter, eggs, flavoring, etc. **7.** (of colors, sounds, smells, etc.) deep; full; vivid. **8.** *Informal.* very amusing. *adj.* —**rich′ly**, *adv.* —**rich′ness**, *n.*

sus pend (səs pend′), **1.** hang down by attaching to something above: *The lamp was suspended from the ceiling.* **2.** hold in place as if by hanging: *We saw the smoke suspended in the still air.* **3.** stop for a while: *suspend work.* **4.** stop payment; be unable to pay one's debts. **5.** remove or exclude for a while from some privilege or job: *He was suspended from school for a week for bad conduct.* **6.** keep undecided; put off: *The court suspended judgment till next Monday.*

On the blank write the entry word and the number of the definition that explains the meaning of the italicized word in each sentence.

The patient *responded* favorably to the new drug. _____

The speech John gave in English class was *condensed* for use on television. _____

Construction work was *suspended* until more steel could be obtained. _____

The writer reached the *peak* of his fame when he was fifty. _____

We could scarcely *distinguish* our house in the fog. _____

The pirate was *brandishing* a gleaming cutlass as he stepped ashore. _____

The music critics were impressed with the *richness* of the violin's tones. _____

The librarian did not realize that the magazine subscription had *expired*. _____

By two o'clock the clouds looked so *menacing* that the picnickers went home. _____

Although he was guilty, the thief quietly but *brazenly* denied the crime. _____

Ann was not asked to welcome the guests because she has the *pettiest* attitude toward strangers of anyone in the club. _____

When Jack saw the empty garage and the drawn shades, he *concluded* that his parents had already left. _____

hat, āge, cāre, fär; let, ēqual, tėrm; it, īce; hot, ōpen, ôrder; oil, out; cup, pút, rüle, ūse; ch, child; ng, long; th, thin; ᴛʜ, then; zh, measure; ə represents *a* in about, *e* in taken, *i* in pencil, *o* in lemon, *u* in circus.

Tune the Definition into the Sentence

Read each sentence and find the meaning of the italicized word. Then rewrite the sentence, substituting all or part of the definition for the italicized word. To fit the definition into the sentence, you may need to add an ending to a word in the definition.

a brupt (ə brupt′), **1.** sudden; hasty; unexpected: *He made an abrupt turn to avoid another car.* **2.** very steep: *The road made an abrupt rise up the hill.* **3.** short or sudden in speech or manner; blunt: *He was very gruff and had an abrupt way of speaking. adj.* —**a brupt′ly,** *adv.* —**a brupt′ ness,** *n.*

clem en cy (klem′ən si), **1.** mercy: *The judge showed clemency to the prisoner.* **2.** mildness: *The clemency of the weather allowed them to live outdoors. n., pl.* **clem en cies.**

con sume (kən süm′), **1.** use up: *A student consumes much of his time in studying.* **2.** eat or drink up: *We will consume at least this much food on our hike.* **3.** destroy; burn up. **4.** waste away; be destroyed. **5.** spend; waste (time, money, etc.). *v.,* **con sumed, con sum ing.** —**con sum′ a ble,** *adj.*

dis tant (dis′tənt), **1.** far away in space: *The moon is distant from the earth.* **2.** away: *The town is three miles distant.* **3.** far apart in time, relationship, likeness, etc.; not close: *A third cousin is a distant relative.* **4.** not friendly: *She gave him only a distant nod. adj.* —**dis′tant ly,** *adv.*

di vert (də vèrt′), **1.** turn aside: *A ditch diverted water from the stream into the fields.* **2.** amuse; entertain: *Music diverted him after a hard day's work. v.*

mu ti ny (mū′tə ni), **1.** open rebellion against lawful authority, especially by sailors or soldiers against their officers. **2.** take part in a mutiny; rebel. 1 *n., pl.* **mu ti nies;** 2 *v.,* **mu ti nied, mu ti ny ing.**

pur loin (pèr loin′), steal. *v.*

va ri e ty (və rī′ə ti), **1.** lack of sameness; difference; variation: *Variety is the spice of life.* **2.** number of different kinds: *The store has a great variety of toys.* **3.** kind; sort: *Which variety of cake do you prefer?* **4.** a division of a species. **5.** *Esp. Brit.* vaudeville. *n., pl.* **va ri e ties.**

wal low (wol′ō), **1.** roll about; flounder: *The pigs wallowed in the mud. The boat wallowed helplessly in the stormy sea.* **2.** live contentedly in filth, wickedness, etc., like a beast; live or continue self-indulgently or luxuriously, as in some form of pleasure, manner of life, etc.: *wallow in wealth, wallow in sentimentality.* **3.** act of wallowing. **4.** place where an animal wallows. 1,2 *v.,* 3,4 *n.*

The ship started to *wallow* in the swirling waters.

Fire *consumes* many valuable trees each year.

The nearest source of water was eight blocks *distant.*

The guide was *diverting* the tourists with tales of his adventures.

When dessert was served, Ann *abruptly* left the table.

The florist had developed a new *variety* of roses.

At the end of the fourth month at sea, the sailors *mutinied.*

The spy *purloined* the secret code.

The island was famous for the *clemency* of its climate.

----

hat, āge, cãre, fär; let, ēqual, tèrm; it, īce; hot, ōpen, ôrder; oil, out; cup, pùt, rüle, ūse; ch, child; ng, long; th, thin; ŦH, then; zh, measure; ə represents *a* in about, *e* in taken, *i* in pencil, *o* in lemon, *u* in circus.

Rewrite each sentence, using the appropriate definition instead of the italicized word.
You may need to change the order of some words to make the sentence read smoothly.

cher ish (cher′ish), **1.** hold dear; treat with affection; care for tenderly: *A mother cherishes her baby.* **2.** keep in mind; cling to: *For many years the old woman cherished the hope that her wandering son would come home. v.*

de light (di līt′), **1.** great pleasure; joy. **2.** thing that gives great pleasure: *Dancing is her delight.* **3.** please greatly: *The circus delighted the children.* **4.** have great pleasure: *Children delight in surprises.* 1,2 *n.*, 3,4 *v.* —**de light′er**, *n.*

en rage (en rāj′), put into a rage; make very angry; make furious. *v.*, **en raged, en rag ing.**

en ti tle (en tī′təl), **1.** give the title of; call by the name of: *A book that explains words is entitled a dictionary.* **2.** give a claim or right to; provide with a reason to ask or get something: *Their age and experience entitle old people to the respect of young people. v.*, **en ti tled, en ti tling.** Also, **intitle.**

ex am ine (eg zam′ən), **1.** look at closely and carefully. **2.** test the knowledge or qualifications of; ask questions of; test. *v.*, **ex am ined, ex am in ing.** —**ex am′in er**, *n.*

in vert (in vėrt′), **1.** turn upside down: *invert a glass.* **2.** turn around or reverse in position, direction, order, etc.: *If you invert "I can," you have "Can I?" v.*

length en (lengk′thən or leng′thən), **1.** make longer: *A tailor can lengthen your trousers.* **2.** become or grow longer: *Your legs have lengthened a great deal since you were 5 years old. v.*

mis lead (mis lēd′), **1.** lead astray; cause to go in the wrong direction: *Our guide misled us in the woods, and we got lost.* **2.** cause to do wrong; lead into wrongdoing: *He is a good boy, but bad companions misled him.* **3.** lead to think what is not so; deceive: *Sometimes advertisements are so exaggerated that they mislead people. v.*, **mis led, mis lead ing.** —**mis lead′er**, *n.*

pon der (pon′dər), consider carefully; think over: *ponder a problem. v.*

ren o vate (ren′ə vāt), make new again; make like new; restore to good condition: *renovate a garment or a house. v.*, **ren o vat ed, ren o vat ing.** —**ren′o va′tor**, *n.*

south er ly (suŦH′ər li), **1.** toward the south: *The windows face southerly.* **2.** from the south. *adj., adv.*

Ted wanted to *examine* the electric dishwasher.

The magician's performance *delighted* the students.

After Mrs. Hill washed the drapes, she had to *lengthen* them.

The cook tried to *invert* the heavy bowl.

The road sign is not clear and may *mislead* you.

The bad news *enraged* the dictator.

The jeweler thought he could *renovate* the watch.

A *southerly* wind brought sweltering heat.

After *pondering* the situation, Ed decided to stay at home.

For months, Sue *cherished* the tiny bird.

His years of service *entitled* the captain to a pension.

----

hat, āge, cāre, fär; let, ēqual, tėrm; it, īce; hot, ōpen, ôrder; oil, out; cup, pu̇t, rüle, ūse; ch, child; ng, long; th, thin; ŦH, then; zh, measure; ə represents *a* in about, *e* in taken, *i* in pencil, *o* in lemon, *u* in circus.

Rewrite each sentence using the definition instead of the italicized word.
You will need to rewrite the definition in your own words to make it fit.
Sometimes you may need to change the words in the sentence, too.

ab sence (ab′səns), **1.** being away: *His absence was caused by illness.* **2.** time of being away: *The sailor returned after an absence of two years.* **3.** being without; lack: *Darkness is the absence of light.* *n.*

ath let ic (ath let′ik), **1.** active and strong. **2.** of, like, or suited to an athlete. **3.** having to do with active games and sports. *adj.* —**ath let′i cal ly,** *adv.*

e quiv a lent (i kwiv′ə lənt), **1.** equal in value, measure, force, effect, meaning, etc.: *Nodding your head is equivalent to saying yes.* **2.** having the same extent: *A triangle and a square of equal area are equivalent.* **3.** something equivalent. 1,2 *adj.,* 3 *n.* —**e quiv′a lent ly,** *adv.*

ex port (eks pôrt′ or eks′pôrt for 1; eks′pôrt for 2, 3), **1.** send (goods) out of one country for sale and use in another: *The United States exports automobiles.* **2.** article exported: *Cotton is an important export of the United States.* **3.** an exporting; exportation. 1 *v.,* 2,3 *n.*

lore (lôr), **1.** facts and stories about a certain subject: *bird lore, Irish lore.* **2.** learning; knowledge. *n.*

om niv o rous (om niv′ə rəs), **1.** eating every kind of food. **2.** eating both animal and vegetable food: *Man is an omnivorous animal.* **3.** taking in everything; fond of all kinds: *An omnivorous reader reads all kinds of books.* *adj.* —**om niv′o rous ly,** *adv.* —**om niv′o rous ness,** *n.*

per son nel (pèr′sə nel′), persons employed in any work, business, or service. *n.*

pop u lar i ty (pop′ū lar′ə ti), being liked by most people. *n.*

teens (tēnz), the years of life from 13 to 19 inclusive. *n. pl.*

ver sion (vèr′zhən), **1.** a translation from one language to another: *a version of the Bible.* **2.** one particular statement, account, or description: *Each of the three boys gave his own version of the quarrel.* *n.*

Jim was interested in bird *lore*.

Much sugar is *exported* from Cuba.

During Jane's *absence*, the club had disbanded.

The *athletic* department awarded letter sweaters to the team.

The boys were all in their *teens*.

The *popularity* of the game increased.

Bob's *version* of the melee was different from Sam's.

Hedgehogs are *omniverous* creatures.

When Mr. Smith returned to the company, he found the *personnel* unchanged.

The German word "Kaiser" is *equivalent* to the Russian word "Czar."

----

hat, āge, cāre, fär; let, ēqual, tèrm; it, īce; hot, ōpen, ôrder; oil, out; cup, pút, rüle, ūse; ch, child; ng, long; th, thin; ŦH, then; zh, measure; ə represents *a* in about, *e* in taken, *i* in pencil, *o* in lemon, *u* in circus.

Homographs

Very often you cannot tell what a word means until you meet it in context. This is especially true of a homograph, or a word that has the same spelling as another, but a different origin and meaning. For example, pitch *can mean "to throw something," or it can mean "a black, sticky substance."*

In each sentence below, the italicized word is a homograph. Read the sentences, look at the dictionary entries at the right, and then answer the questions.

The champ entered in a *blaze* of spotlights.

Which entry for *blaze* is appropriate in this sentence? _____

What part of speech is *blaze* in this sentence? _____

Which definitions would you automatically eliminate? _____

Which definition fits best? _____

Milly recognized the horse by the *blaze* on its forehead.

What part of speech is *blaze* in this sentence? _____

Which entry fits the context? _____

Which definition? _____

The guide *blazed* a trail over the mountain.

What part of speech is *blaze* in this sentence? _____

Which entry and which definition fit best? _____

blaze¹ (blāz), **1.** a bright flame or fire: *He could see the blaze of the campfire across the beach.* **2.** burn with a bright flame; be on fire: *A fire was blazing in the fireplace.* **3.** an intense light; glare. **4.** show bright colors or lights: *On Christmas Eve the big house blazed with lights.* **5.** bright display: *The tulips made a blaze of color in the garden.* **6.** make a bright display. **7.** a violent outburst: *a blaze of temper.* **8.** burst out in anger or excitement. 1,3,5,7 *n.*, 2,4,6,8 *v.*, **blazed, blaz ing. blaze away,** fire a gun, etc.

blaze² (blāz), **1.** mark on a tree made by chipping off a piece of bark. **2.** mark (a tree, trail, etc.) by chipping off a piece of the bark. **3.** a white spot on the face of a horse, cow, etc. 1,3 *n.*, 2 *v.*, **blazed, blaz ing.**

blaze³ (blāz), make known; proclaim. *v.*, **blazed, blaz ing.**

Mrs. Evans' *prize* muffins were prominently displayed at the fair.

What part of speech is *prize* in this sentence? _____

Which entry fits best? _____

Which definition? _____

Mrs. Evans *prized* the award very highly.

What part of speech is *prize* in this sentence? _____

Which entry fits this context? _____

Which definition? _____

The Admiral sailed into the harbor with his *prize* in tow.

Which entry is appropriate in this sentence? _____

prize¹ (prīz), **1.** reward won after trying against other people: *Prizes will be given for the three best stories.* **2.** given as a prize. **3.** that has won a prize. **4.** worthy of a prize: *prize vegetables.* **5.** reward worth working for. 1,5 *n.*, 2-4 *adj.*

prize² (prīz), thing or person that is taken or captured, especially an enemy's ship and its cargo taken at sea. *n.*

prize³ (prīz), **1.** value highly: *She prizes her best china.* **2.** estimate the value of. *v.*, **prized, priz ing.**

"I've gotten into a terrible *snarl* over this algebra," wailed Lorraine.

Which is the appropriate entry? _____

Which definition fits best? _____

The mother dog *snarled* whenever someone tried to fondle her puppies.

What part of speech is *snarl* in this sentence? _____

Which entry fits this context? _____

Which definition? _____

snarl¹ (snärl), **1.** growl sharply and show one's teeth. **2.** a sharp, angry growl. **3.** speak harshly in a sharp, angry tone. **4.** sharp, angry words. **5.** say or express with a snarl. 1,3,5 *v.*, 2,4 *n.* —**snarl er,** *n.* —**snarl ing ly,** *adv.*

snarl² (snärl), **1.** tangle: *She combed the snarls out of her hair.* **2.** confusion: *His legal affairs were in a snarl.* **3.** confuse. 1,2 *n.*, 1,3 *v.*

hat, āge, cãre, fär; let, ēqual, tėrm; it, īce; hot, ōpen, ôrder; oil, out; cup, pút, rüle, ūse; ch, child; ng, long; th, thin; ŦH, then; zh, measure; ə represents *a* in about, *e* in taken, *i* in pencil, *o* in lemon, *u* in circus.

Use both the definitions and the pictures to answer the questions below.

ar ma dil lo (är′mə-dil′ō), any of several small burrowing mammals of South America and some parts of southern North America, with an armorlike shell of bony plates. Some kinds can roll up into a ball when attacked.

Armadillo
(total length 2½ ft.)

bat (bat), a flying mammal with a mouselike body and membranous wings supported on the enormously developed bones of the forelimbs. Bats fly at night. There are over 600 species; most of them are insect-eating but some live on fruit and a few suck the blood of other mammals.

Bat

duck bill (duk′bil′), a small water mammal of Australia and Tasmania that lays eggs and has webbed feet and a beak like a duck; platypus.

Duckbill (about 1½ ft. long)

mon goose or **mon goos** (mong′güs), a slender, ferretlike carnivorous mammal of India, used for destroying rats, and noted for its ability to kill certain poisonous snakes without being harmed.

Mongoose (length, including the tail, about 2 ft.)

sa ble (sā′bəl), **1.** a small flesh-eating mammal valued for its dark brown, glossy fur. **2.** its fur. Sable is one of the most costly furs. **3.** *Poetic.* black; dark: *a widow's sable garments.*

Sable (about 1½ ft. long, without the tail)

sloth (slōth or slôth), **1.** unwillingness to work or exert oneself; laziness; idleness: *His sloth keeps him from engaging in sports.* **2.** *Archaic.* slowness. **3.** a very slow-moving mammal of South and Central America that lives in trees. Sloths hang upside down from tree branches.

Sloth (about 2 ft. long)

wea sel (wē′zəl), a small, quick, sly mammal with a long, slender body and short legs. Weasels feed on rats, birds, eggs, etc.

Weasel (6 to 8 in. long, without the tail)

whale (hwāl), **1.** mammal shaped like a huge fish and living in the sea. Men get oil and whalebone from whales. **2.** hunt and catch whales.

Greenland whale
(about 60 ft. long)

wol ver ine or **wol ver ene** (wùl′vər ēn′ or wùl′vər ēn), **1.** a clumsy, heavily built, meat-eating mammal of northern regions, related to the weasel. **2.** its fur.

Wolverine (2 to 3 ft. long, without the tail)

What is another name for the duckbill? _____

Which animal lives in trees—the mongoose or the sloth? _____

Why isn't the size of the bat indicated? _____

Which is larger—a sable or a weasel? _____

Which two of these animals have meat as their chief food—the sable, the bat, the wolverine? _____

Why do you suppose the whale was included in this group of animals? _____

Could a duckbill move about easily in a cage one yard square? _____

Are the sloth and the armadillo natives of South America? _____

Which two of these animals are about the same size—the sable, the weasel, the duckbill? _____

Is the nose of the duckbill shaped like that of the mongoose? _____

Which of these animals are most similar in appearance and habits? _____

Special Uses of Words

Most English words are shared by all who speak the language. But some words, and some meanings of words, are used only by certain groups of people or on certain occasions. In the dictionary these specialized words and meanings have labels showing how, when, and where they are used. If the use refers to all the meanings of a word, the label is put before all the meanings. If it refers to only one meaning, the label is put between the number and the definition to which it applies. Some of the labels are:

Informal, used in ordinary, everyday speech or writing but not in formal speech or writing.

Slang, not accepted as good English by educated speakers or writers and used only in very informal speech or writing.

Dialect, used only in the speech of a certain geographical area.

Poetic, usually found only in poetry or in prose that is attempting to achieve a poetic effect.

Archaic, used rarely except in old books or in books written in the style of an earlier period.

Trademark, owned by a particular company and used to identify its product.

French, Latin, Italian, etc., foreign words used in English writing and speech but not thought of as English.

Brit., Scottish, U.S., etc., used mostly or only in a particular part of the English-speaking world.

Answer the questions below by referring to these dictionary entries.

a fore (ə fôr′), *Archaic* and *Dialect*. before. *adv., prep., conj.*

ar dor (är′dər), **1.** eagerness; warmth of emotion; great enthusiasm: *the ardor of a saint, patriotic ardor*. **2.** burning heat. *n.* Also, *Brit.* **ardour.**

brae (brā), *Scottish*. slope; hillside. *n.*

dark some (därk′səm), *Poetic*. **1.** dark. **2.** gloomy. *adj.*

hock[1] (hok), joint in the hind leg of a horse, cow, etc., above the fetlock joint. *n.* Also, **hough.**

hock[2] (hok), *U.S. Slang*. pawn. *v., n.*

ko dak (kō′dak), **1.** a small camera with rolls of film on which photographs are taken. **2.** take photographs with a kodak. 1 *n.*, 2 *v.*, **ko daked, ko dak ing.**

Ko dak (kō′dak), *Trademark*. a small camera made by the Eastman Kodak Company. *n.*

plank (plangk), **1.** a long, flat piece of sawed timber thicker than a board. **2.** cover or furnish with planks. **3.** cook on a board: *Steak is sometimes planked*. **4.** article or feature of the platform of a political party, etc. **5.** *Informal*. put or set with force: *He planked down the package*. **6.** *Informal*. pay at once: *She planked out her money*. 1,4 *n.*, 2,3,5,6 *v.*

ram bunc tious (ram bungk′shəs), *U.S. Slang*. **1.** wild and uncontrollable; unruly. **2.** noisy and violent; boisterous. *adj.*

San (sän or san), *Spanish* and *Italian*. Saint. *adj.*

sleep er (slēp′ər), **1.** person or thing that sleeps. **2.** a railroad sleeping car. **3.** a horizontal beam. **4.** *Brit.* tie to support a railroad track. **5.** *Informal*. person, animal, or thing that does very much better in a contest of any sort than was anticipated. *n.*

Would it be legal for you to manufacture a camera and give it the trade name *Kodak?* _____

If you read in a sports magazine that the half-mile race was won by a *sleeper*, which meaning of the word would you think was intended? _____

If you heard a man mention sheep on the *brae*, would you judge that he was French? _____

San Francisco was settled by Spaniards. Did they give the city an English name? _____

The word *afore* might be found in a story written years ago. Where else might it be used?

If a writer spells the word *ardor* "ardour," is he using the American spelling? _____

Might a playground attendant use the word *rambunctious* when telling a friend about the behavior of some children in his care? _____

In what kind of writing would you expect to read about "a *darksome* path"? _____

Would you expect to read in a history book that the Dutch *planked* out twenty-four dollars for Manhattan Island? _____

If a man said that he had *hocked* his watch, which entry's meaning would he be using? _____

Which Pronunciation Is It?

At the right of each sentence you will find pronunciations for two different words.
Refer to the key at the bottom of the page to determine how to pronounce them. Then
underline the pronunciation for the word that belongs in the sentence.

Frank tried to _____ the handle onto the pitcher.   (sod′ər)   (sōl′jər)

The trapper wanted to _____ some furs for a gun.   (bat′ər)   (bär′tər)

Mrs. Harris was _____ when she heard that a theft had taken place.   (dis tôrt′)   (dis trot′)

The sentinel raised his _____ and prepared to fire.   (mus′kit)   (mū′zik)

The _____ for mutiny is a dire one.   (pē′nuk′əl)   (pen′əl ti)

A brilliant _____ went shooting across the dark sky.   (kə mit′)   (kom′it)

The locality was noted for its fine _____ crops.   (bär′li)   (bãr′li)

Owning a helpless little puppy did much to _____ Helen's fear of dogs.   (al′i)   (ə lā′)

The prisoners were placed in _____ that clanked when they walked.   (slak′ənz)   (shak′əlz)

The heavy rain completely obliterated a _____ glued on the side of the barn. (pas′tər)   (pōs′tər)

Underline the pronunciation that correctly answers the question.

Which word means "stiff"?   Which means "pale"?
(rech′id)   (rij′id)   (ri līd′)   (won)   (wun)   (wôrm)

Which means "avoid work"?   Which means "mistakes"?
(shėrk)   (shärk)   (shrēk)   (ar′ōz)   (er′ərz)   (ēr′ əz)

Which could a dress be made from?   Which means "dreamy thoughts"?
(mə tėr′nəl)   (mə tēr′i əl)   (mas′tər fəl)   (rev′ər ənt)   (ref′ər ē′)   (rev′ər i)

Which is a mechanical man?   Which means "famous"?
(rō′bət)   (rab′it)   (rob′ər)   (im′ə nənt)   (em′ə nənt)   (in′ə sənt)

Which shows directions?   Which means "willing to share"?
(kəm pōz′)   (kam′pəs)   (kum′pəs)   (jēn′yəs)   (jen′ər əs)   (jen′ər āt)

hat, āge, cãre, fär; let, ēqual, tėrm; it, īce; hot, ōpen, ôrder; oil, out; cup, pùt, rüle, ūse; ch, child;
ng, long; th, thin; ᴛʜ, then; zh, measure; ə represents *a* in about, *e* in taken, *i* in pencil, *o* in lemon, *u* in circus.

Choose the pronunciation for the name of each object
and underline it. Use the key at the bottom of this page.

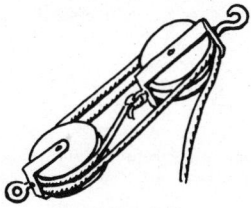

(pŏŏl′ĭz)
(pŏ·lēs′)

(ûrn)
(ī′ērn)

(bärj)
(băj)

(wō′fŏŏl)
(wŏf′′l)

(kûr′nĕl)
(kĕn′ĕl)

(bâr′lĭ)
(bär′lĭ)

(rȧ·vēn′)
(rā′vĕn)

(tôr′tŭs)
(tŏŏr′ĭst)

(bûr′ō)
(bū′rō)

(sĭl′ŏŏ·ĕt′)
(sȧ·lūt′)

(kŏr′ȯ·nā′shŭn)
(kär·nā′shŭn)

(dī′ȧ·mŭnd)
(dĕ·mȧnd′)

(kär′tŏn)
(kär·tōōn′)

(kŏm·pârz′)
(kŭm′pȧs)

(dēr)
(dâr)

(dŏl′ĭ)
(doi′lĭ)

(gŭt′ēr)
(gĭ·tär′)

(jŏŏ′ĕl)
(joul)

(pĕs′tēr)
(pȧs′tŭr)

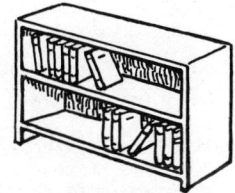

(bōō·kāz′)
(bŏŏk′kās′)

āle, chȧotic, câre, ădd, ȧccount, ärm, ȧsk, sofȧ; ēve, hẽre, ĕvent, ĕnd, silĕnt, makẽr; īce, ĭll, charĭty;
ōld, ȯbey, ôrb, ŏdd, sŏft, cȯnnect; fōōd, fŏŏt; out, oil; cūbe, ŭnite, ûrn, ŭp, circŭs, menü; go;
she; natūre, verdūre; par′don (pär′d′n), eat′en (ēt′′n), e′vil (ē′v′l).

How Much Does a Dictionary Entry Tell You?

Use these definitions to answer the questions about the sentences below.

di shev eled (də shev′əld). **1.** rumpled; mussed; disordered; untidy. **2.** hanging loosely or in disorder: *disheveled hair*. *adj.*

di shev elled (də shev′əld), *Brit.* disheveled. *adj.*

fa cil i ty (fə sil′ə ti), **1.** absence of difficulty; ease: *The boy ran and dodged with such facility that no one could catch him. The facility of communication is far greater now than it was a hundred years ago.* **2.** power to do anything easily, quickly, and smoothly. **3.** something that makes an action easy; aid; convenience: *Ropes, swings, and sand piles are facilities for play.* **4.** easygoing quality; tendency to yield to others. *n., pl.* **fa cil i ties.**

fun da men tal (fun′də men′təl), **1.** of the foundation or basis; forming a foundation or basis; essential. **2.** principle, rule, law, etc., that forms a foundation or basis; essential part. **3.** having to do with the lowest note of a chord in music. **4.** the lowest note of a chord in music. 1,3 *adj.*, 2,4 *n.* —**fun′da men′tal ly,** *adv.*

hi-fi (hī′fī′ for 1, hī′fī′ for 2), *Slang.* **1.** high-fidelity. **2.** high-fidelity reproduction of music or the equipment for this. 1 *adj.*, 2 *n.*

pri or[1] (prī′ər), coming before; earlier: *I can't go with you because I have a prior engagement.* *adj.* **prior to,** coming before in time, order, or importance; earlier than; before.

pri or[2] (prī′ər), head of a priory or monastery for men. Priors usually rank below abbots. *n.*

ret i nue (ret′ə nü or ret′ə nū), group of attendants or retainers; following: *The king's retinue accompanied him on the journey.* *n.*

se ñor (sā nyôr′), *Spanish.* **1.** Mr.; sir. **2.** gentleman. *n., pl.* **se ño res** (-nyō′rās).

sev er (sev′ər), **1.** cut apart; cut off: *sever a rope. The ax severed his head from his body.* **2.** break off: *The two countries severed friendly relations.* **3.** part; divide; separate: *a church severed into two factions. The rope severed and the swing fell down.* *v.* —**sev′er a ble,** *adj.*

The lawyer stated that his client's claim was filed in court *prior* to Mr. Harris' claim.

Which entry for *prior* gives the appropriate meaning for this sentence? _ _ _ _ _ _ _ _ _ _ _ _ _

How would you rewrite the sentence without using *prior?* _

_ _

Rinaldo found that his antagonist had great *facility* with a sword.

Which syllable is accented? _ _ _ _ _ _ _ _ _ _

Which definition fits here? _ _ _ _ _ _ _ _ _

How would you reword the last part of the sentence, using the definition? _ _ _ _ _ _ _ _ _

_ _

Mr. Andrews *severed* all his connections with the company when he retired.

What is the root word? _ _ _ _ _ _ _ _ _ _ _ _

Which definition fits here? _ _ _ _ _ _ _ _ _

Which key word gives the sound for the *e* in the second syllable? _ _ _ _ _ _ _ _ _ _ _ _ _

Jane bought a *hi-fi* set with her earnings.

Is this the kind of word that would probably be used in formal writing? _ _ _ _ _ _ _ _ _ _

Why or why not? _ _ _ _ _ _ _ _ _ _ _ _ _ _ _

What part of speech is *hi-fi?* _ _ _ _ _ _ _ _

The *fundamental* principles of bacteriology were taught in the college course.

What part of speech is *fundamental?* _ _ _ _ _ _ _

Which definition fits here? _ _ _ _ _ _ _ _ _ _ _ _

Which syllable has the primary accent? _ _ _ _

Jim's clothes were dirty and *disheveled.*

On which syllable does the accent fall? _ _ _ _

How would a British writer spell this word?

_ _

Joan was chosen to be a member of the football queen's *retinue.*

How many syllables does *retinue* have? _ _ _ _

What key words give the vowel sound for the last syllable? _ _ _ _ _ _ _ _ _ _ _ _ _ _ _ _ _ _

How would you rewrite the sentence, using the definition? _ _ _ _ _ _ _ _ _ _ _ _ _ _ _ _ _ _ _

_ _

_ _

"Welcome to our home, *señores,*" said the man with great courtesy.

What foreign language does this word come from? _

Is the man speaking to one man or to more than one? _

What is the key word for the vowel sound in the last syllable of *señores?* _ _ _ _ _ _ _ _ _ _ _ _

---

hat, āge, cāre, fär; let, ēqual, tėrm; it, īce; hot, ōpen, ôrder; oil, out; cup, pùt, rüle, ūse; ch, child; ng, long; th, thin; ŦH, then; zh, measure; ə represents *a* in about, *e* in taken, *i* in pencil, *o* in lemon, *u* in circus.

Clues to a Person's Feelings

An author may tell you directly how a character in a story feels, or he may indicate the character's feelings by telling what the person says or does. An author may also let you know how a character feels by describing inner sensations. For example, he might say, Al's skin began to prickle. Or he might describe some observable change in the body, as Al frowned.

In each passage below, underline the phrase that the writer used to show how the person felt.

With a thumping heart, Steve peered into the dark, silent room.

When his teacher said that he was an expert typist, Amos puffed out his chest and pulled in his stomach.

The color faded from Jerry's cheeks when he heard that his dog had been struck by a car.

An icy chill ran up and down Peggy's spine as she listened to the coyotes howling on the lonely prairie outside the cabin.

Mr. Hoffman's eyes were twinkling as he said, "If I were you, boys, I wouldn't worry about finding a new place to practice basketball."

The tightrope walker held her breath as her partner in the act seemed about to lose his balance on the high wire.

Francis tried to answer Miss Lynn's question, but he had to gulp several times before he was able to speak.

As she watched her son start off to school for the first time, Mrs. Madison had a lump in her throat.

Terry began to tremble as he realized that he had stepped on the brake just in time to stop his automobile before it hit the two children playing in the street.

Steve gazed blankly into space, unmindful of the jostling passengers who surrounded him.

When the child was asked what his name was, he only looked at his toes and held tighter to his mother's skirt.

His muscles frozen, Roy stood poised on the diving board, unable to move.

Caroline had a sensation of dryness in her throat as she rose to make her report to the school assembly.

The policeman merely arched his eyebrows when Mr. Dale said, "I didn't notice that I had put my car in a No Parking zone."

As the student pilot waited for clearance from the control tower to take off on his first solo flight, every nerve in his body was tingling.

Harry's eyes narrowed when he noticed a frayed cable on the pulley of the steam shovel.

Mr. Adams breathed a deep sigh as the airplane's faltering engine finally settled down to a steady purring.

As the long, dull speech ran past his dinner hour, Mr. Dean began to tap his foot.

When Susanna momentarily forgot one of her lines during the play, a wave of crimson crept over her face.

As he slowly edged his way across a narrow catwalk on the high scaffolding, Dan kept wiping away the perspiration that ran down his forehead and into his eyes.

While he stared at the algebra problem, Mike wrinkled his brow and tapped his pencil on the desk.

Helen began to hum a song when she noticed that there were only a few more dirty dishes to be washed.

To the Rescue

"Please, Father. Let me come along," Bert begged for the tenth time since he and his father, a wholesale grocer, had begun feverishly to load the big truck with boxes of food.

"No, Bert. You'd only be in the way," said Mr. Daly. "And don't ask me again," he added, pausing to wipe the sweat from his brow. The heat in the warehouse was stifling.

"It was lucky you were in the office when that telephone call came," Mr. Daly went on. "I don't know where I could have gotten any of the men at this hour."

Bert's thoughts sped back over the past half-hour. It seemed only five minutes since he had stopped in at the warehouse, intending to walk home with his father. Mr. Daly had been working late, checking the books.

Then the telephone call had come, and a shaky voice had told the news. Pawnee Falls, thirty miles to the south, had been hit by a freak wind and cloudburst. The dam above the city had given way, and conditions in Pawnee Falls were desperate. Scores of people were hurt, and hundreds had been driven from their homes.

Bert had once seen a flooded town. Many of the houses had been almost covered with water, and Bert had felt sorry for the frightened and homeless people.

Bert thought again of the message. "Send us food and medical supplies. The only way to reach us is by boat. We have made arrangements with the owner of your ferry, the *River Queen*, to make the trip here. He is bringing doctors and will leave in an hour from the Second Street Dock. Can you be there ready to drive your loaded truck on by that time?"

"You can count on me!" Bert's father had promised. Now, good as his word, he was ready to go.

"Close the doors after me, Bert," he called. "And then you might as well go on home."

Bert watched the red tail lights of the truck as his father drove away. Then his heart leaped into his throat. His father was taking the short cut that went under the M & I tracks. Bert had ridden with the regular drivers and knew that the top of the big truck wouldn't clear the underpass. Evidently his father didn't know this.

Bert began to run, shouting wildly as he went. Then he heard a sickening scraping noise. When he arrived at the scene, he heard the engine racing furiously as his father struggled to back the truck out. It was no use. The truck was wedged in tight.

With an exclamation of dismay, Mr. Daly shut off the motor and clambered down out of the big truck.

"Well," he said, "there goes my chance of making the ferry. What a mess! Now we'll have to get the wrecker."

As his father gloomily began looking around for a telephone, Bert had a sudden inspiration.

"Dad, I know a way out! All we have to do is let a little air out of the tires. That will lower the truck enough to do the trick. Then you can back out yourself."

"You're right, Son!" shouted Mr. Daly. "Absolutely right! Let's get busy."

In a few minutes the truck was extricated.

Mr. Daly leaned over and opened the door.

"Get in, Bert," he said. "We'll have to go get more air in these tires. I guess I need you on this trip after all."

Within a short time Bert experienced many different feelings. Explain when he probably felt:

inspired _____

disappointed _____

fearful _____

happy _____

sympathetic _____

How Did the Speaker Feel?

After each incident below, underline the word that best describes the
way the speaker felt when he said what he did.

It was the height of the rush hour when Ed stopped his truck in front of the Crory Building and went in to deliver a package. The street was barely wide enough for two lanes of traffic, and in a few minutes a long line of cars was stalled back of the parked truck.

When Ed returned, a police officer was standing beside the offending vehicle.

"Hey, you!" bawled the officer, his face crimson. "Get this truck out of the way. Who do you think you are?"

The traffic officer felt ____.
enthusiastic   enraged   hysterical   embarrassed

The members of Nick's hiking club had started up the trail shortly after midnight so that they could reach the summit of the mountain before sunrise. As the boys approached the crest, faint streaks of light began to tint the sky. Just as they reached the highest plateau, the sun seemed to burst from the horizon, flooding the earth with rose and golden light.

Nick caught his breath. "Oh, look!" he gasped, gazing into the eastern sky.

Nick felt ____.
horrified   wistful   overawed   hilarious

Lucinda's usually smiling face wore a look of strain these days. Even the fun of trimming the tree, wrapping packages, and decorating cookies failed to lift the weight from her heart. This was to have been the most wonderful Christmas of her life—the Christmas of her first formal dance. But here it was only three days before the party, and Phil still hadn't called her.

Suddenly the phone rang. Lucinda leaped to answer. "You've been sick? . . . Why—why, yes, Phil, of course I'll go with you," she breathed.

Lucinda felt ____.
sad   disgruntled   blissful   uncertain

Ted enrolled for the course in Spanish only because a foreign language was required in his school. The work was difficult for him. He dreaded the first test and studied hard in preparation for it. The day after the test, Miss Ruiz, the teacher, stopped him in the hall to tell him that he had made a high score.

"I made an *A* on the test?" Ted squeaked.

Ted felt ____.
irritable   defiant   curious   incredulous

Dan worked all summer to earn money for a used car. By September he had accumulated enough to purchase an ancient model that he had had his eye on. For a few days the car ran perfectly, but the first time Dan tried to drive to school, it sputtered, coughed, and then jolted to a stop two blocks away from home. Some younger boys walked by while Dan was vainly tinkering with the engine. As the boys passed, they hooted, "Why don't you get a horse?"

The boys felt ____.
mischievous   sympathetic   baffled   ashamed

Mr. Haynes had planned his radio speech so that it would take exactly eight minutes. His secretary had typed the script on easily handled cards that wouldn't rustle when he turned them. The rehearsal went well, and when it was time to go on the air, he had a pleasant feeling of composure. For a few minutes he spoke fluently. Then it happened. As he tried to flip over the next card of his script, the whole handful slipped out of his grasp and scattered to the floor.

There was utter silence for a moment. Then Mr. Haynes stammered, "I g-guess that's all I have to s-say."

Mr. Haynes felt ____.
cheerful   infuriated   disturbed   relieved

A Harrowing Experience

I am an enthusiastic "spelunker"—or at least I used to be. I didn't know what the word meant until I read about it in a story. Then I learned that for several years I had been a spelunker, or speleologist—a person who likes to explore and study caves.

There are many beautiful limestone caverns near our town, and almost every Saturday my best friends, Bill and Olaf, and I went exploring in them. One Saturday, though, Bill and Olaf couldn't go, and so I decided that I would go by myself.

Just as I was about to leave, my sister Mary appeared. "Can't I go with you today, Lem?" she asked.

"I should say not," I told her curtly. Mary always thinks she ought to do everything I do, even though she's a girl and nearly two years younger than I am.

Grabbing up my flashlight, I started over to the caves. Maybe I'd find another new one today. That's what I always tried to do—find a cave I hadn't seen before.

I did, too. As I wandered through a long, meandering passage, I saw a small unfamiliar-looking opening. I crawled through it into the most beautiful cavern I had ever seen. It was full of spectacular rock formations—stalactites hanging from the ceiling like huge icicles, and spirelike stalagmites rising from the floor, all glittering like jewels.

All of a sudden there was a roar right behind me. I turned, terrified, and found that a small avalanche of rocks had fallen across the opening where I had entered. I stood there frozen, too shocked to think for a moment. Then I began to scurry around the cave, looking for another opening. I couldn't find one big enough for a cat to get through.

As I stood shivering with growing terror, I heard another roar. Almost at the same time, I was thrown down violently on my back. The rocks and dirt poured over me, covering me almost to my neck. Of course, I must have been stunned, because at first I felt nothing. Then a terribly sharp pain in my hip made me realize what had happened—the second slide had almost buried me.

Fortunately my head and my right arm were free. And, wonder of wonders, in my right hand was my old flashlight, still burning as brightly as ever. I turned the light down toward my leg and saw the large rock that was causing me so much pain. I pulled and strained, trying to move my leg a little, but it wouldn't budge. I couldn't tell whether or not my leg was broken but the effort certainly made it hurt worse.

I won't try to describe how panic-stricken I was then. After some time I did get control of myself and tried to think about what I'd better do. First I turned off the flashlight. It would do no good to wear out the battery. Then I started shouting. But I soon gave that up, for I realized that probably no one would be looking for me yet, and I might need all the voice I had later. So then there was nothing for me to do but just lie there and wait.

The hours passed like years, and I began to get terribly hungry and thirsty. Finally I decided it must be night, and I began to shout again and to listen between shouts. But I heard nothing except the echo of my own voice in the cavern. The hours wore on. By this time my entire leg was numb. I dozed now and then, but in between times I shouted until I had no voice left. Then I almost gave up hope and lay in a sort of daze.

Centuries afterwards I came to with a start. Had I heard a sound? I listened as hard as

I could. There it was again. "Lem! Lem!" It was Mary's voice.

I yelled, "Here I am!" and quickly turned on the flashlight. High above me, my sister was leaning over the rim of a fissure or opening in the rock that I hadn't noticed before.

"Oh, Lem!" she said tearfully. "I thought we'd never find you. We've looked all night! Are you all right?"

"I don't know. I think my leg's badly hurt. There was an avalanche, and a big rock has pinned my leg down."

"I'll get Dad. He's in another passage," and Mary disappeared.

I hated to have her go because I was afraid she couldn't find that opening again. But in a few minutes there was my father, looking down on me. His face looked happy but very tired.

"Hold on, Lem," he said. "We'll get you out. Just hold on."

Then he was gone, but it was only about a half hour until he returned with some other men.

"We're not going to try to get down to you," my father called, "for fear of starting another avalanche. But we've made a sort of harness with some long ropes attached that we'll hold on to. I'll throw the harness down to you. Get it around your chest—under your arms. Then we'll try to pull you out."

I didn't dare think of how painful that would be. I caught the harness, and after maneuvering for fifteen minutes, got it around me. Then the pulling began. I thought I wouldn't be able to take it, but I knew I had to. Finally I felt the rock on my leg move, and then I was dragged inch by inch out of my painful bed. Slowly I was drawn up the side of the cave, and strong hands pulled me through the opening. From that time on I remembered nothing until I woke up in bed with a huge cast on my leg.

All that was three months ago. Now my leg is almost as good as new.

Mary just breezed into my room. "Will you loan me a dollar, Lem? I'll pay you back as soon as I can."

Mary is extravagant with her money and she borrows on her allowance before she gets it.

"I should say n——" I started to say. Then I changed my mind. "Sure, Mary," I said. "Anything I have is yours!"

Lem experienced different emotional reactions at various times in this story. To answer the first four questions, use any of these words or add some of your own.

terrified	indebted	relieved	elated
self-confident	regretful	hopeless	selfish
awe-struck	courageous	thankful	apologetic

How did Lem feel before he discovered the cavern? ------------------------------

----

How did he feel when he was in the cavern just before the first avalanche? ------------

----

How did Lem feel after the avalanches trapped him? --------------------------------

----

How did Lem feel when he was at home after his rescue? ---------------------------

----

By the end of the story, Lem must have changed his mind about certain things. What do you think these things might be? ---

----

Your Language Gives You Away!

An amusing game with words was introduced over the radio several years ago by Bertrand Russell, a famous British philosopher and mathematician. The game consisted of making up sentences in which the same situation, person, or thing is described in three different ways. The statements vary according to the way the speaker feels. For example:

1. He is firm.
2. He is obstinate.
3. He is a pig-headed fool.

Your attitude toward a person determines whether you call him "firm," "obstinate," or "pig-headed." If you admire the person, he is "firm." If you disapprove of him, he is "obstinate." If he annoys or disgusts you, he is "pig-headed." The language you use depends on your feelings and reveals your attitude.

Number the statements in each group below in correct order. Make the most approving statement number 1, the most disapproving one number 3.

____ This is a nondescript animal.

____ This is an unusual-looking dog.

____ This is just a mongrel.

____ He's fat.

____ Hm! He'd better watch his diet.

____ He's cute and chubby.

____ She's very sincere.

____ She's brutally frank.

____ She's outspoken.

____ He might have made his talk shorter.

____ He bored us to death.

____ He discussed the subject in detail.

____ She has a regal manner.

____ She's a stuck-up snob.

____ She seems rather haughty.

____ What an idiotic grin!

____ He had a foolish smile on his face.

____ His expression was genial.

____ He's terribly conceited.

____ He is justifiably proud.

____ It's gone to his head a bit.

____ It was just a little lapse.

____ He should have been more careful.

____ He certainly bungled it.

____ She's extremely competent.

____ She's always trying to boss things.

____ Why doesn't she let others help?

____ She was sneering at him.

____ She was laughing at him.

____ She wore a look of affectionate amusement.

____ She's rather inquisitive.

____ She's very solicitous about her friends.

____ She's nosy.

____ She's a docile child.

____ She tends to withdraw into herself.

____ She always seems sulky.

____ They frequently argue.

____ They don't always see eye to eye.

____ They're constantly wrangling.

____ He is rather extravagant.

____ He is very generous.

____ Money just burns a hole in his pocket.

Read each paragraph. Then decide which of the words below the paragraph best describes the feeling that the person undergoing the experience probably would have, and underline that word.

The farmer stood motionless, watching the scene before him. As mysteriously as it had come, the horde of grasshoppers was leaving. No longer was the earth covered with millions and millions of hungry jaws devouring everything in sight. Hiding the sun like a great cloud, the insects were sweeping eastward. Desolation lay everywhere. Nothing green remained. A stench rose from the stream, which was solidly filled with drowned grasshoppers already rotting in the intense heat.

indifference   despair   optimism

On the end of the upturned boat, a sailor sat looking out over the wide expanse of ocean. He seemed not to notice the crab crawling laboriously from rock to rock at his feet. His eyes saw only the distant ship—his ship—just disappearing over the horizon. To what strange lands would it go this time, and what wonderful sights would it see? Slowly he shook his head, and shaded his eyes with his rope-calloused left hand for a moment. Then he rose, and with the rolling gait of a man unused to land, began walking back toward the village. The empty right sleeve of his jacket swung back and forth with the motion of his steps.

disdain   sullenness   regret

The boy had left his companions near the summit of the lonely mountain and gone on by himself to scale the highest point. He didn't linger long at the top, for a thick mist blotted out the view below, and icy blasts tore at his clothing. As he started back down, his teeth chattered uncontrollably. He had gone hardly a dozen yards before the smoke-gray clouds enveloped him in swirling mist. He stumbled, feeling his way. The going seemed rougher than it had been on the way up. And those boulders that kept looming in the path—he didn't remember them at all. Why didn't he find the other boys? He shouted, but there was no answer, only the whining of the wind among the rocks.

speculation   alarm   exhilaration

On the warm sand by the stream the boy lay resting. Before his eyes a pair of blue-winged ducks floated on the surface of the gently moving water. They seemed to know they were safe. A yellow-and-black butterfly hovered over the white clusters of chokecherry blossoms, then drifted lazily upward and disappeared from sight. On the other side of the water wild roses reflected the flush of the setting sun. From the dark spruces rose the sleepy twittering of birds settling down for the night.

peacefulness   joviality   apprehension

Fifty degrees below zero! The dry snow creaked and crunched under the explorer's heavy boots. The sky was unusually clear and bright that night, so bright that one could have read a newspaper easily. Overhead the stars glistened frostily. In the north a luminous glow lay just above the horizon. As the man looked, wide-eyed, waving streamers of rainbow light formed and danced across the sky. Suddenly great beams like searchlights shot upward. First one and then another burst into skyrocket brilliance and then faded away a few seconds later. The air was filled with a curious sense of waiting—as if something wonderful were about to happen.

apathy   amusement   awe

The exhausted man gathered his strength for a last frantic effort to escape from the blackness of the narrow, underground passage. Then, unmindful of the sharp rocks that slashed his clothing, he pushed onward. One last lunge—he was no longer hemmed in. He could touch nothing but the rocks beneath him! His flashlight trembled in his hand as he examined the vast cavern. Weirdly shaped stalactites were mirrored in an inky lake. Bats, alarmed at his presence, flew around him, their wings brushing his face. The flashlight fell with a clatter; the man cried out as blackness again enveloped him. Then he sank down and covered his ears to shut out the terrible reëchoing sound.

remorse   aggravation   horror

Because of their differing feelings about a long-standing tradition, two former friends find themselves in a conflict highly charged with emotion.

Malemute Mail

by Charles Coombs

"Ah-Kah! Ah-Kah!"

The Eskimo driver's hoarse shout to his dog team echoed across the snow of the Alaskan river trail. Ever since Mayak had left the small trading post of Bettles two hours before, the going had been hard, for the warm breath of a chinook had softened the surface of the snow. Even the ice on the Koyukuk River was uncertain. Twice Polar, the lead dog, had broken through.

Mayak was a proud member of the Kobuk Eskimos, whose men for three generations had delivered the mail along the Koyukuk River. Now he was on the final leg of the seven-hundred-mile Koyukuk River Mail Run that went from Nome to the remote outpost of Wiseman.

Mayak glanced at a small box strapped far forward on the sled and marked RUSH . . . FRAGILE.

"It's some kind of serum," Joe Pipaluk had said when the mail was being transferred from his sled to Mayak's. "They're waiting for it at Wiseman. The fever has hit an Indian village a day's drive from there—hit it bad. There's a missionary doctor with the sick folks. But if he doesn't get this serum soon——" His voice had trailed off. Then he added, "Maybe someone should have flown the serum in."

"Flown it in!" Mayak's dark eyes sparkled fire. "How can you—a Kobuk—say that!"

Now, making slow progress along the winding trail, Mayak thought about Fred Miller, a young pilot he had met that summer when he was working as a ground mechanic at the Nome airport. Mayak recalled how hard Fred had been trying to get the contract for the Koyukuk River Run.

"In my Fairchild I could deliver that mail in a day," Fred had said to Mayak. "What have you got against airplanes, anyway? Especially when you're so interested in them. Anyone who studied aircraft mechanics the way you did at White Mountain, and then worked at the airport. . . . Say, we ought to make a good team."

"Look, Fred," Mayak had interrupted. "I haven't a thing against airplanes. But my duty is to my people. The mail run is the only way they have of earning the money they must have for medicines and such things."

"Sure—but look how long it takes for the trip."

"What's so urgent about time out here?"

"OK, Mack—forget it. But—well, I've been scouting around in that country. I can land my Fairchild within a mile of every trading post along the Run. I'd like to get that mail haul, Mack. It would help me pay for my plane."

"You lay off!" Mayak had snapped. "There's no place on the Koyukuk for your plane."

The breach in his friendship with Fred had grown steadily wider. Mayak hadn't seen the pilot since he had been back on the Run. But several times he had seen the Fairchild cruising above the Koyukuk.

An hour later, as Mayak guided the dogs around a dangerous-looking soft place, he heard the drone of an airplane overhead. Then he saw its blinking lights just over the treetops.

A wave of anger surged through Mayak as he recognized the Fairchild. "Fred's been out campaigning again among the traders along the trail!"

Suddenly the plane dipped sharply, then leveled off and landed on a long patch of smooth snow. Fred climbed down from the cabin.

"Hi, Mack," he called cheerily. "Bet you weren't expecting company way out here."

"What do you want?" Mayak asked curtly.

"I wanted to be sure that nothing had happened to you. And also, I wanted to offer my help in getting that serum through to Wiseman."

"I'll have that serum in Wiseman by noon tomorrow," said Mayak shortly.

"Noon?" Fred protested. "That's nearly twenty hours away. And then it'll have to be taken on to the Indian village. I could have it there—all the way—in an hour or less."

"*If* you got there, Fred," Mayak said. "Too many things can happen to a small plane like yours. My dog sled is the sure way, and that's what counts." Then his face darkened. "You were just waiting for something like this to happen! Don't think for a minute that I haven't seen those gasoline drums at the trading posts along the river. They're yours, aren't they?"

"I didn't intend to disclaim them," said Fred. "I'm a firm believer in open competition."

"Which means that you intend to take over this mail run, no matter how you do it!" Mayak accused. Then he shook his head and sighed. "Look, Fred, I'm only doing what I think best."

"Sure, Mack. Well, I'll go on to Wiseman and tell them when to expect you. When you *do* get there, I can fly the serum on to the village. That will save another day's dog sledding."

Fred put a lot of meaning into his last remark, and for a moment Mayak began to doubt his own judgment. Was he wrong in trying to hold back progress?

As the sound of the plane faded in the distance, Mayak thought he noted a slight falter in the purr of the engine. But he couldn't be certain.

During the next few hours, the going became increasingly difficult. The Eskimo driver had just finished rescuing Polar from a fourth break through the ice, when he began to admit to himself that he could never make it to Wiseman without giving the dogs a rest. As he was looking for a suitable spot to stop, he saw a dark figure standing beside the trail.

"It's me," the figure called.

"Fred! What in the world——"

"The engine failed. Water got into the carburetor. The gas I got at the last trading post must have been improperly handled. I came down all right, on the river, but one ski broke through the ice. So—do you mind if I trail you to Wiseman? I can hire some fellows to come back with me and get the plane up onto the ice."

Mayak was busy with his thoughts. "How bad is the plane wrecked?" he found himself saying.

"It's not wrecked at all, Mack. And while I was waiting for you, I got the carburetor cleaned out. The engine works fine now."

"Maybe—maybe we could pull the plane out with the dogs," Mayak said softly. "I—the dogs —need a rest. I'm afraid we wouldn't make it to Wiseman by noon tomorrow, Fred. You were right. That serum's got to get there in a hurry."

"You mean——"

"Let's try it by plane, Fred." As Mayak went forward to unhitch the sled's towline, he thought about the importance of what he was going to do.

If Fred flew the serum to Wiseman, the news would spread quickly. This would mean the end of dog sleds on the Koyukuk River Mail Run.

But now it seemed to Mayak that one should think of something more than tradition. Even the fact that the Fairchild's engine had failed momentarily couldn't wipe out the realization that Fred had brought the plane down to a safe landing.

Then, too, Fred had complained about the careless way in which his drums of gasoline had been handled. Why couldn't the Kobuks be responsible for running well-managed fueling depots along the Run? With airplanes becoming so necessary in the north country, servicing them could become a new occupation for his people.

But right now, getting the serum to Wiseman was the main problem. He led the dogs across the ice; then he carefully hitched the towline to the plane ski that hadn't broken through the ice.

Half an hour later, the straining dogs had managed to pull the Fairchild onto solid ice.

"Boy, what dogs!" cried Fred. "I see now why you Kobuks have so much pride in——"

"I'm afraid this Kobuk has had too much pride and not enough common sense," Mayak cut in. Then he ran back to the sled and returned with the small box.

A few minutes later, Mayak watched the Fairchild take off. Fred's smiling face and cheery wave of farewell warmed Mayak's heart. He leaned down and patted Polar's shaggy neck.

"Big boy," he said soberly, "you've done your work well—but it looks as if you and your pals are in for a nice long rest."

On a separate sheet, answer these questions:

1. Why did Mayak dislike the idea of Fred's taking over the mail run in his plane?

2. What facts suggest that Mayak was not blindly opposed to all modern progress?

3. Why did Fred want the mail contract?

4. What were Fred's motives in coming out to meet Mayak on the trail to Wiseman?

5. Why did Mayak at first refuse to give the serum to Fred? Why did he change his mind?

6. Do you think Mayak betrayed his people when he let Fred take the serum? Why or why not?

This article is from a biography of the famous author and doctor, Oliver Wendell Holmes.

A Doting Father

by Catherine Drinker Bowen

Dr. Holmes' son, Oliver Wendell, Jr., was about as different from his father as it is possible to be, but he, too, became world famous. At the relatively early age of forty-one he was appointed judge of the Supreme Court of Massachusetts. Later he became a justice of the United States Supreme Court. Yet the doctor fondly continued to treat him as though he were still a child. When a friend wrote to congratulate the doctor on his son's appointment to the Massachusetts high court, the doctor replied, "Thank you for all the pleasant words about the Judge. To think of it —my little boy a Judge, and able to send me to jail if I don't behave myself!"

Not long after young Holmes became a judge, he was guest of honor at a dinner. The Mayor of Boston was there, and seated next to this dignitary was Dr. Holmes. The doctor was in fine fettle; he laughed, joked, talked incessantly. On both sides of him, men leaned forward to catch what he was saying.

Mr. Justice Holmes sat observing this scene as the table was cleared, the cigars lighted, and men pushed back their chairs. From time to time he had caught his father looking at him, and there was no mistaking the gleam in that parental eye. Young Holmes had seen it too often. His father was going to make a speech—and this time the son feared he was to be the subject.

Mayor Palmer rose and introduced the doctor. Instantly Dr. Holmes was on his feet, beaming. From his hand trailed a long slip of paper. The company applauded whole-heartedly. Adjusting his spectacles, Dr. Holmes threw an arch glance at his son. The guests, catching that look, applauded more heartily than ever. Clearing his throat, the doctor began reading aloud:

> "The justice who, in gown and cap,
> Condemns a wretch to strangulation,
> Has scratched his nurse and spilled his pap,
> And sprawled across his mother's lap
> For wholesome law's administration. . . ."

The audience howled delightedly, its eye moving from the poet to the Judge. Wendell Holmes, smiling carefully, looked at the tablecloth.

The poem went on and on. If his father left out the war, Wendell thought, he could forgive all this. He could almost enjoy it. . . . Amazing how the old man could make a roomful of hard-headed businessmen respond to this kind of thing! That high old voice had all the inflection of an actor's. But his father would never be able to resist the war. Ah, here it was!

> "The fearless soldier who has faced
> The serried bayonet's gleam appalling,
> For nothing save a pin misplaced,
> The peaceful nursery has disgraced
> With hours of unheroic bawling."

Beneath the table, Wendell gripped his napkin in both fists. Looking up, he caught the eye of a Harvard professor fixed on him quizzically.

> "The whirligig of time goes round
> And changes all things but affection. . . ."

The audience suddenly ceased smiling and began to look sentimental.

> "You did not come to weep,
> Nor I my weakness to be showing;
> And these gay stanzas, slight and cheap,
> Have served their simple use—to keep
> A father's heart from overflowing."

Finally the high, soft old voice stopped. Dr. Holmes sat down. There were cheers, calls for a reply from the Judge. Mr. Justice Oliver Wendell Holmes, Jr., rose slowly to his feet and faced the assemblage.

In the situation described here, young Wendell Holmes' feelings were quite different from those of his father. Put 1 by the feelings that you think were those of the son. Put 2 by those of the father.

- - -dread   - - -pride   - - -resignation

- - high spirits   - - -delight   - - -satisfaction

- - -embarrassment   - - -eagerness   - - -exasperation

- - -grudging admiration

Adapted from *Yankee from Olympus* by Catherine Drinker Bowen: copyright, 1943, 1944, by Catherine Drinker Bowen; reprinted by permission of Little, Brown & Company and Ernest Benn, Ltd.

Prefixes Have Meanings

be-, prefix meaning:
1. thoroughly; all around: *Bespatter = spatter thoroughly or all around.*
2. at; on; to; for; about; against: *Bewail = wail about.*
3. make; cause to seem: *Belittle = cause to seem little.*
4. provide with: *Bespangle = provide with spangles.*

co-, prefix meaning:
1. with; together: *Coöperate = act with or together.*
2. joint; fellow: *Coauthor = joint or fellow author.*
3. equally: *Coextensive = equally extensive.*

dis-, prefix meaning:
1. opposite of, as in *discontent.*
2. reverse of, as in *disentangle.*

inter-, prefix meaning:
1. together; one with the other: *Intercommunicate = communicate with each other.*
2. between: *Interpose = put between.*
3. among a group: *Interscholastic = between or among schools.*

non-, prefix meaning: not; not a; opposite of; lack of; failure of, as in *nonbreakable, nonconformity, nonpayment.*

out-, prefix meaning:
1. outward; forth; away, as in *outburst, outgoing.*
2. outside; at a distance, as in *outbuilding, outfield, outlying.*
3. more than; longer than, as in *outbid, outlive.*
4. better than, as in *outdo, outrun.*

over-, prefix meaning:
1. too; too much; too long, etc., as in *overcrowded, overfull, overburden, overpay, oversleep.*
2. extra, as in *oversize, overtime.*
3. over, as in *overflow, overlord, overseas, overthrow.*

super-, prefix meaning:
1. over; above, as in *superimpose, superstructure.*
2. besides, as in *supertax.*
3. in high proportion; to excess; exceedingly, as in *superabundant, supersensitive.*
4. surpassing, as in *superman, supernatural.*

ultra-, prefix meaning:
1. beyond, as in *ultraviolet.*
2. beyond what is usual; very; excessively, as in *ultraexclusive, ultramodern.*

un-¹, prefix meaning: not; the opposite of, as in *unfair, unjust, unequal.*

un-², prefix meaning: do the opposite of; do what will reverse the act, as in *undress, unlock, untie.*

under-, prefix meaning:
1. on the underside; to a lower position; from a lower position; below; beneath, as in *underline.*
2. being beneath; worn beneath, as in *underclothes.*
3. lower, as in *underlip.*
4. lower in rank; subordinate, as in *undersheriff.*
5. not enough; insufficiently, as in *underfed.*
6. below normal, as in *undersized.*

Rewrite the italicized part of each sentence below, using the correct form of the two words suggested. Use the definitions of the prefixes to help you decide.

disloyal   ultraloyal

The *servant who was not loyal* allowed the thieves to enter his master's house.

----

overplayed   outplayed

The Lockport team *played better than* the Somerset squad in every respect.

----

overexposed   underexposed

The last roll of film had been *exposed to the light for too short a time.*

----

coexisting   nonexisting

Susan was amazed to find ripe fruit, green fruit, and flowers *existing at the same time* on the orange trees.

----

uncritical   ultracritical

Since her teacher was *extremely critical*, Tina worked on the notebook until after midnight.

----

nonsecret   supersecret

Mr. Robertson is working on a *highly secret* project for the government.

----

undersized   oversized

The clown looked ludicrous in a tiny hat and *white shoes that were much too large for him.*

----

disappearance   nonappearance

The *failure of the star to appear* one night in the play caused consternation in the audience.

----

beclouded   unclouded

When the astronomer saw that the moon was *hidden by clouds*, he knew that he could not perform his experiment.

----

interlocked   unlocked

Kerry was unable to figure out how the parts of the puzzle *joined with one another.*

The italicized words in each paragraph start with the same letters. One is an English word with the prefix be-, co-, dis-, fore-, im-, in-, mis-, pre-, re-, super-, or un- added. Decide which word is an English word plus a prefix and write it on the dotted line.

Joe dug his nails into the palms of his hands as he waited *impatiently* at the starting line. He was the first runner on the relay team, and he realized that a good start was very *important* if his team were to win.

The exhibit of *precious* stones included some of the largest and most famous diamonds in the world. On Sunday afternoon about a hundred people attended a *preview* of this exhibit.

There was an *impish* gleam in Dick's eyes as he put the finishing touches on the comical poster. He was sure that it would be *impossible* for anyone to figure out who had made it.

Sue was *supersensitive* about the low grade she got on the Latin test. She kept insisting that something was wrong with the test because she had had *superior* grades on all the other tests.

Dave reached for the dictionary and looked up the word *missile*. He sometimes *misspelled* the word, but this time he wanted to make sure he wrote it correctly.

After Howard learned that the bus service had been *discontinued*, he called his friend Bob to *discuss* what they should do.

As she looked through her desk drawers for the play tickets, Mary *realized* that everything was in a mess. She decided then and there to spend next Saturday morning cleaning out the desk and *reorganizing* the contents.

In the *forenoon* Mr. Stone took us to see the harbor area. While there we watched one of the *foreign* freighters unload cargo.

The farmer and his wife *befriended* the man whose car had stalled in the high snowdrifts. They immediately gave him a hot *beverage* to drink and offered him food.

"If the weather is cool, the *uniforms* of the marching band are fine," Ned told his mother. "But if it's a hot day, we're really *uncomfortable* in them."

Gordon's brother Philip, who was a *copilot* on a transatlantic passenger plane, always had some funny stories to tell us about his experiences. One story that we especially liked was about a *colonel* in the army.

"Sometimes I think this *index* is *inaccurate*," muttered Nancy. In her haste to finish her homework before it was time for the party, she had turned two pages at once and missed the *J*'s completely.

Since the *unique* wood carvings Jim had found in Germany were priceless, he *unpacked* them with the greatest of care. Then he put them in a glass display case.

"We'd better *invite* Lola's twin sister to the party, too," suggested Anne. "She isn't in our class, but I have noticed that the two girls are *inseparable*."

Suffixes

A root word and two of its derived forms are listed above each paragraph. The root word is a noun and the derived forms a verb and an adjective:

1. verbs are formed by adding the suffixes -fy, -ize, -en, or -ate;

2. adjectives are formed by adding the suffixes -y, -al, -ous, -ic, -ful, or -ible.

Complete each paragraph below by writing the correct words on the dotted lines.

beauty   beautify   beautiful

Mrs. Holt worked hard to _____ her back yard, but she had no idea that she would win a prize in the contest for the most _____ homes.

critic   criticize   critical

The music _____ wrote an unfavorable report of the spring concert. He was especially _____ of the numbers sung by the mixed chorus.

origin   originate   original

Ray was unable to find any information about the _____ of the town's name, for all the records of the _____ settlers had been destroyed in a fire.

type   typify   typical

This book is a _____ story about the courageous men and women who settled the western part of our country. The two main characters _____ early pioneers.

center   centralize   central

The mayor planned to _____ the city government still further by moving the offices of all the city officials to a new building in the _____ of town.

heart   hearten   hearty

The captain thought the warm weather would _____ the sailors, but he did not hear their _____ laughter again until land was sighted.

sympathy   sympathize   sympathetic

Mrs. Wilson was very _____ when James told her about his problem. Her _____ seemed to cheer him, for he went back to his work with a smile.

glory   glorify   glorious

When Ann saw the sunset _____ the valley, she realized that all she had heard about the beauty of the resort was true. It was indeed a _____ sight.

office   officiate   official

Many voters were pleased to learn that Mr. Hill was a candidate for the _____ of sheriff. They knew that he was honest and that he would perform his _____ duties in a capable manner.

colony   colonize   colonial

When they decided to _____ the island, the Spanish traders did not realize that it contained valuable mineral deposits. The _____ was in existence more than a year before any precious ore was found.

apology   apologize   apologetic

Sam wanted to _____ to Mrs. Brown for stepping in her flower bed. He had rehearsed the _____ many times, but whenever he thought of actually ringing her doorbell, his knees turned to jelly.

terror   terrify   terrible

The news of the approaching hurricane struck _____ into the residents of the small town. They remembered the storm of the past year and the _____ damage and suffering it had caused.

A root word and two of its derived forms are listed above each paragraph. The root word is a verb and the derived forms a noun, an adjective, or an adverb:

1. nouns are formed by adding the suffixes -er, -ence, -ment, or -ion;

2. adjectives are formed by adding the suffixes -ive, -ent, -able, -less, or -al;

3. adverbs are formed by adding the suffix -ly.

Complete each paragraph below by writing the correct words on the dotted lines.

count   counter   countless

Ellen could not imagine how any one could ever .... all of the stars. To her, the sky was filled with .... numbers of them.

persist   persistently   persistence

Jane wanted a flower garden, but she wasn't willing to fight the weeds .... Because she lacked ...., the garden was an unsightly jungle by mid-July.

manage   manageable   management

John was secretly pleased when the coach asked him to .... the baseball team during his absence. He knew that the boys trusted him and that their .... would be no problem.

conclude   conclusive   conclusion

The judge felt that the evidence presented in the case had been very .... As he watched the members of the jury leave the room, he hoped that they had reached the same .... that he had.

apply   applicable   application

When Miss Ray went to .... for the job she had seen advertised in the paper, she took her social security number with her. She knew that she would need it to complete her ....

erupt   eruption   eruptive

When ominous signs convince people living on the side of a volcanic mountain that the volcano is about to ...., they flee. They know that their lives may be endangered by hot lava when the .... takes place.

operate   operation   operational

The president of the railroad wanted a complete report on .... expenses for one month. He also asked for a list of the men required to .... the trains.

defend   defender   defensive

People were able to .... their cities in olden times by building walls around them. Such .... methods would have little value today.

excel   excellence   excellent

Mr. Brown complimented the girls who had prepared the lunch on the .... of the food. He said that he had eaten six of the .... biscuits.

educate   educationally   education

Mr. Williamson realized the value of a good .... He knew that successful job experience is important, but he knew that a good worker needs to be .... qualified first of all.

protect   protection   protective

Like other members of the cat family, lynx and ocelots have a .... attitude toward their young. In times of crisis they will .... their babies even though they may have to battle larger and more ferocious animals to do so.

imagine   imagination   imaginatively

As Josie walked through the cathedral, she began to .... all the renowned men and women who had once crossed its worn threshold. The throng that Josie had created in her .... seemed so real that she involuntarily stepped aside to let them pass.

Most of the words in the "poem" below are pure nonsense. Yet, as you read it, you have the feeling that it almost makes sense. This is because the endings on the nonsense words are familiar. Put 1 over the nonsense words that seem to name something (nouns). Put 2 over words that seem to indicate action (verbs), and 3 over words that apparently describe something (adjectives).

A Warning

A sindy naction draced the stoniment
Around a vindable tabanation.
Then later it groted in squellish glee
And bantified our daliration.

Alas, we mafinized in vain
And never brotted the olorous thing!
So don't you vernify a naction
Or you may calisize its sting.

After each sentence below, write the meaning of the italicized word. Wherever possible, use the root word in your definition. If the word form is unfamiliar, your knowledge of the meaning and function of word endings should help you.

1. The Sarasota Pharmacy put on an intensive advertising campaign to *popularize* its new brand of vitamins.

- -

2. Mrs. Burke's face was doleful as she surveyed the desolate *wintry* landscape.

- -

3. Davy felt queasy at the very thought of taking the *nauseous* medicine.

- -

4. "Don't hurry. We like standing in the cold," said Joel *sarcastically.*

- -

5. Sudden gusts of wind made the kite dance *erratically* on its string.

- -

6. When Jacobus wanted to change his name to John, he had to go to court to *legalize* it.

- -

7. As the roaring of the waters *intensified*, the boys realized they must be nearing the rapids.

- -

8. Kate often spoke *flippantly*, but she actually felt shy and frightened.

- -

9. After the doctor had set Hiram's broken leg, the pain was more *tolerable.*

- -

10. The vase was made of some kind of opaque material that gave out a *metallic* sound when Mary tapped it.

- -

11. Sitting in a hot stuffy room for hours will *stupefy* even the most alert person.

- -

12. William knew that the water in the radiator would *solidify* unless he used antifreeze.

- -

Which italicized words are verbs? (Indicate by number.) -
Which are adverbs? -
Which are adjectives? -

What Do Story Beginnings Reveal?

What do you learn from this opening paragraph?

"The day of the catastrophe began much like any other. Carlos watched the sunrise paint the mountain peaks lavender and pink and then turn the roof of the old Spanish church to gold. Before the day ended, the church would be demolished, the yard strewn with wreckage."

You learn that this story takes place in mountainous country, probably in Latin America. The time is early morning. The main character is probably a man or a boy. A disaster will destroy a church.

Below are the beginnings of five other stories. After each, write what it tells you about the story. If you need more space, write on a separate sheet.

1. Through the oppressive heat of the afternoon the *Araby* lay at anchor in Bolong Bay while sweating Filipinos loaded Manila hemp into her forward hold. Even when the sun sank behind the rim of the Sulu Sea, the decks were still warm, the cabins stifling.

In the officers' saloon Captain Jarvis pushed back his plate. "Too blamed hot to eat," he said. "Maybe it's just as well our planter didn't come aboard for supper."

Howard Pease, "The Silver Outrigger"

----

2. Day had broken cold and gray when the man turned aside from the main Yukon trail and climbed the high earth bank, where a dim and little-traveled trail led eastward. The bank was steep, and the man paused for breath when he reached the top.

The time was nine o'clock. There was no sun, though there was not a cloud in the sky. Over the face of things lay a gloom that made the day dark. That was due to the absence of sun. This did not worry the man. He was used to the lack of sun.

Jack London, "To Build a Fire"

----

3. I had called upon my friend Sherlock Holmes upon the second morning after Christmas, with the intention of wishing him the compliments of the season. He was lounging upon the sofa in a purple dressing-gown, a pile of crumpled morning papers, evidently newly studied, near at hand. Beside the couch was a wooden chair, and on the angle of the back hung a hard-felt hat, much the worse for wear. A lens and forceps lying upon the seat of the chair suggested that the hat had been suspended in this manner for examination.

A. Conan Doyle,
"The Adventure of the Blue Carbuncle"

----

4. The worst crime a gun-bearer can commit is to run away from his *bwana* in a crisis. I have had many gun-bearers; and all of them, with a single exception, stayed with me even though an elephant, a rhino, or a lion was charging. That one exception proved the rule and almost cost me my life. It came about in this way.

Theodore J. Waldeck, *On Safari*

----

5. We had now reached the summit of the loftiest crag. For some minutes the old man seemed too much exhausted to speak.

"Not long ago," he said at length, "I could have guided you on this route as well as the youngest of my sons; but, about three years past, there happened to me an event such as no man ever survived to tell of—and the six hours of deadly terror which I then endured have broken me [up] body and soul."

Edgar Allan Poe, "A Descent into the Maelstrom"

Which story beginnings:
give the clearest idea of what will happen? ____
tell you little about probable story events? ____

Each incident below might be the beginning of a story in which someone learns the meaning of responsible behavior. Read the incidents and then answer the questions.

1. Mark's family had just moved to the neighborhood, and for the tenth time that day he wished they hadn't. As he silently took his seat in the unfamiliar classroom, he was startled to feel a nudge on his shoulder.

"Are you interested in coin collections?" asked the boy who sat behind him.

"Some," Mark replied shyly. "Why?"

"Two other fellows and I meet once a week at my house and compare ours. Why don't you come to our meeting after school today?"

"I'd like to," Mark answered. "My dad has a big collection of coins, all catalogued from 1900. In fact, he has some albums that are complete. He started his collection years ago when he was in school. He also has a glass case filled with unusually rare coins. Once I showed some of his coins to a hobby club."

"That's terrific!" said his new friend. "Bring one of the albums over with you today, will you?"

"Okay," Mark promised eagerly. "Fine!" As he walked home from school, however, Mark began to regret his promise. It was true that he had shown some of the coins at his other school. However, he had neglected to say that he had lost a coin from its slot in one of the books on his way home. Besides, it was a coin that could not be replaced. After that sad experience, Mark had promised his father that he would never again take the coins out of the house.

What will be the problem in this story?

Assuming that Mark is a conscientious boy, what do you think he will do?

___ take one of the coin books to the meeting and hope that his father will never find out

___ phone and say he's ill and can't come

___ attend the meeting and say that the entire collection has been sent to a hobby show

___ invite the boys to his home after the meeting to see the coins

___ ask his mother to go with him and take one of the books

2. "How's it going?" Mr. Timson asked Evelyn, the feature editor of the high-school newspaper. "Is your section ready to be mimeographed?"

"Not quite," Evelyn said. "But it will be."

As the teacher nodded and walked away, Evelyn looked around frantically. "Where *is* he?" she moaned. "Where *is* that boy?"

She was waiting for John Taylor, who was to have turned in a full-column humorous story by noon. John was a very clever writer, but deadlines meant nothing to him. Today the paper had to be "put to bed" at exactly three o'clock. It was ten minutes after one already.

Just then Pat Field sauntered in. "Hi, Editor! Any last-minute item you want me to write?"

Evelyn shook her head. "N-no." Then she bit her lip and said, "Yes, yes, there is. I've got a column to fill. Can you think of something?"

"Sure!" Pat said. He strode off, grabbed some paper, and sat down at the back of the room. Evelyn sighed. Maybe Pat's article wouldn't be brilliant, but it would fill the space.

It was two-thirty when Pat handed in his story. It told of ways to look for after-school jobs in the neighborhood. It was nicely written, and it would fit into the space almost exactly.

Evelyn was pasting the marked copy on the layout form when John Taylor strolled in.

"Here you are," he drawled as he dropped some papers on the desk. "Better late than never."

What will be the problem in this story?

Assuming that Evelyn is a girl of strong character, what do you think she will do?

___ use John's story because more readers would enjoy it

___ use Pat's article because he coöperated in an emergency, and John needed to be taught a lesson

___ use John's story because he might decide not to write more funny articles for the paper

___ ask the boys to shorten their articles so that she can put both articles in the paper

First Hunt

His father said, "All set, boy?" and Joe nodded, picking up his gun with awkward mittened hands. His father opened the door, and they went out into the cold dawn together, leaving the snug security of the shack, the warmth of the kerosene stove, the companionable smell of bacon and coffee.

Not that Joe had eaten much breakfast. It had stuck in his throat, and his father, noticing this, had said, "Just a touch of buck fever, Son; don't let it bother you." And he added, almost wistfully, "Wish I were your age, getting ready to shoot my first duck. You're luckier than you realize, boy."

They stood for a moment in front of the shack. Ahead of them was only flatness; not a house, not a tree, nothing but the vast expanse of marsh and water and sky. Ordinarily Joe would have been pleased by the arrangements of black and gray and silver that met his eye. Ordinarily he would have asked his father to wait while he fussed around with his camera, trying to record these impressions on film. But not this morning. This was the solemn, long-awaited morning when he was to shoot his first wild duck.

This was the morning. And he hated it, had hated the whole idea ever since his father had bought him a gun, had taught him to shoot clay pigeons, had promised him a trip to this island in the bay, where the shooting was the finest in the state.

He hated it, but he was grimly determined to go through with it. He loved his father and wanted his approval more than anything in the world. Joe knew that if he could conduct himself properly this morning, he would get it.

He thought of what his father had said to his mother after the first lesson in shooting: "You know, Martha, Joe's got the makings of a fine wing shot. He's got control, timing, and nerve."

They came to the blind, a narrow pit facing the bay. In it was a bench, a shelf for shotgun shells, nothing else. Joe sat down tensely and waited while his father waded out with an armful of decoys to lure the birds. Light was pouring into the sky now. Far down the bay a string of ducks went by, outlined against the sunrise. Watching them, Joe felt his stomach constrict.

To ease his feeling of dread, he picked up his camera and took a picture of his father silhouetted against the quicksilver water. Feeling guilty, he put the camera hastily on the shelf in front of him and picked up his gun again.

His father came back and dropped down beside him, boots dripping, hands blue with cold. "Better load up. Sometimes they're on top of you before you know it. I'll let you shoot first," he said, "and I'll back you up if necessary." He loaded his own gun, closed it with a snap. "I've been waiting a long time for this day," he said happily. "Just the two of us, out here on the marshes. We——"

He broke off, leaning forward. "Look! There's a flight now, headed this way. They'll come in from left to right, against the wind, if they give us a shot at all. Keep your head down; I'll give you the word."

Joe kept his head down. Behind them the sun had cleared the horizon, flooding the marshes with tawny light. He could see everything with an almost unbearable clearness: his father's face, tense and eager, the white frost on the gun barrels. His heart was thudding wildly. *No*, he prayed, *don't let them come. Make them stay away, please!*

But they kept coming. "Four blacks," his father whispered. "Keep still!"

Joe kept still. He heard the whistle of wings as the flight went over, swung wide, began to circle. "Get set," Joe's father breathed. "They're coming."

In they came, heads raised alertly, wings spread in a proud curve. Light flashed from the gleaming feathers around the leader's neck and glinted on his breast. Down dropped his bright orange feet, reaching for the steel-colored water. Closer, closer . . .

"Now!" roared Joe's father, jumping to his feet, gun ready. "Take the leader!"

Joe felt his body obey. He stood up, leaned into the gun the way his father had taught him. Under his finger the trigger curved, smooth and deadly.

From "First Hunt" by Arthur Gordon, first published in *This Week Magazine*. Used by permission of *This Week Magazine*; copyright © 1955, by United Newspapers Magazine Corporation.

In the same instant, the ducks saw the gunners and flared wildly. Up went the leader as if jerked by an invisible string. For half a second he hung there, poised against wind and sun, balanced between life and death. *Now*, said something in Joe's brain, *now!* And he waited for the slam of the explosion.

But it didn't come. Higher still went the duck, out of range, out of sight.

There was no sound, then, except the faint rustle of the grasses. Joe stood there, gripping his gun.

"Well," his father said at last, "what happened?"

The boy did not answer. His lips were trembling.

His father said, in the same controlled voice, "Why didn't you shoot?"

Joe thumbed back the safety catch. He stood the gun carefully in the corner of the duck blind. "Because they were so alive," he said and burst into tears.

He sat on the bench, face buried in his hands, and wept. All hope he had of pleasing his father was gone. He had had his chance, and he had failed.

Beside him his father crouched suddenly. "Here comes a single. Looks like a pintail. Let's try again."

Joe did not lower his hands. "It's no use, Dad. I can't."

"Hurry," his father said roughly, "or you'll miss him altogether. Here!"

Cold metal touched Joe. He looked up unbelieving. His father was offering him the camera. "Quick, here he comes. He won't hang around all day!"

In swept the big pintail, right into the decoys. Joe's father clapped his hands. The splendid bird soared upward. One instant he was there, not thirty yards away, feet drawn up, head raised, wings beating. Then he was gone, whistling like a feathered missile downwind.

Joe lowered the camera. "I got him!" His face was beaming. "I *got* him!"

"Did you?" His father's hand touched his shoulder. "That's good. There'll be others along soon; you can get all sorts of shots." He hesitated, and Joe saw that there was no disappointment in his eyes, only pride and sympathy and love. "It's OK, Son. I'll always love shooting. But that doesn't mean you have to. At times it takes just as much courage not to do a thing as to do it. Think you could teach me to work that gadget?"

"Teach you?" Joe felt as if his heart would burst with happiness. "There's nothing to it. Here, I'll show you——"

Underline the sentence:

that first tells you Joe is worrying about a problem. Put *1* beside it.

that first tells you definitely what the problem is. Put *2* beside it.

that tells you Joe thought his father did not approve of his interest in photography. Put *3* beside it.

that first tells you Joe failed to do what his father expected of him. Put *4* beside it.

that gives you the first hint that Joe's father may have begun to understand his son's viewpoint. Put *5* beside it.

Where are you *sure* of the father's change of heart? Underline and put *6* beside the sentences that tell you.

What It Takes

by Captain Burr Leyson

A deadly menace lay in wait over the polar ice-cap. For days Jack Haly, a young meteorologist attached to the Air Forces arctic weather patrol, had charted the position of the storm on his maps. He was worried. The emergency airstrip from which the patrol operated was hundreds of miles from civilization and was not equipped for instrument landings. And there were no other airports so equipped within the limited range of planes stationed there. If a plane were trapped aloft by a sudden storm, it would have to make a crash landing in the barren wastes of the North.

Daily, Jack had warned the flight crews of the danger. But they always responded, "Don't worry about us, Kid. You play with your maps, and we'll take care of the flying!"

Because Jack's duties as meteorologist kept him on the ground, he was not accepted into the close companionship of the members of the flight crew. Theirs was a world of action, excitement, adventure. Courage, the ability to see it through, to ride it out in the air, was their measure of a man. How could Jack, a groundling, ever hope to measure up to such a standard?

Today, as more reports of the brewing storm came in, Jack forgot his personal worries. The storm would break any minute and might trap one of the planes. Late in the afternoon it happened. A plane reported, "Visibility closing in. Winds intense." This was it!

All the men at the airstrip were packed into the radio tent, waiting for word from the flight. The plane, they knew, had little time to fight its way clear. The next report on its position showed that heavy gusts of wind had carried it thirty miles south of the airstrip, beyond a rugged height of land. The only break in that height of land was a narrow gorge cut by the river that ran beside the airstrip. Impassable rapids filled the gorge.

"Crash landing! Get fix on position!"

The men watched tensely as the radio operator typed another message: "See ground near gorge. Will need doctor. . . ." Then all was silent.

"Kid! Where's that kid?" a pilot shouted. Jack pushed his way through the crowd.

"When's this weather going to break so we can send out a search flight?"

Jack hesitated. It was like passing a sentence of doom. "Forty to forty-eight hours, at least."

Until the storm moderated, there was no hope of rescuing the plane's crew. Jack stood with the other men looking at the point on the map where the gorge was marked "Impassable." Suddenly he turned to Dennison, the chief pilot and senior officer present.

"Captain," Jack began, "you can't get a flight out until day after tomorrow. But if you'll let me try, I'm pretty sure I can get through."

Dennison whirled on Jack, his eyes blazing. "Goin' to grow wings, I suppose? Don't bother me, Kid. If *we* can't get through, no one can."

"Listen!" Jack said. "I may be young and I'm no airman, but Dad taught me to handle a canoe in some mighty rough water. I'm willing to try to get through the gorge to those men. We don't have canoes, but we do have rubber rafts. They'll ride even better!"

Before Dennison could speak, "Doc" Martin, the unit medic, broke in. "Maybe the youngster has an idea. I'm willing to go with him."

There was nothing Dennison could do but agree. The risk was high, but this was the only possible chance of rescuing the downed crew.

Doc hurriedly selected some medical supplies. Then he and Jack fought their way through the storm to the river, where the rubber life raft was waiting for them. An outboard motor was fitted to a board lashed across the rim.

Two hours later, when Jack and Doc were approaching the high cliffs that marked the entrance to the gorge, darkness was falling. The current was picking up speed. They felt the raft bound into the air as it passed over the first of the huge waves thrown up by underwater obstacles. The raft was heading directly into the rapids.

Hastily Jack cut the motor switch, tore at the fastenings that held the engine, and cast it overboard. From now on its weight would be but an added hazard. Jack passed a canoe paddle forward to Doc.

"Get ready to paddle, Doc! I'll tell you when." Both men inflated their life jackets. The water was oil-slick now and running with dizzy speed.

The narrowing gorge ahead was a mass of jagged boulders, foaming waves, and hissing spray. There lay the greatest danger. Time and time again they avoided disaster by a hairbreadth. Jack's arms felt leaden from the effort of paddling. Fighting clear of one rock, the men found themselves hurtling down on a mass of roaring foam that hid some huge obstruction. Jack started to warn Doc to hold on to the safety rope, but his words were lost in a choking sheet of spray. The raft spun and tilted to one side. Then the dashing waters caught it and heaved it far into the air.

Jack felt his body swing out of the raft. He shot out an arm and his fingers closed on the collar of Doc's jacket. Then both men struck the water with a sickening jar. Jack felt a stunning blow on his back as the waters smashed him against a huge rock. Vaguely he fought his way to the surface. Then he knew no more.

His next thought was of pain. His body was one great aching mass. Then he realized that water was gently lapping his face. He was floating in the shallows near the bank. Beside him was Doc, floating on his back. Jack struggled ashore, dragging Doc behind him, and then fell on the bank.

As Jack fought his way back to full consciousness, his strength gradually returned under the urge of his anxiety to drive ahead. Doc moved and groaned, then worked himself to his knees. The two men looked around. They were on a flat, boulder-strewn shore. Upstream they could hear the rumble of the rapids in the gorge. They were clear—they had made it! Now, where was the crash? Jack fumbled for his oilskin-wrapped revolver and fired three shots, the wilderness signal of distress. Would the plane crew be near enough to hear? Would they be able—— Before he could complete the thought, he heard answering shots. The two men set off in a stumbling run.

Not five minutes later they heard shouting. Then they saw a light, and the next moment they stood beside the crashed plane.

For the next hour Jack obeyed Doc's commands as he aided the injured men. All would survive, but only Doc's presence had saved two of them.

Almost forty hours to the minute from the time Jack had predicted the break, the storm lessened and then ceased. Within an hour a plane from the Unit circled low overhead to drop emergency supplies and a message saying that a helicopter was on the way to fly them out.

Late that afternoon the helicopter arrived. The most seriously injured men were taken out first. The last flight carried only Jack and the pilot. Weary and sore, Jack relaxed as best he could. Finally he saw the airstrip and a crowd waiting near the mess tent. As Jack stumbled out of the copter, he felt hands grab him and half carry him into the tent. Dennison, standing at the head of the long table, stretched out his hand.

"Swell show, Jack!" Then, motioning him to a seat at the head of the table, he shouted, "Move over, gang! Give the man a seat!"

As Jack sat down, looking into the smiling faces of the crew, he suddenly realized that he was no longer an outsider. He was one of them. The "Kid" had proved himself.

What does the first paragraph lead you to think the story problem will be? _____

_____

What does the third paragraph lead you to think the story problem will be? _____

_____

At what point do you feel that Jack perhaps will get the flight crews' respect? _____

_____

At what point do you feel fairly sure that he will get the crews' respect? _____

_____

At what point do you know that he got the crews' respect? _____

_____

Rescue in the Clouds

*by Captain Lloyd Reinhard
as told to Michael Duball*

Our Convair was up around 7000 feet over Paterson, New Jersey, and still climbing, when I began making a position report to the airline company station. As we moved through a small break in the clouds, a plane streaked into view. I did a quick "double take."

"New York," I snapped over the mike, "there's a T-33 jet trainer at my altitude!"

It was moving by so close that I could make out every detail. The pilot seemed to be wiggling his wings at me, and I thought he was in trouble.

"I'll try to contact him on military frequency," I said, and that was the last contact I had with our New York office.

We had taken off from La Guardia at 11:48 A.M. with nineteen passengers and a crew of three. The weather was 800 feet overcast with rain, and we were on a routine instrument flight from New York to Buffalo and Toronto—or what started out to be routine until the jet showed up.

"Hold a straight course on up," I said to my copilot, who was flying the plane. I didn't know where the jet was or what he was going to do, and for some reason I couldn't make contact with him. Then at 10,500 feet we broke out on top, into a deep-blue, cloudless sky, and I saw that the jet was still with us and closing the gap between us.

It came abeam of me, about fifty feet, and the pilot put his hand to his mouth, touching the microphone on his face mask. He tapped his earphones and then made a throat-slitting motion, indicating that his radios were dead. I realized that he didn't know where he was and that he couldn't use his electrically controlled flight instruments to go down because his batteries were dead.

I tried to "raise" him on my radio anyway, since we were so close. I called out his number, which was plainly to be seen: "Jet 353. . . . Air Force Jet 353. . . . Do you read me?"

He couldn't, but Stewart Air Force Base heard me calling and checked through to me, establishing that the jet was their plane. "He seems to be lost," I told them. "I'll try to bring him back to you."

As we headed over to Stewart, which is in the Catskill Mountains, the jet hugged close to me. I switched on the public address system and told the passengers what was happening. Thirty-eight miles and ten minutes later I flew over Stewart, having picked up the range beam without any trouble. The tower let me know that there was a 400-foot broken ceiling with a 700-foot overcast. A landing there was out of the question.

I circled around a couple of times, and then I caught the jet boy's frantic hand signals as he tapped his back chute and raised his hand toward the canopy. He was telling me that he was going to bail out. I waved him back, shaking my head, hoping for a lucky break in the weather.

It wasn't forthcoming, and with Stewart right up in the mountains, it was a good place for me to stay away from. The pilot started his bail-out motions again, and I signaled him "No! No! Sit tight. We'll take care of you!"

"Stewart tower!" I snapped. "The man wants to jump. I've got to do something in a hurry. I'll try to get him into La Guardia."

I motioned to the jet to come in closer on our 62-mile course from Stewart to La Guardia. As we came in over White Plains, Yonkers, New Rochelle, and the most heavily populated area in the upper Bronx (it was all happening fast, bing—bing—bing!), the pilot pointed anxiously at his wing-tip fuel tanks. I thought he was trying to tell me they were empty. I didn't know until later that with his electrical power out, he couldn't operate his fuel pumps and use this auxiliary fuel supply.

"I'm going over the side" his gestures said.

I thought of where that plane might crash, with homes and apartment houses crammed in below us. I knew that I must get through to the pilot. I pointed to him and to myself and then I put my hands alongside each other, letting him know that I would fly in with him, make the landing with him. Then I pulled a cigarette out of my pocket and held it to the window, as if to say "Calm down."

Later he described the kind of sunglasses I was wearing. He was that close.

I radioed La Guardia tower, and they hit me back fast: "You're in the clear and number one to approach from 11,000."

I couldn't believe that I was hearing right and asked for a repeat. But it was OK. They were clearing all other aircraft out of the entire area so that I could lead the jet down fast.

We began descending at about 190 miles per hour, and as we left the top layers, it was like dropping into a bowl of pea soup.

Heavy gray-black cloud masses engulfed the craft and momentarily blotted out our own wing tips. The thought flashed through my mind—what was I letting myself in for? And yet I couldn't leave that man stranded out there. I had prevented him from jumping, and I felt that I was personally responsible for his life.

The passengers knew what was going on, and I was pretty sure that a lot of prayers were being said back in the cabin.

I saw the jet about five or six feet away from our wing tip. I was losing the plane and catching it again in flickering glimpses. I lit the wing navigation lights and our leading edge light. That seemed to help him fly formation with us. Then we broke out under the soup at 800 feet and went charging over the airport range station.

"Where's the jet?" came a voice over my radio. The Air Force craft was hugging me so close that the men in the tower couldn't see it!

"He's on my left," I said, and by that time we had covered another quarter of a mile.

"Land southeast on Runway 13," the voice came in, clipped and clear.

I signaled the information to the jet pilot and let him know he was number one to land. But we had passed the end of the runway, and still he didn't break off. I pointed to him frantically. He was riding my wing so tight he hadn't seen the field! Then he took a quick look, and I saw his eyes—the only feature showing above his mask—light up as if he'd seen a vision of heaven.

He made one circuit and came back in for a landing. We went right in after him, and I felt my stomach easing down into place again.

I was pulled off the flight for a relief replacement. Before I left the plane, I told the passengers that the jet had landed safely. They burst out with spontaneous applause. I was embarrassed—but it was a moment I'll never forget.

Later I met the pilot, Lieutenant Preston Maddocks, up in the airlines office. "I had just five minutes to go on fuel," he said, "and when I landed, my knees were so rubbery I could hardly press the brake pedals to stop the plane. Boy! Was I glad to see that 8000-foot runway!"

"Lieutenant," I told him, "for your information, that runway is 5900 feet long!" He grabbed hold of the edge of the desk, and his knees buckled. A jet normally requires a longer run.

Where do you first learn that Captain Reinhard thinks something unusual is happening? Put *1* by the sentence that tells you.

Where does the captain learn what the jet's difficulty is? Write *2* beside the paragraph.

Where does the captain learn that there is something else adding to the jet pilot's dilemma? Write *3* at this place.

Where does Captain Reinhard indicate that he is not so calm as he tries to make the jet pilot believe he is? Put *4* by three such places.

Where do you get the first hint of how the story problem may be solved? Put *5* at this place.

Where do you know that La Guardia tower realizes the urgency of the situation? Put *6* at this place.

Where does Captain Reinhard realize that the jet pilot finally understands how he is to be saved? Put *7* at this place.

Where does the suspense for Captain Reinhard finally end? Put *8* at this place.

Every Dog Should Own a Man

by Corey Ford

Every dog should have a man of his own. There is nothing like a well-behaved person around the house to spread the dog's blanket for him or bring him his supper when he comes home man-tired at night. Properly trained, a man can be a dog's best friend.

I happen to belong to a medium-sized English setter, who acquired me when he was about six months old and has been training me quite successfully ever since. He has taught me to shake hands with him and fetch his ball. I've learned not to tug at the leash when he takes me for a walk, and I make him a devoted companion. In fact, my setter has broken me so thoroughly that I have decided to set down a few of his basic rules of man-handling, as a guide for other dogs.

The first problem for a dog is to pick out the right man. A dog should exercise great care in making his choice, since he is apt to become quite attached to the man and will find it hard to get rid of him later if he proves unsatisfactory.

The next question for a dog to decide is whether he and the man should share the house together. Some dogs prefer a kennel, but my setter decided to move right in the house with me. I can get into any of the chairs I want except the big over-stuffed chair in the living room, which is his.

It is a great mistake for a dog to break a man by using force. Punishment should be used rarely, and then only in cases of deliberate disobedience. More can be accomplished by a reproachful look than by a fit of temper. My setter has never raised a paw to me, but he has almost cured me of the habit of running away. When he sees me start to pack my suitcase, he just lies down on the floor with his chin on his forepaws and gazes at me sadly. Usually I wind up by unpacking the suitcase and turning in my train reservations.

In training a man, diet is very important. The average man has a tendency to gobble everything in sight. The dog should exercise a restraining influence on his appetite by eating all the leftovers in the house before the man gets a chance at them.

Last but not least, it is up to the dog to see that his man has the right companions. If the dog does not approve of a guest who has been invited to the house, he should express his dislike by removing a small section of the visitor's trouser leg as a gentle hint. Personally, I look forward to seeing the milkman these days, because he is practically the only person my dog will let in the house.

Training a man takes time, of course. A dog should realize that man does not possess a dog's instincts, and it is not the man's fault when he fails to understand what the dog desires. Men are apt to be high-strung and sensitive, and a dog who loses his temper will only break the man's spirit. A dog must be patient and understanding, and not fly off the handle if his man cannot learn to chase rabbits as well as a dog does.

After all, as my setter says, it's hard to teach an old man new tricks.

What sensible rules for a happy relationship between man and dog is the author of this humorous article suggesting? Write at least three such rules on the lines below.

Smithtown Defeated by Frankville in One of the Season's Fastest Games

Frankville Scores Needed Runs in Ninth Inning

In the opinion of the excited crowd who watched Frankville beat Smithtown yesterday afternoon, it was one of the season's most thrilling games. Under perfect weather conditions the Frankville team showed a ninth-inning burst of speed that practically cinched the state title.

Unfortunately for Smithtown, Ed Hill, Frankville's captain and star pitcher, was in top form and allowed the visiting team only three hits. Unfortunately also for Smithtown, Frankville's leading batter, Hal Tracy, was able to play again, after having spent the past two weeks recovering from a sprained ankle. On the shoulders of these two men rests most of the honor of yesterday's victory for Frankville.

During the first three innings Hill allowed the opposing team no hits, but in the fourth inning Smithtown's best batters came to bat and got two hits. Gray, the Smithtown catcher, then hit a home run that scored three runs.

The score stood at 3 to 0 in Smithtown's favor until the ninth inning, when the Frankville men hit their stride. They scored four runs in quick succession, and the game came to a triumphant end for Frankville.

Smithtown Scores in the Fourth Inning But Loses to Frankville in Ninth

Rookie Pitcher Hurls Shut-Out Ball Until Ninth Inning

On one of the most disagreeably hot days of the summer, a small crowd watched Smithtown lead Frankville for eight innings yesterday, only to lose the game in the ninth. This unexpected setback somewhat endangers Smithtown's prospects for winning the state championship this year, though it is not too late in the season for Smithtown to recover its lead.

Harry Bauman, veteran pitcher for Smithtown, was out of the game with a broken finger, and the Smithtown rooters staked their hopes on young Jim Brisbane. Brisbane, who joined the team last spring as a southpaw rookie, proved his worth by hurling shut-out ball until the ninth inning.

In the fourth inning things began to happen fast for Smithtown when Tom Mills and Fred Spencer both hit singles. They were followed to the plate by Jimmy Gray, Smithtown's efficient and popular catcher, whose timely home run brought in two other players.

Brisbane held the score at 3 to 0 in favor of Smithtown until the last inning. Tired by this time, and facing Frankville's first-string batters, the young pitcher allowed the opposing team four runs. Final score: Frankville 4, Smithtown 3.

The two articles on this page both describe the same baseball game. One article appeared in the *Frankville Sun*, and the other appeared in the *Smithtown Times*. Underline the sentences or phrases in each article that describe:

> the crowd
> the weather
> the state championship
> the fourth inning
> the last inning

The article on the _____ side of the page appeared in the *Smithtown Times*.

Different Viewpoints

*Four people were asked whether they thought the deer-hunting season
should be extended so that more deer would be destroyed. Each person's
answer reflects a different viewpoint.*

1

"I think deer have a right to live, but there are so many of them around here that they've become a nuisance.

"Not a day passes that I don't see three or four—not off in the distance, but right here on my farm. Last year they ruined my garden by getting into it every night. A fence high enough to keep them out would cost me more than the garden crops are worth. Deer have stripped the leaves from my apple trees as high as they can reach. They feed themselves daily in my fields of hay.

"I wouldn't want the deer to disappear completely, as they probably would if there were no restrictions at all on hunting, but I do believe the hunting season should be extended to get rid of some of them."

2

"I believe that absolutely all hunting should be stopped. No wild creature should be the prey of men with guns.

"When I think of the shy, graceful deer being shot down by cruel hunters, it makes me ashamed that I am a human being. These gentle creatures have surely done nothing to deserve such a dreadful fate!

"It is bad enough that many of these forest friends are killed outright, but all too frequently hunters only wound them. The animals may escape the hunters, but they go off to die a slow and painful death from their injuries.

"If no hunting were allowed, the woods would become much more interesting to tourists and nature lovers."

3

"As nearly anybody who knows me can tell you, there is no activity that I enjoy quite so much as deer hunting. All during the year I look forward to late November, when I take off for the north woods for a weekend of shooting. I only wish I could stay longer.

"There's no thrill like the one I get when a deer appears and I am able to kill it with my first shot.

"Once I spent all day in the woods without seeing a single buck or doe. I don't want the season extended or the number of deer reduced. I would rather see the number increased. It costs time and money to come here for a couple of days, and I want to get a deer!"

4

"There are more deer in the state today than there were when the pioneers settled here.

"Fifty or sixty years ago, deer had become so scarce that the state passed game laws and provided special shelter areas for them. The wild animals that were the natural enemies of the deer have been almost completely destroyed. Under these conditions, deer have increased so rapidly that there simply isn't sufficient food for all of them.

"In a heavy snowfall or an unusually severe spring, as many as half the number in some herds may die of exposure or starve to death. The deer that remain are frequently in a weakened condition.

"I feel that the number of deer should be reduced, and shooting is kinder than letting them die a lingering death."

Which statements show an interest in the well-being of the deer? _____

Which statements express opinions that obviously were influenced by the writer's personal experiences? _____

Which statement has the most impersonal and factual tone? _____

Which statement is based entirely on the selfish desires of the speaker? _____

This selection is from the autobiography of a man who spent his childhood on a homestead in Oklahoma. At that time the state, formerly Indian Territory, was just beginning to be settled by white people.

Oklahoma Wasn't "Civilized"

by Marquis James

When I was about seven years old, my biggest problem was to get my hair cut. My mother's reason for keeping my hair long was that "civilized" little boys wore their hair that way. I knew her to be right enough about that. It was all too plain from the pictures in the magazines that came from the East, *Scribner's Monthly* and the *Youth's Companion*.

But then everything was different in the East. There were streetcars and stores ten stories high and the greatest houses that you ever heard tell of. These houses were lighted by something that was called gas. Everyone had a piano—in a room called the parlor. The only parlor I knew of was Mills's Tonsorial Parlor in Enid, where if it hadn't been for Mama I could have had my hair cut. And then in all these houses there were bathtubs to take baths in, though they didn't look like tubs. They looked like watering troughs. I would see pictures of these things, and Mama would tell me their names and all about them.

In these pictures the men wore different clothes from the ones worn in Enid. Ever so many wore stovepipe hats. Mama said that back East Papa had always worn such hats. That struck me as funny. I told Papa I bet he looked funny in one of those stovepipe hats, and he said in his slow way, "I expect I did."

The ladies all wore different clothes, too. Even Mama said she used to wear them. Upstairs was a leather-covered trunk with a broken hinge. In it were dresses that looked sort of like the ones worn by ladies in *Scribner's Monthly*. Mama cut them up finally to make quilts.

When these people in the pictures rode horses, they dressed even more outlandishly and had the queerest saddles, like racing saddles. But mostly they went about in carriages or funny little two-wheeled rigs that Mama called hansoms. They rode on railroads and on steamboats. Mama used to take a steamboat from Cincinnati to St. Louis to see her folks in Missouri. I yearned to ride on a steamboat. I'd never even seen any kind of boat, and I couldn't remember having had a ride on a railroad train.

Mama was always ready to answer my questions about the magazine pictures because she said she wanted me to know about civilized things. And although the pictures brought a breath of novelty to our house, what Mama said about "civilization" was a little disturbing. Until then I had thought the whole world lived in sod houses on endless plains or in little towns like Enid. I had believed, too, that people everywhere dressed and acted like the settlers, cowboys, stagecoach drivers, outlaws, storekeepers, Indians, and Mexicans that I saw in Enid. The ideas introduced by Mama and by *Scribner's Monthly* made the world a much more complicated place to live in.

This article is written from the viewpoint of:

___ a person who had lived in many different kinds of places.

___ a person whose entire life up to then had been spent in a frontier area.

Unless you read the article carefully, you are apt to make some false generalizations because of the writer's viewpoint. Read the generalizations below and check the ones that you think are correct.

___ All homestead mothers wanted their children to be "civilized."

___ Everyone in the East had a piano, a front parlor, and a big house.

___ Life in Oklahoma in the early 1890's was not representative of life in the eastern states.

___ At first all the homesteaders lived in sod houses or rough shacks.

___ Eastern boys all had long hair.

___ In the 1890's the United States was largely an uncivilized country.

___ People in Oklahoma dressed differently from people in the East.

___ The homesteaders did not take baths.

___ All eastern men wore stovepipe hats.

Watching Baseball

by Robert Benchley

Eighteen men play a game of baseball and eighteen thousand watch them, and yet those who play are the only ones who have any official direction in the matter of rules and regulations. This is, of course, ridiculous. A set of official rulings for spectators at baseball games is therefore reproduced herewith.

In the first place, there is the question of shouting encouragement, or otherwise, at the players. There must be no more random screaming. It is of course understood that the players are entirely dependent on the advice offered them from the stands, and how is a batter to know what to do if, for instance, he hears a man in the bleachers shouting, "Wait for 'em, Wally!" and another man in the south stand shouting, "Take a crack at the first one, Wally!"?

The official advisers in the stands must work together. Before each player goes to bat, there should be a conference among the fans, and as soon as a majority have come to a decision, their advice should be shouted to the player in unison under the direction of a cheer-leader. If there are any dissenting opinions, they may be expressed in a minority report.

In the matter of hostile remarks addressed at an unpopular player on the visiting team it would probably be better to leave the wording entirely to individual fans. Each man has his own talents in this sort of thing. If it should become necessary to rattle the opposing pitcher or prevent the visiting catcher from getting a difficult foul, all considerations of good sportsmanship should be discarded. The game must be kept free from all such softening influences.

One of the chief duties of the fan is to engage in arguments with the man behind him. An ardent supporter of the home team should be prepared to take offense. He should be equipped with a stock of ready sallies that can be used regardless of what the argument is about, such as: "Oh, is that so?" "How do you get that way?" "So are you." "Oh, is that so?" "Who says so?" "Oh, is that so?" Any one of these, if hurled with sufficient venom, is good for ten points.

For those fans who are occasionally obliged to take inexperienced lady-friends to a game, a special set of rules has been drawn up. These include the compulsory purchase of tickets in what is called the "Explaining Section." The view of the diamond from this section is not very good, but it doesn't matter, as the men will be too busy explaining to see anything of the game anyway, and the women can see just enough to give them material for questions.

Absolutely no gentlemen with uninformed ladies will be admitted to the main stand. In order to enforce this regulation, a short examination on the rudiments of the game will take place at the gate, in which ladies will be expected to answer briefly the following questions:

1. What game is being played on this field?
2. How many games have you seen before?
3. What is a pitcher? a base? a bat?
4. What color uniform does the home team wear?
5. What is the name of the home team?
6. In the following sentence, cross out the incorrect statements, leaving the correct one: The catcher stands (1) directly behind the pitcher in the pitcher's box; (2) at the gate taking tickets; (3) behind the batter; (4) at the bottom of the main aisle, selling ginger-ale.
7. What again is the name of the game you expect to see played?
8. Do you cry easily?
9. Is there anything else you would rather be doing this afternoon?
10. If so, please go and do it.

At what habits of baseball fans is Mr. Benchley poking fun? _____ _____ _____ _____ _____ _____

The main humorous device he uses is (underline one): wild exaggeration . . . . use of funny made-up words . . . saying the opposite of what he really means . . . . putting together things that are inappropriate or incongruous.

Adapted from *Love Conquers All* by Robert Benchley; copyright, 1922, by Harper & Brothers; copyright, 1950, by Gertrude Benchley; reprinted by permission of Harper & Brothers and John Lane the Bodley Head, Ltd.

The introduction to a book usually presents the viewpoint of the author and tells why he wrote the book. The two prefaces below are from books about horses that you might enjoy reading. One is from Will James' book, Smoky. The other, by Wesley Dennis, introduces his collection of stories, Palomino and Other Horses.

1. To my way of thinking there's something wrong, or missing, with any person who hasn't got a soft spot in their heart for an animal of some kind. With most folks the dog stands highest as man's friend, then comes the horse, with others the cat is liked best as a pet, or a monkey is fussed over; but whatever kind of animal it is a person likes, it's all hunky-dory so long as there's a place in the heart for one or a few of them.

I've never yet went wrong in sizing up a man by the kind of a horse he rode. A good horse always packs a good man, and I've always dodged the hombre what had no thought nor liking for his horse or other animals, for I figger that kind of gazabo is best to be left unacquainted with. No good would ever come of the meeting.

With me, my weakness lays towards the horse. My life, from the time I first squinted at daylight, has been with horses. I admire every step that crethure makes. I know them and been thru so much with 'em that I've come to figger a big mistake was made when the horse was classed as an animal. To me the horse is man's greatest, most useful, faithful, and powerful friend. He never whines when he's hungry or sore-footed or tired, and he'll keep on a-going for the human till he drops.

The horse is not appreciated and never will be appreciated enough—few humans, even them that works him, really know him, but then there's so much to know about him. I've wrote this book on only one horse and when I first started it I was afraid I'd run out of something to write, but I wasn't half thru when I begin to realize I had to do some squeezing to get the things in I wanted; and when I come to the last chapter was when I seen how if I spent my life writing on the horse alone and lived to be a hundred I'd only said maybe half of what I feel ought to be said. . . .

From *Smoky* by Will James; copyright, 1926, 1954, by Charles Scribner's Sons; copyright, 1954, by Auguste Dufault. Reprinted by permission of the publisher.

2. I've always been crazy about horses and horse stories, so it has been a real pleasure to collect these favorites of mine and to illustrate them as well.

The horses in this book are old friends, as courageous, honest, deceitful, high-spirited, or loyal as many people I know. Whether it's Chapo the Faker or Coaly-bay the outlaw, or Harum Scarum or a horse called Pete, I've known horses like these on my ranch, and loved them all.

People who admire horses don't always realize that the horse has evolved in much the same remarkable way as man. The first known horse was about the same size as a fox. That was millions of years before the Ice Age—before man, even. But since then he has grown into an animal useful and beloved. Since the Indians trained the wild horses descended from the steeds of the Spanish invaders, the horse has been an important part of American life—particularly in the West where the mustang of the Great Plains, because of his smartness and endurance, became the equivalent of the cowboy's sixth sense.

These stories are about all kinds of horses: circus horses, thoroughbreds, mustangs, outlaws—but horses are horses, and whether you ride in a saddle or a rocking chair, I know you will love the proud, fiery, beautiful beasts in these pages the way I do.

Underline the correct answer.

Both men have great love for horses. Yes No

Both men seem to feel that horses are friendly, helpful, and courageous. Yes No

Both introductions tell something about the early history of the horse. Yes No

One introduction goes beyond judging horses and judges the men who ride them. Yes No

Both authors seem to be defending the horse as an almost perfect creature. Yes No

One author has chosen to include stories about many different types of horses. Yes No

One introduction gives a better insight into the author's personality than the other. Yes No

The style of both introductions is approximately the same. Yes No

On Ice

by Denzil Batchelor

A hockey fan will tell you that the first and greatest thrill of the game is its speed. But hockey has grace as well. If you were to watch twelve swallows dip and swoop, swerve and skim hither and yon about a confined space, you would see something about as fast and elegant as hockey players in action. The rhythmic pattern of the swallows would be a delight to the eye; but it would be pattern and nothing else.

Hockey players have the grace and beauty of the swooping, wheeling swallows; but they add point and purpose to the pattern because they are playing a game. The puck is bandied back and forth as the players swoop and wheel. Then the pass is made. The forward floats toward the net. He shoots, the goalie stops and clears—then the play flashes off, sixty yards away, and blazes up around the opposite goal.

Hockey*

by John Kieran

I'm a fairly peaceful man, and an old-time baseball fan,
  You can hear me yell when Heilmann hits the ball;
And I howl when Ty Cobb stabs one, and I growl when
    Speaker grabs one,
  And I roar when Babe Ruth's homer clears the wall.
But the diamond sport is quiet to that reeling rousing riot,
  To a slashing game of hockey at its prime;
It's a shindig wild and gay; it's a battle served frappé;
  Give me hockey—I'll take hockey—any time!

Once, when crazy with the heat, I coughed up to buy a seat,
  Just to see a pair of robbers grab a purse.
It was clinch and stall and shove, and "Please excuse my
    glove,"
  Till I blessed them with a healthy Irish curse.
But for fighting, fast and free, grab your hat and come with me,
  Sure the thing that they call "boxing" is a crime,
And for ground and lofty whacking, and enthusiastic smacking,
  Give me hockey—I'll take hockey—any time!

I've an ever-ready ear for a rousing football cheer,
  And I love to see a half-back tackled low.
It's a really gorgeous sight when the boys begin to fight
  With a touchdown only half a yard to go.
But take all the most exciting parts of football, baseball, fighting,
  And then mix them up to make a game sublime,
Serve it up with lots of ice, you don't have to ask me twice,
  Give me hockey—I'll take hockey—any time!

Yes, for speed and pep and action, there is only one attraction,
  You'll see knockouts there a dozen for a dime,
When the bright steel blades are ringing and the shinny sticks
    are swinging,
  Give me hockey—I'll take hockey—any time!

What aspects of hockey appeal most to the writer of the article? ------------------------------
to the poet? -- Which ideas does the picture on
this page illustrate—those in the poem or those in the article? ------------------------------

WHAT A SHIP CAN SEE

How the ships look on a radarscope

10 miles

10 miles

20 miles

30 miles

The Accident That Couldn't Happen

For those who navigate ships or airplanes, radar operates as a sixth sense. Like the other senses that help man keep his course in the world, it is taken for granted until something goes wrong. Then come the questions.

After the tragic collision on July 25, 1956, that sent the prow of the Swedish liner *Stockholm* knifing into the Italian ship, *Andrea Doria*, one nagging question persisted: What happened to radar on the ships?

A radar transmitter sends out brief, intense pulses of radio energy that bounce back when they strike an object. The echo is recorded on an indicator. This is usually a round radarscope on which spots of light called "pips" appear to indicate a floating iceberg or a passing ship.

The *Stockholm* and the *Andrea Doria* both had two sets of shipboard radar. Under normal conditions, any of these sets should have been able to detect an object as massive as an ocean liner at the distance of twenty or thirty miles.

In the confusion following the sinking of the *Andrea Doria*, a number of theories were offered to account for the prolonged navigational blindness of the two liners. The most unlikely is that the radar failed. The two radar sets aboard the *Stockholm* had been inspected the day before she sailed from New York. Presumably, those on the *Andrea Doria* had been checked when she left Genoa. The chances of a simultaneous failure of all four sets are very small.

A somewhat more believable theory is based on the fact that the radar instrument sometimes gives misleading information. Violent magnetic storms, low-lying fog blankets that trap the beam, radio interference, and a host of other factors can seriously disturb the operation of radar.

Unfortunately, one bit of evidence casts doubt on this general theory. The French liner *Ile de France*, which raced to the disaster in the same dense fog, had no trouble in picking up a completely clear picture of the area. Not only could the French captain plot the position of the two wounded liners and a couple of rescue ships, but he was able to use his radar for "strategic maneuvering" as he closed on the scene.

In the absence of any good explanation for the ineffectiveness of the radar, most observers have settled on human error as the reason for the collision. A radar expert suggested that a common fault among officers on the bridge is failure to keep an adequate plot or diagram of the "pips" on the radarscope that indicate moving objects. If this had been done, he maintained, the accident probably would not have occurred.

Who knows what really happened? Actually, the explanation of the tragedy may be as simple as that offered by one naval officer: "It's something like two people nearly colliding on the sidewalk. In an effort to avoid each other, they may turn into each other's path."

This article appeared in the "Science" section of a weekly magazine. Check the statement that best expresses the point of view of the writer.

---- He has doubts about the value of mechanical devices.

---- He respects mechanical marvels but recognizes that their value depends upon the skill and alertness of the people who operate them.

---- He thinks it is useless to try to explain an accident, because "accidents just happen."

*Below is a report of a true incident as it appeared in a
news magazine. After reading the article, consider how you
might rewrite the information in various other forms.*

Mystery Voice

Recently a comedian on a British Broadcasting Company television channel had viewers convulsed with laughter. Suddenly the comedian's punch lines were drowned out by a burst of squeaks, squawks, and crackles. These sounds were followed by a deathly silence. Then an eerie voice with an unfamiliar accent flooded English living rooms with a strange request.

The mystery voice ordered somebody named Mac to proceed to an address in a place called Flatbush and pick up three people. Then the mystery voice faded, and the voice of the English comedian was heard again.

Hundreds of angry—and frightened—British televiewers immediately flooded the BBC TV studios with telephone calls. The BBC launched an investigation at once. Were its televiewers picking up broadcasts from Mars?

As it turned out, the mystery voice didn't come from Mars but from Brooklyn, New York! BBC investigators soon discovered that Channel 1 and a New York taxi company both used the same shortwave frequency. But they had done so for years without conflict, for the taxi company's radio had a range of only 10 miles. What, then, had flipped the taxi company's radio signals all the way across the Atlantic?

Scientists had a ready answer. Sunspots were to blame. Sunspots are violent storms of electrical gases that whirl through the sun's atmosphere. These storms radiate enormous amounts of magnetism. And when sunspots are particularly active, they sometimes cause freakish results in radio reception on the earth.

Check the phrase that you think best completes each statement below.

1. If I were writing up this episode in the form of a short story, using a British televiewer as my main character, I would emphasize:

---- the weather and atmospheric conditions present that evening.

---- the reactions of the taxi dispatcher when he discovered that his message had been heard in England.

---- the kind of television show that was being broadcast at the time.

--- the emotional reactions of the televiewer.

2. If I were writing up this incident for a science magazine, I would emphasize:

---- how an actual broadcast from Mars might originate.

---- the behavior and effects of sunspots.

---- the development of radio-operated taxicabs.

---- a do-it-yourself plan for getting rid of interference in TV reception.

3. If I were reporting this incident from the point of view of a BBC investigator, I would emphasize:

---- the time and money lost through such interference in TV reception.

---- the step-by-step procedures involved in locating the source of the mystery voice.

--- the listening-audience rating of the comedy program.

---- the source and wording of the inquiries about the phenomenon that came into the BBC switchboard.

Clues to an Accented First Syllable

dol′lar   pep′per   com′mon   les′son

sum′mon   dif′fer   stub′born   bliz′zard

let′ter   shal′low   glit′ter   gal′lon

1. In each of these two-syllable root words the two like consonant letters following the first vowel letter are a clue to an accented first syllable and to a short vowel sound in that syllable.

pock′et   jack′et   pack′age   crack′le

jock′ey   reck′on   wick′ed   tack′le

chick′en   stock′ing   sock′et   buck′le

2. In each of these two-syllable root words the letters *ck* following the single vowel letter are a clue to an accented first syllable and to a short vowel sound in that syllable.

sin′gle   bub′ble   ea′gle   cir′cle

daz′zle   cat′tle   can′dle   tur′tle

ma′ple   peo′ple   nee′dle   thim′ble

3. In each of these two-syllable root words the final *le* preceded by a consonant is a clue to an unaccented final syllable.

Read each sentence. Then mark the accented syllable in the word below. Which of the three numbered statements applies to it? The first one is done for you.

George changed the typewriter ribbon before he started to work on the letter.

      r i b′ b o n __1__

"I'll press out the wrinkles in this dress before I wear it," said Judy.

      w r i n k l e s _____

For many years a large bell had hung in the steeple of the old colonial church.

      s t e e p l e _____

As she whirled around and around on her ice skates, Susan became quite dizzy.

      d i z z y _____

Mr. Roberts began to chuckle because the TV program made him think of his own family life.

      c h u c k l e _____

The shock of the tragic accident caused Ben to stutter for several months.

      s t u t t e r _____

The geologist found some fossils of prehistoric animals embedded in the rock.

      f o s s i l s _____

"I would certainly like to hear your angle on this dispute," remarked Mr. Green.

      a n g l e _____

Since the rocket has been improved, it has become an effective weapon of warfare.

      r o c k e t _____

Henry lost a nickel down the drain of the sink, and he could not retrieve it.

      n i c k e l _____

Clues to an Accented Final Syllable

in vite′	sup pose′	dis play′	be tween′
ex treme′	a muse′	a fraid′	ap proach′
es cape′	de fine′	re peat′	ex claim′

1. In each of these two-syllable root words the silent vowel in the final syllable is a clue to an accented syllable and a long vowel sound in that syllable.

ad vice′ — no′tice	en rage′ — man′age	be have′ — oc′tave
dis grace′ — sur′face	o blige′ — car′tridge	re vive′ — na′tive
en tice′ — of′fice	ar range′ — or′ange	ar rive′ — mo′tive

2. In these pairs of two-syllable words ending in final *e* preceded by *c*, *g*, or *v*, final *e* is not necessarily a clue to accent nor to a long vowel sound. However, it is a clue to the soft sound of *c* or *g*.

o mit′ted	for got′ten	re gret′ted	oc cur′rence
e quip′ping	per mit′ted	for bid′ding	pre fer′ring
be gin′ner	up set′ting	ex pel′ling	re cur′ring

3. In each of these two-syllable root words the two like consonant letters before the ending or suffix are a clue to an accented final syllable in the root word. They are also a clue to a short vowel sound in that syllable, except when the vowel is followed by *r*.

Read each sentence and mark the accented syllable in the word below. Write the number of the above statement that applies.

Robert tried to conceal the tear in his sleeve.

c o n c e a l _____

Lightning hit the transmitter and damaged it.

t r a n s m i t t e r _____

The boys had precise orders to be home by ten o'clock on Thursday night.

p r e c i s e _____

"Will this sweater retain its shape when it is washed?" asked Marjorie.

r e t a i n _____

John studied the newspaper reports that told about the rebellion on the island.

r e b e l l i o n _____

Caesar announced that his army had brought back a thousand captives.

c a p t i v e s _____

Mr. Welles decided to exchange his tractor for a trailer, and tour the country.

e x c h a n g e _____

James was mistaken in inferring that he could use the car any time he wished.

i n f e r r i n g _____

Several fire trucks blocked the main street, compelling all motorists to detour.

c o m p e l l i n g _____

"Do not confuse the issue with misleading statements," said the judge.

c o n f u s e _____

Other Clues to Accent

ar rive′ — ar riv′al   mis take′ — mis tak′en   dis pute′ — dis put′ed
po lite′ — po lit′est   ex plode′ — ex plod′ed   a maze′ — a maz′ing
de cide′ — de cid′ed   pro vide′ — pro vid′er   re fuse′ — re fus′al

1. In these words the single consonant letter following the single vowel before an ending or suffix is a clue to (a) a dropped final *e* in the root word, (b) an accented final syllable in the root, and (c) a long vowel sound in the accented syllable.

fo′cus — fo′cus ing   thun′der — thun′der ing   hu′mor — hu′mor ous
piv′ot — piv′ot ed   an′swer — an′swer ing   cho′rus — cho′rus es
fe′ver — fe′ver ish   spon′sor — spon′sor ing   bor′der — bor′der ing

2. These words show that a single consonant following a single vowel before an ending or suffix may also be a clue to a schwa sound in the unaccented final syllable of the root word.

Read each sentence. Then write in the blank the number of the above statement that applies to the italicized word.

Howard was *describing* a newspaper article he had read about the laws that had been passed at the last session of Congress. _____

The girl sat *cowering* in the corner, trembling at the angry threats of her older brother, who had discovered her deceit. _____

The young man stepped over to the clerk and asked whether he had any *blossoming* plants for sale at this time. _____

The *customer* looked carefully at every plant in the flower shop before finally deciding on one she wanted. _____

The students *promoted* the idea of having a Career Club as a means of learning about different kinds of work. _____

Everyone agreed that Bill's *proposal* was a good idea, although it might be difficult to work out the practical details. _____

Andrew, who was usually very quiet, made a bold and *surprising* suggestion at the meeting of the Glee Club. _____

"What is *happening!*" exclaimed June, looking up from her work. "What is that ripping sound coming from the next room?" _____

A flier who had *piloted* jet planes spoke at the second meeting, and he was applauded most enthusiastically by the boys. _____

Many people *paraded* up and down the wide boardwalk, enjoying the summer sunshine and the gaiety of the amusement park. _____

Mrs. Henderson put up a screen to serve as a *divider* between the breakfast nook and the cooking area in her kitchen. _____

Just as Elizabeth was *completing* the final chapter of the thrilling mystery, the electricity went off, leaving her in the dark. _____

Below are seven visual clues that help you determine which syllable is accented in a two-syllable root word (either with or without an ending or a suffix). Read the clues. Then mark the accented syllable of each widely spread word below and give the number of the clue that told you where the accent falls. The first one is done for you.

Clues to an *accented final syllable* in a two-syllable root word:

1. As in *re tain* (ri tān′): two vowel letters together

2. As in *for gave* (fər gāv′): two vowel letters, one of which is final *e*

3. As in *com pel ling* (kəm pel′ling): two like consonant letters before an ending or suffix

Clues to an *accented first syllable* in a two-syllable root word:

4. As in *pen nant* (pen′ənt): two like consonant letters following the first vowel letter

5. As in *pock et* (pok′it): the letters *ck* preceded by a single vowel letter

6. As in *hur dle* (hėr′dəl): a final syllable ending in *le* preceded by a consonant

Clues that must be checked by context:

7. As in *con fid ing* (kən fīd′ing) or as in *pi lot ing* (pī′lət ing): a single consonant letter following a single vowel letter before an ending or suffix may be a clue to either an *accented final syllable* or an *accented first syllable*.

__1__ showed great   r e s t r a i n t′

____ a jar of homemade   j e l l y

____   l a d l e   the soup out

____   m o r o s e   because he is bedridden

____   p e r v a d i n g   air of boredom

____ heart-shaped   l o c k e t

____ a   t a p e r i n g   roof

____   e x c e l l i n g   in eloquence

____ impetuously pressed the   t r i g g e r

____   s w e l t e r i n g   in the sun

____ a   m a m m o t h   undertaking

____   c o n s u m i n g   the available oxygen

____   r e p e l l i n g   the barbaric tribe

____   r e n o u n c e   a claim

____   c a s c a d i n g   waterfall

____ kick to the   c o f f i n   corner

____ white   p i c k e t   fence

____   d e p l e t e   the supply of muffins

____ a distinctive   t i t l e

____ remove the   b l i s t e r e d   paint

____   r e v e a l   his hiding place

____ predicament gave me the   j i t t e r s

____   g a m b o l i n g   lambs

____   r e f e r r i n g   to the dictionary

____ a   c o n c i s e   criticism

____   m a r s h a l i n g   the routed troops

____ saw the puck   n e s t l e   in the net

____ a   r e p r o a c h   to the team

____ captive in   s h a c k l e s

____   t a m p e r i n g   with the explosives

Meaning and Pronunciation

Use the dictionary definitions to answer the questions about the italicized word in each sentence below. Then mark the accented syllable.

con duct (kon′dukt for 1, 3, 6; kən dukt′ for 2, 4, 5, 7, 8), **1.** behavior; way of acting: *Her conduct was inexcusable.* **2.** act in a certain way; behave: *She always conducts herself like a lady.* **3.** direction; management: *the conduct of an office.* **4.** direct; manage: *conduct the affairs of a business.* **5.** direct (an orchestra, etc.) as leader. **6.** leading; guiding. **7.** lead; guide: *Conduct me to your teacher.* **8.** transmit (heat, electricity, etc.): *Those pipes conduct steam to the radiators upstairs.* 1,3, 6 *n.,* 2,4,5,7,8 *v.*

con test (kon′test for 1, 3, 5; kən test′ for 2, 4, 6, 7), **1.** trial to see which can win. A game or race is a contest. **2.** try to win. **3.** fight; struggle. **4.** fight for; struggle for: *The soldiers contested every inch of ground.* **5.** argument; dispute. **6.** argue against; dispute about: *The lawyer contested the claim and tried to prove that it was false.* **7.** take part in a contest. 1,3,5 *n.,* 2,4,6,7 *v.* —**con test′a ble,** *adj.*

es cort (es′kôrt for 1,2; es kôrt′ for 3), **1.** one or a group going with another to give protection, show honor, etc.: *an escort of ten airplanes. Her escort to the party was a tall young man.* **2.** act of going with another as an escort. **3.** go with as an escort: *Warships escorted the troopship.* 1,2 *n.,* 3 *v.*

es say (es′ā for 1; e sā′ for 2; es′ā or e sā′ for 3), **1.** a literary composition on a certain subject. An essay is usually shorter and less methodical than a treatise. **2.** try; attempt. **3.** a try; an attempt. 1,3 *n.,* 2 *v.*

for bear[1] (fôr bãr′), **1.** hold back; keep from doing, saying, using, etc.: *The boy forbore to hit back because the other boy was smaller.* **2.** be patient; control oneself. *v.,* **for bore, for borne, for bear ing.** —**for bear′ing ly,** *adv.*

for bear[2] (fôr′bãr), forebear; ancestor. *n.*

prog ress (prog′res for 1, 3; prə gres′ for 2, 4), **1.** advance; growth; development; improvement: *the progress of science.* **2.** get better; advance; develop: *We progress in learning step by step.* **3.** a moving forward; going ahead: *make rapid progress on a journey.* **4.** move forward; go ahead: *The war has progressed some time.* 1,3 *n.,* 2,4 *v.*

re ject (ri jekt′ for 1, 2, 4; rē′jekt for 3), **1.** refuse to take, use, believe, consider, grant, etc.: *He rejected our help. He tried to join the army but was rejected.* **2.** throw away as useless or unsatisfactory: *Reject all apples with soft spots.* **3.** a rejected person or thing. **4.** vomit. 1,2,4 *v.,* 3 *n.* —**re ject′er,** *n.*

sus pect (səs pekt′ for 1-4; sus′pekt for 5; sus′pekt or səs pekt′ for 6), **1.** imagine to be so; think likely: *The old fox suspected danger and did not touch the trap.* **2.** believe guilty, false, bad, etc., without proof: *The policeman suspected the thief of lying.* **3.** feel no confidence in; doubt: *The judge suspected the truth of the thief's excuse.* **4.** be suspicious. **5.** person suspected: *The police have arrested two suspects in connection with the bank robbery.* **6.** open to suspicion; suspected. 1-4 *v.,* 5 *n.,* 6 *adj.*

"Put the *rejects* on this pile at the left," the foreman of the factory directed.

Which meaning of *reject* is used in this sentence? (Indicate by number.) _ _ _ _

Which part of speech is this meaning? _ _ _ _ _ _ _ _

When the guide *conducted* sightseers through the caverns, he called attention to and described many of the unusual rock formations.

Which meaning of *conduct* fits here? _ _ _ _

Which part of speech is this meaning? _ _ _ _ _ _ _ _

As the term project *progressed*, the students learned to organize their plans efficiently.

Which meaning does *progress* have here? _ _ _ _

Which part of speech is it? _ _ _ _ _ _ _ _ _ _ _

Joan finally decided that she would enter her *essay* in the contest.

Which meaning of *essay* fits here? _ _ _ _

Which part of speech is it? _ _ _ _ _ _ _ _ _ _ _

One of George's *forbears* had owned a ship that plied between Boston and Singapore.

Which entry of *forbear* fits here? _ _ _ _ _ _ _ _ _ _

Which part of speech is it? _ _ _ _ _ _ _ _ _ _ _

Joe, who was president of the student council, *escorted* the queen to her throne and placed the crown on her head.

Which meaning does *escort* have here? _ _ _ _

Which part of speech is it? _ _ _ _ _ _ _ _ _ _ _

"We have several good *suspects* in this case," the police chief told the reporter from the evening paper.

Which meaning of *suspect* fits here? _ _ _ _

Which part of speech is it? _ _ _ _ _ _ _ _ _ _ _

Everyone at the meeting was given an opportunity to *contest* the committee's proposals.

Which meaning does *contest* have here? _ _ _ _

Which part of speech is it? _ _ _ _ _ _ _ _ _ _ _

In many two-syllable root words having both noun and verb meanings, the _ _ _ _ _ _ syllable is accented when the word is used as a noun. The _ _ _ _ _ _ syllable is accented when the word is used as a verb.

hat, āge, cãre, fär; let, ēqual, tėrm; it, īce; hot, ōpen, ôrder; oil, out; cup, pút, rüle, ūse; ch, child; ng, long; th, thin; ŦH, then; zh, measure; ə represents *a* in about, *e* in taken, *i* in pencil, *o* in lemon, *u* in circus.

Patterns of Accent in Longer Words

In words of three or more syllables one of the first two syllables is accented. Mark the accented syllable in these words. The first two are done for you.

oc'to pus	tor na do	mu se um	mis er a ble
oc ca'sion	dis as ter	hos pi tal	po ta to
ve hi cle	mer cu ry	fur ni ture	op er ate
con di tion	em bar rass	com mis sion	va ca tion
fas ci nate	dec o rate	ex per i ment	com mu ni ty
mos qui to	ther mom e ter	hor ri ble	cel e brate
in ci dent	mi cro phone	moc ca sin	to bog gan
ho ri zon	a rith me tic	re mem ber	mes sen ger
ri val ry	im me di ate	ac ci dent	par tic u lar
im ple ment	cor du roy	ca tas tro phe	a pol o gy

Read each sentence. Then mark the accented syllable in the word printed below the sentence.

The severe windstorm damaged the television antenna on top of the house.

an ten na

"Today's game will determine whether or not we go to the state finals," said Rob.

de ter mine

After tasting the salad, Susan decided to add some more vinegar to it.

vin e gar

Charles noticed that there was a leak in the aluminum pan he had filled with water.

a lu mi num

Mr. Richards recommended Bob for the job because he knew he was a capable person.

ca pa ble

George got plenty of exercise when he helped his brother mow the lawn and rake the grass.

ex er cise

David was surprised that a wrecking crew could demolish a building so quickly.

de mol ish

Mrs. Stoner asked Bill not to cut down the asparagus plants growing near the fence.

as par a gus

The freezing temperature damaged many of the oranges on the trees.

tem per a ture

"This watch has never kept accurate time," Phil told the repairman.

ac cu rate

Primary and Secondary Accent

Some words in our language have two accented syllables. If a word has two accented syllables, you usually stress one of these syllables more than the other when you say the word. We call this stronger stress a primary accent. The lighter stress we call a secondary accent. In many words the secondary accent falls on either the first or second syllable, and there is only one unaccented syllable between the secondary and the primary accent.

Mark the primary and the secondary accent in each of these words. Then find the key word at the bottom of the page that has the same vowel sound that you hear in the syllable with the primary accent. Write the key word on the dotted line. The first two are done for you.

ag′ri cul′tur al .... *cup* ....

i mag′i na′tion .... *āge* ....

pa tri ot ic ....

rep re sent ....

veg e ta tion ....

sat is fac to ry ....

en er get ic ....

ap pli ca tion ....

hor i zon tal ....

re spon si bil i ty ....

Mas sa chu setts ....

hes i ta tion ....

man u fac ture ....

ex ag ger a tion ....

con sci en tious ....

vis i bil i ty ....

hip po pot a mus ....

in stru men tal ....

tel e scop ic ....

pos si bil i ty ....

a pol o get ic ....

Cin cin nat i ....

dis ap point ment ....

kan ga roo ....

in ter rup tion ....

sci en tif ic ....

hu mil i a tion ....

lo co mo tive ....

des per a tion ....

o ver whelm ....

au to mat ic ....

un du la tion ....

Phil a del phi a ....

in dis tinct ....

veg e tar i an ....

mu nic i pal i ty ....

ad mi ra tion ....

dis be lief ....

math e mat ics ....

cul ti va tion ....

hat, āge, cãre, fär; let, ēqual, tėrm; it, īce; hot, ōpen, ôrder; oil, out; cup, pu̇t, rüle, ūse

Word Quiz

Check the correct statement below each word.

counterfeit

This word has three syllables.
This word has four syllables.

decree

The first syllable in *decree* is *dec*.
The first syllable in *decree* is *de*.

cowslip

The first syllable rhymes with *thou*.
The first syllable rhymes with the last syllable of
   bestow.

where

This word rhymes with *sneer*.
This word rhymes with *snare*.

invincible

The *c* is pronounced like the *c* in *diplomacy*.
The *c* is pronounced like the *c* in *coarse*.

tassel

The *a* is pronounced like the *a* in *staff*.
The *a* is pronounced like the *a* in *dame*.

nourish

The first syllable rhymes with *our*.
The first syllable rhymes with the first syllable
   of *herbage*.

challenge

The *ch* is pronounced like the *ch* in *chute*.
The *ch* is pronounced like the *ch* in *wrench*.
The *ch* is pronounced like the *ch* in *chord*.

restitution

This word has three syllables.
This word has four syllables.

retreat

The first syllable is accented.
The last syllable is accented.

writhe

The *th* is pronounced like the *th* in *thence*.
The *th* is pronounced like the *th* in *thud*.

mutton

The first syllable is accented.
The last syllable is accented.

brigand

The *g* is pronounced like the *g* in *gem*.
The *g* is pronounced like the *g* in *gourd*.

subtle

The *b* is pronounced like the *b* in *embank*.
The *b* is silent like the *b* in *numb*.

refine

This word rhymes with *famine*.
This word rhymes with *define*.

neigh

This word has the same vowel sound as *pate*.
This word has the same vowel sound as *height*.

staff

This word rhymes with *chafe*.
This word rhymes with the last syllable of *telegraph*.

compress

The man placed a cold *compress* on his head.
The word is pronounced kom′pres.
The word is pronounced kəm pres′.

fable

The first syllable is accented.
The last syllable is accented.

rigorous

This word has three syllables.
This word has two syllables.

convert

The missionary tried to *convert* the pagan.
The word is pronounced kon′vĕrt.
The word is pronounced kən vĕrt′.

Organizing Your Ideas

The Parthenon

Since the age when Greece was at the height of her glory, long before the birth of Christ, much of mankind has admired and copied her beautiful buildings.

The Parthenon in Athens, the most famous of these buildings, was a temple for the goddess Pallas Athena. It might not seem large to us today, as it was only about sixty feet high, but its perfect design made it an impressive structure. Forty-six columns surrounded the building and supported the roof.

To build the Parthenon, the Greeks used a beautiful white marble obtained from their own mountains. They did not like the glaring whiteness of the marble, however, so they tinted it a warm ivory color. The band above the columns was skillfully carved by Greek artists and painted in brilliant reds and blues.

Inside the Parthenon stood a great statue of Pallas Athena, covered with gold leaf and reaching almost to the roof.

Today the Parthenon, though in ruins, retains the beauty of form and line that you see in the model pictured above.

The Lincoln Memorial

The Lincoln Memorial in Washington, D.C., was erected by the United States as a tribute to one of its most beloved presidents. This noble structure, completed in 1922, is visited each year by thousands of people who honor the memory of Abraham Lincoln.

Many people consider this the most beautiful memorial building in America. Rising eighty feet above a base composed of three stone platforms, the building is made of white marble and is located in beautifully landscaped Potomac Park. The design of the structure is similar to that of a Greek temple.

The thirty-six columns surrounding the memorial represent the thirty-six states that made up the Union in Lincoln's time. The names of these states are carved between linked wreaths on a band of marble just above the columns.

When a visitor enters the columned inner room of the memorial, his attention is focused upon a majestic statue. It is Abraham Lincoln seated on a large chair. This statue is in perfect harmony with the serene beauty and dignity of the building.

Read the articles and study the pictures. Then list below on the left-hand side three ways in which the buildings are alike. On the right-hand side, list three ways in which they are different.

1. _____

2. _____

3. _____

1. _____

2. _____

3. _____

Can You Make an Outline?

The United States Coast Guard

The men in the Coast Guard service have a full-time job seeing to the safety of all who navigate rivers, lakes, and the oceans that border the United States and its possessions. One duty of the Coast Guard is to try to prevent marine accidents. Another duty assumed by the Coast Guard is rescuing the shipwrecked.

One way in which the Coast Guard prevents accidents is by regularly checking freighters to make sure that they are in shipshape condition. Inspectors examine the hull, the machinery, safety devices, and the rest of the ship's apparatus to see that nothing is out of order.

In the North Atlantic Ocean, there is a special Coast Guard "ice patrol" that cruises about watching for floating ice. At night and in stormy or foggy weather, the enormous chunks of ice are almost impossible to see. Ships in the area keep in radio contact with the "ice patrol" and thus know the precise location of floating ice.

Another section of the Coast Guard handles the "weather patrol" stations in the Atlantic and Pacific oceans. This patrol broadcasts frequent on-the-spot weather reports. The information alerts crews on ships and planes so they can prepare for severe gales or alter their courses to avoid unusually bad storms.

Navigational aids operated by the Coast Guard include lighthouses on the coasts, lightships in the water, and foghorns. In the darkness and during storms, the boom of the horns and the flashing beam of the lights caution ships' pilots to watch out for dangerous reefs.

Occasionally an accident does occur. In such a situation the Coast Guard is instantly available to aid the victims.

If planes or ships at sea are reported missing or are long overdue, the Coast Guard is notified and quickly goes into action. Its men comb the seas until the plane or ship is finally located.

When a shipwreck occurs, men of the Coast Guard make every effort to rescue the victims. This work calls for brave, well-disciplined men who must be able to handle small boats in the midst of wild storms.

The Coast Guard pioneered in saving lives by using helicopters. With these "whirly-birds," emergency cases of the injured and ill can be rushed from ships to the shore and be under medical care in a short time.

Each year thousands of people remember with gratitude the services performed by the many loyal young men who have enlisted for duty in the United States Coast Guard.

Write the following subheads under the appropriate main heads in the outline:

Rescuing shipwreck victims
Locating floating ice
Rushing ill and injured to shore
Broadcasting weather reports
Inspecting freighters
Hunting missing or overdue ships and planes
Operating lighthouses, lightships, and foghorns

I. The Coast Guard helps prevent accidents by
  A. _____
  B. _____
  C. _____
  D. _____

II. The Coast Guard saves victims of accidents by
  A. _____
  B. _____
  C. _____

Careers in Conservation

This article discusses a few of the jobs available in the field of conservation. Read the article; then fill in the outline with the duties of the various kinds of jobs.

If the exciting life of a forest ranger appeals to you, remember that your job will go beyond the fighting of disastrous forest fires. As a forest conservationist you will also wage a defensive war against hordes of tree-killing insects. You will be responsible for the removal of diseased timber that might infect a large area. You will be in charge of reforestation projects.

Just as important as the forester is the soil conservationist. Every year millions of tons of fertile soil are blown away or carried away as silt by heavy spring rains or by autumn floods. Much of this tragic loss can be prevented by damming of streams, scientific planting of trees, and proper use of land to arrest erosion. As a soil conservationist, you will study and map soil areas so that farmers will know what regions are suitable for cultivation, grazing, or forest land. You will advise farmers on the kinds of crops to plant and help them with such problems as land leveling, strip plowing, and terracing.

Fighting to preserve the forests and soil is only a part of the conservation war, however. There is also a great need for the conservation of wildlife.

As an animal conservationist, your job will be to protect game from reckless hunters, to seek to increase the number of fur-bearing animals, and to curb the destruction done by such animals as coyotes, wolves, and even rabbits.

If you decide to become an expert on fish life, you can work on restocking lakes and streams. You will also see to it that these waters are kept pure so that fish will not be poisoned and die.

You might also become the kind of animal conservationist who studies the habits and diseases of birds. One of his jobs is to protect the birds that devour harmful insects. Or, if insects are your particular interest, you might learn how to control those that do damage and foster those, like the bee and the silkworm, that have proven valuable to mankind.

I. Forest conservationist

   A. _____

   B. _____

   C. _____

   D. _____

II. Soil conservationist

   A. _____

   B. _____

   C. _____

III. Animal conservationist

   A. _____

   B. _____

   C. _____

   D. _____

   E. _____

   F. _____

   G. _____

   H. _____

The Pattern of a Hurricane

by Hart Stilwell

The feel, the sound, and the sight of a hurricane are terrifying. The whole earth seems to come to life, to shudder and groan, to twist and struggle, to lie deathly still, and then to slowly revive and go its normal way again.

However, these terrifying storms always give advance warnings. The veteran of one hurricane knows when a new one is bearing down on him. He can see it. He can feel it. And there are people who insist that they can *smell* an approaching hurricane.

The people on the seacoast need not bother to look at the sky to know when a hurricane is approaching. The water warns them in two ways. The tide is unusually high; and huge, racing hurricane waves appear far in advance of the storm.

At almost the same time there will probably be advance warnings in the sky. The first hint is a change in the color of the light. An odd, yellowish haze appears. If it is near the end of the day, a brilliant red sunset may be noticed. If it is night there may be a circle around the moon.

The barometer begins falling. The air becomes damp and uncomfortably still. There is a definite feeling that something is going to happen. The animals, birds, fish, and insects are keenly aware of the meaning of this change. They instinctively start moving toward shelter.

Another unmistakable warning of an approaching hurricane is the appearance of light, low, racing clouds that seem to be skimming along barely above the tops of trees and buildings. Light rain may fall from some of these clouds. Occasional sharp gusts of wind will swirl along, followed by periods of quiet.

As the storm draws closer, the racing clouds become heavier, the periods of sunlight shorter. The haze in the sky is more pronounced. The wind begins to blow more steadily, increasing both in sound and in fury. Then comes the dreaded monster itself.

When the full force of the hurricane wind sweeps over the land, the whining and sighing and whistling of the wind change to a rumbling roar that builds up to occasional shrieks. The storm lashes, whips, and drives across everything in its path.

The sky grows darker until it seems that night is approaching, though it may be noon. A weird, bluish-gray light breaks through at intervals. The stinging rain seems not to fall but to race along with the storm, moving horizontally.

The wind is so powerful that a person facing into it cannot breathe.

The wind may build up to heights of even 180 miles an hour. Mingled with the roar of the wind and the roar of the seas are overtones of tearing and breaking and crashing. Roofs are picked up and tossed about like giant leaves. Buildings sway and quake; some are demolished. People who try to move in the face of the blow must get down on all fours and crawl. Ancient trees are ripped apart or uprooted. Strangely, the palm, its long slender trunk reaching far into the sky, seems best able to withstand the fury of the storm. It bows before the force of each gust of wind, but clings stubbornly to the soil.

For a period of four to twelve hours the wind screams and rages, the sea pounds the shore, and the rain pours down. Then, suddenly, the wind ceases. If it is daytime, sunlight may break through. If it is night, stars may become visible.

The inexperienced person begins to hope that the storm is over. The hope is false. The huge "eye," or center of the hurricane, has settled on the weary, battered land. All around this area of calm the storm is still raging.

The calm may last as long as three hours, if the hurricane is a big one. Being in the dead-calm "eye" is the weirdest sensation that a person experiences in a hurricane—the eerie feeling of being in that calm and knowing that all around it the winds are tearing along at 150 miles or more an hour.

There is a feeling of relief when the "other half" of the blow suddenly strikes. Though the wind's viciousness seems worse than anything before, its shrieking now indicates that the storm will soon be over.

The storm moves slowly inland, after it passes the coast, and gradually loses its power. It will finally break up when it reaches hills. On its way inland the hurricane continues to pour out tremendous torrents of water as it dies, or "dries out" as weathermen say. Left behind it is a wreckage-scarred area that looks as though it would never rise from the catastrophe.

The ideas in this article fall under two main headings. After you have read the article, complete the outline below.

I. Advance warnings of the hurricane

    A. _____

    B. _____

    C. _____

    D. _____

    E. _____

    F. _____

    G. _____

    H. _____

    I. _____

II. Stages of a hurricane

    A. _____

    B. _____

    C. _____

    D. _____

School for Survival

Stranded in the arctic! Imagine yourself as a member of a flight crew forced to bail out of a damaged plane crossing the top of the world. How long could you remain alive in that cold, dreary, empty land?

The answer would depend on your training. Nowadays, the chances are that you would be able to survive until rescued. That is, if you had attended a "school for survival." The Air Force sponsors such schools to teach its men the fundamentals of survival in the wilderness. One such school is located in the frozen wastes of northern Alaska.

Instructors in this school are all veterans of the arctic; some are natives of the region. They teach their students by taking them into the wilderness for a week at a time—first to the wind- and snow-swept tundra, then to an ice pack—and letting them learn through actual experience.

The first thing a student learns is how to build a suitable shelter. On the tundra, a satisfactory tentlike shelter can be made by lacing a parachute to a framework of willow branches. On the ice pack, the men learn to build igloos by cutting blocks of snow and fitting them together. Snow houses are made doubly strong and warm by causing the inside walls to melt slightly and then freeze over again into solid ice.

Food is vital for survival, and not often easy to find in the frozen North. The men learn how to trap or snare small animals, how to fish through the ice, and how to net crabs. The instructor also points out roots and plants that are edible. After a rough day in the arctic cold, even a root and seaweed stew tastes good!

Each student is provided with a survival kit—the same sort that he would probably have if he were actually forced to parachute from a crippled plane. The kit contains such things as a vacuum-packed sleeping bag, five days' concentrated rations, snares for catching game, fishing tackle, hatchet, a hunting knife, and a compass. There is also an extra pair of socks—something that could save a man's life if he happened to get his feet wet in below-freezing temperatures.

Most of the men are amazed at the usefulness of their parachutes. Just a few of the things that can be made from parachute parts are bedrolls, tepees, blankets, slingshots, fishhooks and lines, nets, splints, bandages, and snowshoes.

But equipment and information alone are not enough to enable a stranded airman to survive in the arctic. He must also learn to keep his head. As one instructor told his group, "Your greatest enemy is not hunger, not cold, not the terrain. It is fear." For no matter how much a man knows, if he becomes panicky he may do some silly thing that will cost him his life.

After the men have completed their short but grueling course in the arctic, they can feel a new confidence in their ability to survive in the wilderness. For some of them—those who actually do use the training later—this school may be the most important one they've ever attended. But all the men agree on one thing. The lessons they have learned are some they don't ever *want* to have to use.

Put the main heads and subheads given below into their proper places in the outline form.

Because of special skills needed for survival
How to keep their heads
What students learn
How to build suitable shelters
Why survival schools were established
Through instruction by veterans of the arctic
How training is given
Because of possible crashes in the arctic
How to find food
Through practical experience
How to improvise equipment

I. _____
   A. _____
   B. _____
II. _____
   A. _____
   B. _____
III. _____
   A. _____
   B. _____
   C. _____
   D. _____

The history of the automobile has been one of constant improvement and change. Modern cars have many features that early models did not. Most of the changes have increased

1. ease of driving
2. safety of the rider
3. comfort of the rider

Before each statement below, place 1, 2, or 3 to show whether the feature mentioned increases ease of driving, safety, or comfort. If the statement may apply to more than one of these points, put more than one number before it.

____ Modern cars have shatterproof glass that may crack when struck but will not fly in all directions.

____ Modern cars have a hydraulic-brake system powerful enough to stop a car within a comparatively short distance after the brake is applied.

____ Instead of hard seats, modern cars have luxurious seats with box springs.

____ Cars have various devices designed to keep the windshield clear of rain, snow, and ice.

____ Early cars had wheels like buggy wheels edged with a strip of hard rubber, but modern cars have balloon tires.

____ Safety belts that prevent the driver and the passengers from being thrown out of the car are available.

____ The rear-view mirror is sometimes mounted on a ball-swivel joint so that the driver may adjust it easily.

____ Some of the modern cars have the gear-shift mounted on the steering post.

____ In 1915, when a tire was punctured, the driver had to stop and mend it. Now, a spare tire mounted on a wheel is part of a car's equipment, and the entire wheel can be replaced at once and the tire repaired later.

____ Present-day cars contain heaters. Some are also air-conditioned.

____ The heavy, low, steel bodies of modern cars are stronger and less likely to be crushed in a collision than the older, lighter cars.

____ Some modern cars are equipped with a photoelectric cell that acts as an electric eye, automatically dimming the headlights when approaching another car.

____ Sun visors, mounted above the windshield in modern cars, prevent the blinding effect of glare.

____ During recent years, the automatic transmission has been devised, relieving drivers of the need to shift gears by hand.

____ The windows in some models of cars today can be raised or lowered by push button.

____ Early cars were usually open models with canvas tops. For protection against weather, the driver had to put up side curtains. Now cars are enclosed or are quickly converted from open to closed models by pressing a button.

____ Recent models have turn indicators that flash the parking lights on the side in which the driver intends to turn.

____ Early models had to be cranked by hand to start the motor. Today the driver merely presses a starter or turns a key.

____ The "wrap-around" windshield of most modern cars gives the driver clear vision to the sides as well as straight ahead.

Like the writer of this article, most of us at some time have felt the lure of adventure in the wilderness. Mr. Handel is an experienced woodsman who has traveled thousands of miles by canoe in the Canadian wilds.

High Adventure Still Lives
by Carle Walker Handel

We sat around the fire, using a candle in a tin bucket for a light, and pored over a blueprint map. All day we had paddled our way through a lake, taking advantage of islands, promontories, and cliffs. We had waited in the lee of rocky islands for the strong head wind to let up a little so that we could make the open passages. Then we had carefully continued our way toward the end of the big lake, anxiously watching the sky and mountaintops for weather signs. We had kept track of bays, islands, hills, and other landmarks. We had watched the sun, the direction of the wind, and the streaks made in the water by the current. We had checked our compass regularly, using the age-old navigation trick of looking back at regular intervals to check our "wind drift" and "headway."

Anyone who has traveled in wild country knows that to keep your sense of direction you must keep your eyes and ears open to signs along the way, such as a flock of fish ducks flying nose into the wind, their beaks pointing its source like the needles of a floating-dial compass. You must carefully note any change in your direction of travel. And you must "hindsight" regularly so as to know what the trail looks like should it be necessary to backtrack.

With our map fastened under a couple of pack straps and placed so that its directions north,

south, east, and west corresponded with the directions indicated by the compass tied on top, we had worked down to the bay from which issued the outlet of the lake. But upon arriving at this bay, we were perplexed at not seeing that telltale break in the skyline that usually indicates the outlet of a large lake.

We had then skirted several small bays, with no success. To the west, a mountain rose a sheer thousand feet like a great wall, defying human efforts to pass it. It was late, so we had chosen a campsite on a shelving rocky island. (Sand beaches are usually to be avoided in July, since they contain more biting pests at that season than do rocky surfaces.) We had made camp, building beds of balsam on which we had pitched our two wedge tents. One canoe had gone out with instructions to troll with a copper line and an archer spinner over a shoal lying between our island and one about a mile to the northwest. We had noted two loons diving over the water. This indicated the presence of shiners, sometimes called pin herring, which are natural food of lake trout. As we had expected, the canoe trip produced two lake trout, twenty pounds in all, plus the usual fish stories that accompany such incidents of wilderness life.

With four motions of the hunting knife, each trout had been boned and skinned. The pink meat had been cut in chunks and dropped into a pot of boiling salted water on the fire, where, along with a slice of good old raw onion, it had cooked for three minutes. The shredded potatoes also took three minutes to cook, dried spinach the same. Bannock (a kind of camper's biscuit), tea, and applesauce made of dried apples had completed an excellent meal.

By the time the canoes had been dragged onto the shore, food cached, extra wood brought in, and dishes washed, it was time to gather around the fire to talk over the day and swap stories.

The problem of finding the outlet to the lake was the major topic of conversation. The blueprint indicated that we were in the bay that led into the river, but every landmark visible to us seemed to indicate otherwise. Ordinary maps of wilderness country are designed to give only the general lay of the land, lakes, and rivers. So

Adapted from *Canoe Camping* by Carle Walker Handel; copyright, 1953, by The Ronald Press Company.

we dug into one of the duffel bags for a more accurate geological map. In many respects it varied from the blueprint map, but it, too, showed that the river flowed out of this particular bay. After an hour's discussion, the candle burned out, and one by one tired travelers retreated to their blankets.

Finally the guide and I were the only ones left by the fire. After we each had a cup of tea, we walked down to the lake's edge. The wind had long since died, the brilliant stars had come out, and the ghostly flickers of the northern lights were just beginning to appear under the Big Dipper. We stood on the shore for a long time. A white-throated sparrow's sleepy song drifted over the water, a sweet interlude in that great silence.

Then suddenly it came—a sound, at first like a faint whisper, then louder, then fading out only to rise again, a sound that was like the distant exhaust of steam or the whispering of a breeze in a Norway pine. The guide's hand pressed my arm as we both listened intently. We knew what the sound was. From the southwest, under the brow of the mountain, it came—the unmistakable sound of rapids, perhaps a mile or two away. We rolled into our sleeping bags, secure in the knowledge that we had located the passage.

Finding this passage was typical of a thousand experiences in wilderness travel. Many would call it luck, but the wise know that it is based on geographical knowledge of one's surroundings.

If anyone thinks that La Salle, Daniel Boone, Davy Crockett, Jim Bridger, and Lewis and Clark were "just plain lucky," he is far from right. These men survived the wilderness because they took advantage of the wisdom and knowledge gleaned from the Indian trail blazers who preceded them. They used the best equipment available in their day and observed good health habits. Before adventuring forth, they gathered all the information possible, as is shown by the crude maps they drew before starting into the wilds and then corrected en route.

The fine art of wilderness travel today is not just for the few, but for the thousands of us who have the blood of adventuring forefathers in our veins. Once you have experienced such an adventure, you will never quite forget it. When you catch the whiff of wood smoke, see the haze on the hills, hear the geese high in the sky or a train whistle far away in the night, there comes crowding a medley of memories of adventurous days on the wilderness trail, of nights under the stars. Then that deep vibrant urge rises within you to be off to faraway places again.

1. In this article, the author tells an incident of wilderness travel and at the same time tells you, directly or indirectly, many things a woodsman should know. Put X beside paragraphs or sentences that interrupt the story to explain something to the reader.

2. List below at least five good pointers that you could get from this article on how to find your way in the wilds: _____

_____

_____

_____

_____

_____

3. List at least four good rules for choosing a campsite and making camp that you learned from the article: _____

_____

_____

_____

_____

Key Words

An index in a book helps you locate facts quickly. After certain key words, an index gives the pages on which information on a subject may be found. Suppose you wanted to answer the question "Did people travel by stagecoach in colonial days?" You might look in the index for the key words stagecoach *and* travel.

Read each question below. Then list the key words under which you might find information in the index of an encyclopedia or a history of the American colonies.

1. What was the population of New York City by the year 1700?

----

2. In 1673 was Harlem a separate town or part of New York City?

----

3. What was the climate of Connecticut like during the summer?

----

4. Did people in the colony of Virginia raise tobacco on their plantations?

----

5. Did the American colonies carry on trade with the Chinese people?

----

6. In what year did Governor Lovelace become governor of New York?

----

7. What farm products were raised in Connecticut in colonial days?

----

8. Was most clothing in colonial days made of homespun cloth?

----

9. Did the city of Philadelphia have an organized police force by the year 1700?

----

10. Did sailing ships from England make regular trips to New York City in 1673?

----

11. What foods did the people in the colonies learn about from the Indians?

----

12. Was folk dancing one of the amusements enjoyed by the colonists?

----

13. Did the American colonists use whale-oil lamps as well as candles for lighting?

----

14. How were Christmas and New Year's Day celebrated in the colonies?

----

15. What tools were used in building the houses in colonial days?

----

16. Could the children in the colonies have received their education in free public schools?

----

17. When did the people of the colonies begin to coin their own money?

----

18. What was the population of Newport, Rhode Island, in the year 1690?

An Index

The section of an index that is printed below is like those found in many encyclopedias. The set of books from which the index might have been taken contains one volume for each letter of the alphabet. The letter after each heading in the alphabetical list below Puerto Rico shows in which volume or volumes the desired information can be found. The numbers tell you the page or pages to look for in that volume. The words picture, color picture, map, *or* table *indicate where illustrated material on a particular subject may be found.*

Read each question below the index and decide where you would look first to try to find the answer. Put the volume letters and page numbers on the dotted lines. The first one is done for you.

Puerto Rico (pwer′tō rē′kō), formerly **Porto Rico,** island of West Indies, transferred to U.S. by Spain in 1898; 3435 sq. mi. (with nearby islets); population 2,210,703; capital San Juan: P-374–9, *map* N-361, *pictures* P-374–9
animals P-375–6
children P-375–6, *color pictures* P-375
cities P-379
citizenship of natives C-216, P-375
climate P-374–5
education P-376

electric power P-375
farming P-377
flag F-267, *color picture* F-263
forests P-376
government P-378
history P-376–7; U.S. acquires S-271
hospitals P-379
language P-375
people P-375; how the people live P-375–6
population problem P-375, *table* P-374
products P-376, *picture* P-375
shelter P-375, 377

What implements might be used by the workers on a sugar-cane plantation?   _P-377_

What happened to the forests that once covered most of the island? _____

At what cities are the bananas, limes, oranges, and other fruits loaded for shipment to other countries? _____

What does the flag of Puerto Rico look like? _____

Why do the people of Puerto Rico eat so little meat? _____

Where could you find a map showing all of Puerto Rico? _____

Are the Puerto Rican people allowed to vote for the officials of their government? _____

Why do the plantation owners grow rice on terraced ground? _____

Why do many of the natives speak Spanish instead of English? _____

Do the houses in the Puerto Rican cities have adobe walls and patios? _____

Are the Puerto Rican schools like those in the United States? _____

Are there any skyscrapers in the capital city? _____

Do all Puerto Ricans use charcoal-burning stoves and kerosene lanterns instead of electric lights and stoves? _____

What animals other than donkeys are used by the farmers? _____

Why does the island of Puerto Rico have a temperate climate even though it is in the torrid zone? _____

Who discovered Puerto Rico? _____

What Is Science Fiction?

The term "science fiction" is often used loosely to cover almost any unreal thriller based on some element of science or pseudo science. However, many writers think the term should be used only to describe a specific type of story.

For example, Robert A. Heinlein, one of the most successful writers of modern science fiction, thinks that science fiction should deal only with things that, while they do not happen now, *may* very well happen in the future. A writer of science fiction, he says, must use the known facts of science as a basis for his predictions as to what may someday come about.

To make his ideas clear, Mr. Heinlein explains what kinds of books are *not* science fiction. Fantasies like the Oz books do not qualify, nor do books about things that are impossible on the basis of modern scientific knowledge, such as rocket ships that make U-turns, or plant men of Arcturus that live on human flesh. He would also disqualify the wildly romantic sort of stories in which the dashing hero rescues the Martian princess from the villain by means of sheer grit and superscience of a sort unrelated to any science as we know it today.

Read the book descriptions that follow and then answer the questions at the bottom of the page.

1. LUCKY STARR AND THE BIG SUN OF MERCURY by *Paul French*

An interplanetary detective story of sabotage on a mysterious project on Mercury, with exciting action and accurate astronomical information.

2. THE LAST BATTLE by *C. S. Lewis*

The setting of this story is Narnia, a mystic land inhabited by men and talking beasts and ruled by the great lion Aslan. When Shift the ape and Puzzle the donkey enslave the animals and imprison the young king, the children from the "land beyond the world's end" come to their rescue.

3. THE SEARCH FOR THE LITTLE YELLOW MEN by *Macdonald Hastings*

The lure of Africa is beautifully stated in this factual account of the expedition of an Englishman who sets out to locate and study the remaining group of light-skinned pygmies living in a vast desert in Central Africa.

4. SPACE PLATFORM by *Murray Leinster*

Joe Kenmore, by helping make the delicate pilot gyro and by preventing sabotage to the project, is instrumental in getting the first space platform into the sky. Both plot and characters are stock, but the story is full of action, and the scientific detail has been checked by experts.

5. THE SECRET OF SATURN'S RINGS by *Donald Wollheim*

Dr. Rhodes, in an attempt to prove his theory that atomic energy can destroy the earth and its people, makes a trip to Saturn's rings to collect evidence. Various efforts to delay the trip, along with the natural dangers encountered, add excitement and suspense.

6. THE STOLEN SPHERE by *John Keir Cross*

Sartine, the great music hall magician and head of an international spy ring, is brought to justice by a family of trapeze artists. The setting is Europe.

7. EXPLORATION OF MARS by *Willy Ley and Wernher von Braun*

The first half of the book is a brief survey of opinions, theories, and actual observations of Mars through the centuries. The second half discusses possibilities of future flight to Mars with explanations of problems involved and informed guesses as to what the planet may offer.

8. MISS PICKERELL AND THE GEIGER COUNTER by *Ellen MacGregor*

In attempting to get her cow to the veterinarian, Miss Pickerell finds herself substituting for a sheriff with the measles and quite inadvertently discovers a new deposit of uranium.

9. STRANGEST CREATURES ON EARTH by *Edward M. Weyer, Jr.*

Here is another of those strange-fact books that fascinate the youth of today. It tells of the "incredible giraffe," diving spiders, the "rattlesnake of the sea," four-eyed fish, and such oddities. Illustrated with photographs and drawings.

10. THE SHY STEGOSAURUS OF CRICKET CREEK by *Evelyn Sibley Lampman*

The apprehension of a thief is only one of the exciting things that happen after two children discover the last living dinosaur on their ranch. They name the stegosaurus George, and have wonderful conversations with him about such new ideas as money and machines. The story presents many scientific facts that the children glean from a digging professor as well as from George.

11. ROCKET TO LUNA by *Richard Marsten*

Teen-age Ted Baker, a senior at the Air Force Academy, unexpectedly finds himself aboard the first space ship for the moon. The plot is not unusual, but scientific accuracy and superior writing make this a better-than-average book. Six scientists are given as authorities.

Which books are fantasies, or stories dealing with things that, as far as we know today, couldn't possibly exist? _____ Which are nonfiction books of scientific or other information? _____ Which are stories of adventure that might really have happened? _____ Which books seem to meet Mr. Heinlein's standards for science fiction? _____

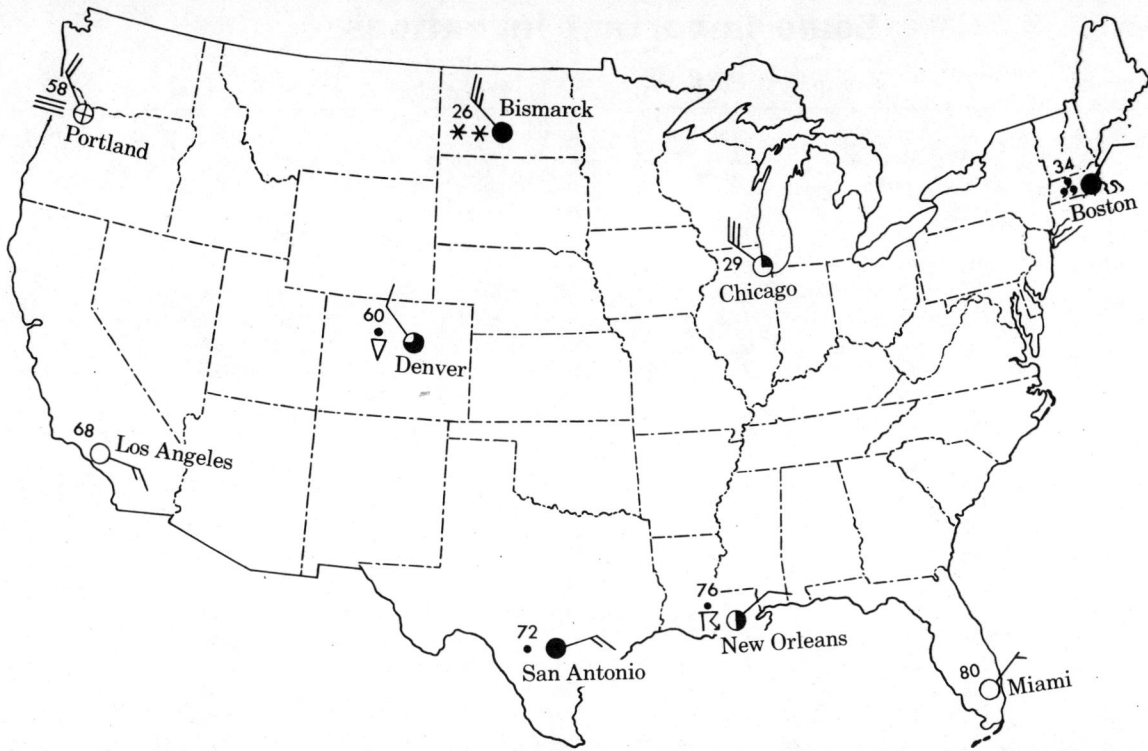

WEATHER SYMBOLS
≡ fog, sky not visible
ɔ⁹ɔ continuous moderate drizzle
• occasional light rain
✳✳ continuous light snow
↧ light rain shower
ʀ̄ thunderstorm with rain

WIND SYMBOLS
west wind   east wind

Speed in Miles Per Hour
◎ calm   9-14   26-31
— 1-4   15-20   32-37
5-8   21-25   38-43

SKY SYMBOLS
○ no clouds
◔ one quarter covered
◑ one half covered
◕ three quarters covered
● all covered
⊗ sky obscured

Early each morning the United States Weather Bureau in Washington, D.C., issues a weather map showing information reported from hundreds of observation stations all over the country. This map is a valuable tool in forecasting weather.

Each weather station gives a complete report, including such information as temperature, amount of clouds, direction and speed of winds, visibility, present weather, barometric pressure, and the amount of precipitation in the past six hours.

The map above is a greatly simplified version of a weather map and includes only a few of the weather stations, which are indicated by circles.

Beside each circle there is usually a symbol that shows the weather at the time the map was made. The numbers show the temperature.

Use the weather map to answer the following questions.

1. What is the speed of the wind at Chicago?
_____

2. Which city on the map has the highest temperature? _____

3. Which city has the lowest? _____

4. Which city is having a thunderstorm with rain? _____

5. At which cities is the wind less than fifteen miles per hour? _____
_____

6. At which city is it snowing? _____

7. At which cities is there precipitation?
_____
_____

8. At which cities is the sky clear? _____
_____

9. At which city is the sky hidden by heavy fog?
_____

10. Are any cities having a wind from the southwest? _____

11. From what direction do the strongest winds seem to be blowing? _____

Some Important Inventions

INVENTION	DATE	INVENTOR	COUNTRY	INVENTION	DATE	INVENTOR	COUNTRY
adding machine	1642	Pascal	France	match, friction	1827	Walker	Britain
adding machine, recording	1888	Burroughs	U.S.	match, phosphorous	1831	Sauria	France
airplane	1903	Jatho	Germany	match, phosphorous	1836	Phillips	U.S.
airplane, experimental	1896	Langley	U.S.	microphone	1877	Berliner	U.S.
airplane, jet engine	1930	Whittle	Britain	microscope, compound	1590	Janssen	Netherlands
airplane, with motor	1903	Orville & Wilbur Wright	U.S.	oleomargarine	1868	Mège-Mouriez	France
airplane, hydro	1911	Curtiss	U.S.	pen, fountain	1884	Waterman	U.S.
airship, nonrigid dirigible	1898	Santos-Dumont	Brazil	pen, fountain	1885	Wirt	U.S.
airship, rigid dirigible	1900	Zeppelin	Germany	phonograph	1877	Edison	U.S.
autogiro	1920	de la Cierva	Spain	photography	1826	Niepce, Sr.	France
automobile, differential gear	1885	Benz	Germany	photography	1835	Fox-Talbot	Britain
automobile, electric	1892	Morrison	U.S.	photography	1837	Daguerre	France
automobile, experimental	1875	Narkus	Austria	photography	1839	Niepce, Jr.	France
automobile, gasoline	1887	Daimler	Germany	steamboat, experimental	1783	Jouffroy	France
automobile, gasoline	1892	Duryea	U.S.	steamboat, experimental	1787	Rumsey	U.S.
automobile, gasoline	1894	Krebs	Germany	steamboat, experimental	1788	Miller	Scotland
automobile, gasoline	1895	Selden	U.S.	steamboat, experimental	1803	Fulton	U.S.
automobile, steam	1889	Roper	U.S.	steamboat, experimental	1808	Stevens	U.S.
balloon	1783	Montgolfier	France	steamboat, practical	1801	Symington	Scotland
balloon, with motor	1852	Giffard	France	steamboat, practical	1807	Fulton	U.S.
clock, pendulum	1657	Huygens	Netherlands	submarine, torpedo	1775	Bushnell	U.S.
Diesel engine	1895	Diesel	Germany	submarine	1881	Holland	U.S.
evaporated milk	1856	Borden	U.S.	submarine, even keel	1897	Lake	U.S.
helicopter, experimental	1907	Bréguet	France	telescope	1608	Lippershey	Netherlands
helicopter, practical	1937	Sikorsky	U.S.	telescope	1609	Galileo	Italy
ice-making machine	1851	Gorrie	U.S.	telescope	1611	Kepler	Germany
linoleum	1860	Walton	Britain	thermometer	1593	Galileo	Italy
				thermometer, mercury	1714	Fahrenheit	Germany
				typewriter	1864	Mitterhoffer	Austria
				typewriter	1868	Sholes	U.S.

Answer the following questions on the basis of the information in the table above.

Many portraits of George Washington were painted in his lifetime. Washington died in 1799. Was he ever photographed? _____

What inventions were developed in different countries at approximately the same time?

What two nations led in the invention of steam-powered water transport? _____

What other means of transportation were invented between 1783 and 1937? _____

Could enlisted men have been classified as clerk-typists in the War of 1812? _____

How many years passed between the first experimental steamboat and the first practical one? _____

In 1863 Lincoln delivered a famous address at Gettysburg. Could he have written his speech with a fountain pen? _____

Tall, pendulum clocks called grandfather clocks are precious heirlooms in many families. Were any of these clocks brought over on the *Mayflower* in 1620? _____

Were matches included in the equipment issued to soldiers in the American Revolution? _____

In 1869 Jules Verne, father of science fiction, wrote *20,000 Leagues Under the Sea*, a story of a submarine voyage. By how many years did Verne anticipate Holland's submarine? _____

Have men been making ice for as long as they have been measuring temperature? _____

Readers' Guide to Periodical Literature

A great deal of valuable information appears in weekly and monthly magazines, and most libraries keep files of back issues for many years. To locate material on a particular subject, you use the *Readers' Guide to Periodical Literature*. This is an index to articles and stories that have appeared in magazines.

The *Guide* lists magazine articles under both author and subject. (Stories and plays are listed by title, too.) Each entry gives additional information in abbreviated form. For example:

> **PHOTOGRAPHY**
> Camera trails. E. H. Evans and W. J. Evans. il Nature Mag 39:440-1 O '46

"Camera trails" is the title of the article. E. H. Evans and W. J. Evans are the authors. "il" means that the article contains illustrations. "Nature Mag" is the abbreviation for *Nature Magazine*, in which the article was published. The number before the colon, "39," is the volume number. This is important if the magazine has been bound, as periodicals often are in libraries. The numbers after the colon, "440-1," tell the pages where you will find the article. "O '46" means October 1946, the date of the magazine. These and all other abbreviations used in the *Readers' Guide* are explained on its inside front cover.

On this page is a small section from the *Readers' Guide*. Below it is an explanation of abbreviations used. Answer the questions by referring to this material.

1. Which headings are names of people? (Underline last name in each case.) --------------------------------------

----

2. What is the title of the *Newsweek* article about Warren Spahn? --------------------------------------

3. Under what heading would you expect to find material on travel to Venus? --------------------------------------
In what magazine is there an article on this subject?----
-------------------------------- What date? ----------
On what pages? ------ Is the article illustrated? ------

4. What is the title of a play about space travel? -----

Who is the author? --------------------------------------
Under what entries will you find this play listed elsewhere?

----

5. What is the number of the bound volume of *Time* in which the article "Practical spacemen" is found? --------------

6. Where would you look for an article on space stations?

SOWELL, Arnie
Hustlers. il por Time 69:83 F 18 '57
SPAAK, Paul Henri
Madmen, accidents, and a blueprint for peace; interview. por Newsweek 49:58 My 6 '57
Mr Europe surveys the future. W. H. Waggoner. pors N Y Times Mag p 14+ Ap 7 '57
NATO, new man. il por(cover) Newsweek 49:56-7 My 6 '57
SPACE (architecture)
Architecture as space, by B. Zevi. Review Sat R il plan 40:16+ Ap 13 '57. M. James
Here is space that lifts your spirit like a song. il House B 99:107-14 Mr '57
Interior space, key that unlocks architecture; excerpt from Architecture and space. B. Zevi. il House B 99:118-19+ Mr '57
New kinds of living spaces for your future. C. Besinger. il House B 99:115-17+ Mr '57
SPACE drama
Visit to the planets. H. K. Melchior. Plays 16:37-44 My '57
SPACE flight
Astronomer looks at space travel. V. M. Blanco. il diag Sky & Tel 16:312-16 My '57
Crews must be born on space ship to stars. Sci N L 71:66 F 2 '57; Same abr. Sci Digest 41:47 My '57
Flight to moon 90 per cent reality. Sci N L 71:131 Mr 2 '57
Hypersonic glider studied as manned missile hope. J. S. Butz, jr. il diag Aviation W 66:72-3+ Mr 18 '57
Ion, photon power space travel hope. Aviation W 66:103-4+ Mr 4 '57
Making way for travel in outer space. il Bsns W p70-1+ Mr 2 '57
Party of one. C. Fadiman. il Holiday 21:6+ My '57
Practical spacemen. Time 68:94 Mr 4 '57
Race into space: can we win? R. K. Winslow. il diag Newsweek 49:66+ Mr 4 '57; Same abr. Sci Digest 41:5-9 Je '57
Security in space. il Time 69:44+ Mr 11 '57
Space travel. Sci N L 71:127 F 23 '57
Taxi to Venus? T. E. Stimson, jr. il diags Pop Mech 107:124-8+ Mr '57
Will reds be first to reach the moon? H. Simons. il Sci Digest 41:93-4 Ap '57

Physiological aspects
Can man survive in space? excerpt from Satellite. E. Bergaust and W. Beller. il Sci Digest 41:33-9 Mr '57
Health in the sky. R. K. Winslow. Newsweek 49:70 Mr 4 '57
Race into space: can we win? R. K. Winslow. Newsweek 49:70 Mr 4 '57; Same abr. il Sci Digest 41:5-9 Je '57
Tranquilized in space. Time 69:56 Ap 8 '57
SPACE stations (proposed) See Artificial satellites
SPAHN, Warren Edward
I say Milwaukee will win the pennant; ed. by F. Bisher. pors Sat Eve Post 229:36+ Ap 20 '57
Plight of the pitchers. por Newsweek 49:72+ My 13 '57
SPAIN, Nancy
War of the writers. por Newsweek 49:108 Mr 11 '57

KEY TO ABBREVIATIONS

+	continued on later pages of same issues
abr	abridged
Ap	April
diag	diagram
ed	edited, edition, editor
F	February
il	illustrated, illustrations, illustrator
Je	June
Mr	March
My	May
por	portrait

Aviation W—Aviation Week
Bsns W—Business Week
House B—House Beautiful
NY Times Mag—New York Times Magazine
Pop Mech—Popular Mechanics
Sat Eve Post—Saturday Evening Post
Sat R—Saturday Review
Sci Digest—Science Digest
Sci N L—Science News Letter
Sky & Tel—Sky and Telescope

Interpreting a Bar Graph

In textbooks and reference books, as well as in magazines and newspapers, factual information is often presented by means of graphs. On this page is an example of a bar graph, a type frequently used. This particular example was taken from a textbook in social science. Answer the questions on the basis of the information you learn from the graph.

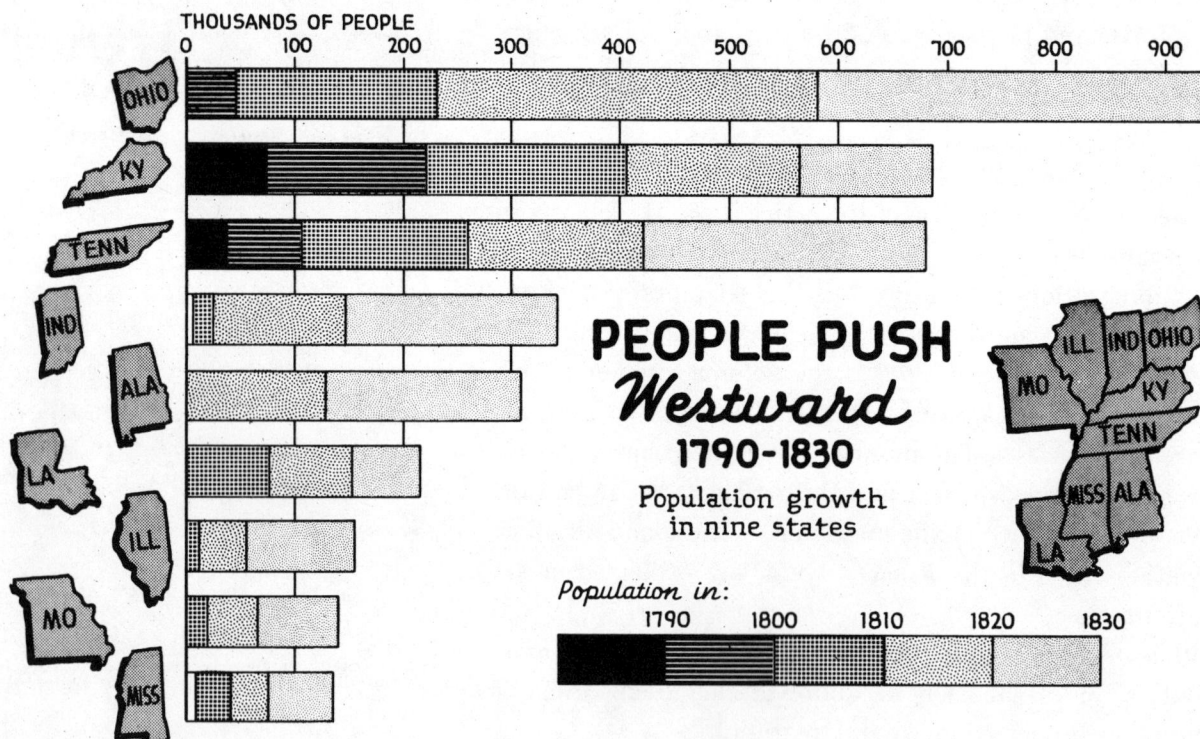

THOUSANDS OF PEOPLE

PEOPLE PUSH
Westward
1790-1830
Population growth
in nine states

Population in:
1790 1800 1810 1820 1830

Which of the states included in the graph had the largest population in 1830? _____

Approximately what was this state's population at that time? _____

Which state had the smallest population in 1830? _____

Was the population of this state less than 100,000 in 1830? _____

Which states were settled before 1790? _____

Which additional states were settled by 1800? _____

Which state had the smallest population in 1820? _____

Which of the states on the graph was settled most recently? _____

Check the things below that you can learn from this graph:

1. The approximate population of a number of states at ten-year intervals between 1790 and 1830.

2. The exact population of any of these states in any given year.

3. The period when appreciable numbers of people began to settle in each of these states.

4. The relative growth of population within a state in different ten-year periods.

5. The comparative number of people in the various states on certain dates.

6. The population of the states today.

Where Can You Find Out?

In your school or public library are many sources of information about modern wonders and the men and women who developed them. Each type of reference material meets a particular need. For example, if you wanted detailed information and background material on a subject, you might go to an encyclopedia. For certain specific bits of information you might consult a dictionary, an almanac, or *Who's Who*.

Among the reference materials found in most libraries are the following:

1. A set of *encyclopedias* containing fairly detailed articles, many of them illustrated, dealing with all fields of knowledge.

2. *Dictionaries.*

3. *Science textbooks.*

4. A *picture-history of science and invention*—including biographies of famous scientists and inventors; pictures, diagrams, and explanations of important inventions; and historical background.

5. An *almanac*—a brief general reference book published every year, listing major events of the year, statistics of many kinds, and a great variety of useful facts and dates.

6. *Who's Who in America*—containing brief biographical information about important living Americans. A new volume containing up-to-date facts is published every year.

7. A *nature atlas*—containing pictures and descriptions of rocks and minerals, trees and wildflowers, birds and animals found in different parts of the country.

8. *Biographies* of scientists and inventors.

9. *Technical and scientific magazines*—containing news and informative articles about current research and scientific discoveries.

In addition, a library usually contains two important "tools" that are designed to help you find particular kinds of materials:

10. The *card catalog*—a card file listing every book in the library by title, author, and subject.

11. The *Readers' Guide to Periodical Literature*—a monthly index to articles in current magazines, listed by subject and author.

Which of the sources of information listed above would you go to first *if you wanted to answer the following questions?* (Indicate by number.)

Is Dr. Jonas Salk still alive and doing medical research? ----

Was dynamite the first explosive invented? ----

Are boils, abscesses, and carbuncles somewhat alike? ----

Were daguerreotypes shown at the Philadelphia Centennial Exposition in 1876? ----

What becomes of the wax when a candle burns? ----

What did the first steam engines look like? ----

What books about railroading does your public library contain? ----

Suppose you have been reading a story about the Frenchman who built the Eiffel Tower. Are the main facts in this book true? ----

What are the distinguishing characteristics of shale, granite, marble, and limestone? ----

What part of all the freight shipped in the United States is carried by trucks? ----

What kind of person was Thomas Edison? ----

What are the newest developments in space travel? ----

What magazine articles dealing with atomic research have been published in the last month? ----

What were the major scientific discoveries made last year? ----

A

Jim realized that the grain was ripe enough to ____.
harness   harvest   harbor

Clowns look awkward but they are actually ____.
graceful   graceless   grateful

Eighty acres of the ranch were used for ____.
greasing   grazing   guessing

Ruth saluted the flag and gave the pledge of ____.
amazement   enchantment   allegiance

B

The factory was closed during the holiday ____.
secret   sensation   season

A faithful Indian scout delivered the ____.
manner   mischief   message

At dusk the nurse awakened, refreshed and ____.
alert   accurate   asleep

The mare's whinny echoed through the ____.
cannon   canyon   coyote

C

The late spring blizzard had halted all ____.
trifles   thicket   traffic

When Rover saw the kennel, he snarled in ____.
disaster   defiance   difference

Ann rode in an old-fashioned ____.
visor   vehicle   vacuum

Frank was not aware that his life was in ____.
peril   plot   pliers

D

A sheriff investigated the abandoned car ____.
modestly   thoroughly   conveniently

Instructions were given for mixing the ____.
implements   ingredients   ignorance

The students greeted the composer with wild ____.
applesauce   apprentice   applause

Ed found the information about coffee in a ____.
magazine   provision   flourish

E

The mechanic advised Jill to have the brakes ____.
consisted   adjusted   elapsed

Some lines were horizontal and others were ____.
typical   critical   vertical

Jean won the scholarship by a unanimous ____.
decision   audition   performance

Bulletins were issued hourly by the weather ____.
barrier   bureau   temperature

F

The villagers viewed the wreckage ____.
sparsely   lustrously   despondently

Ray admonished his sister for her absurd ____.
antics   hazards   attics

Transatlantic flights are now a commonplace ____.
assistance   disturbance   occurrence

Her jaunty manner indicated that Sue felt ____.
confident   conscious   convicted

G

Adequate equipment is essential to a good ____.
laggard   latitude   laboratory

The paragraph about tax laws was long and ____.
rotated   complicated   extricated

Only a scoundrel would defile a religious ____.
havoc   shrine   circuit

The couch was cluttered with record ____.
albums   autocrats   admirals

H

A perfect replica or reproduction is called a ____.
manuscript   facsimile   tributary

The terms of the treaty were divulged by the ____.
emissary   attribute   enormity

Al concluded that the labyrinth of vines was ____.
incompetent   irresolute   impenetrable

The knave was greeted with jeers of ____.
distortion   dedication   derision

A

High waves forced Don's cousin to run his craft onto the beach near a fisherman's hut.

Who landed on the beach?

Don   a fisherman   Don's cousin

What was he riding in?

airplane   motorboat   automobile

Where did the fisherman live?

in a shack   in a mansion   in a hotel

B

On the tropic isle the palm trees were swaying gently in the moonlight.

On what kind of island were the trees located?

chilly   warm   barren

When did this take place?

in the morning   at noon   at night

What caused the trees to move?

a windstorm   a breeze   an atom bomb

C

While Edna watched the sunset during the train's delay at Cedar, she heard someone say that the track had been washed out just before noon.

What happened first?

--- Edna watched the sunset.

--- The train stopped at Cedar.

--- Edna learned that the track was washed out.

When did Edna hear the news of the washout?

before noon   in the night   at dusk

D

"Congratulations!" said Dick, grasping David's hand. "That pole vault will set a record!"

What expression did Dick have on his face?

impatience   admiration   amusement

If Dick had used a complete sentence when he said "Congratulations!" what would he have said?

--- "Thank you for the congratulations!"

--- "I like congratulations!"

--- "I want to congratulate you!"

E

Just after Tom snatched the child from the curb, the careening truck overturned.

When did Tom grab the child?

--- after the truck overturned

--- before the truck overturned

--- at the same instant

What was Tom trying to do?

frighten the child   play games   save the child

F

If Ann had known that a completed project was necessary to be eligible for the trip, she might have been more interested in finishing her sewing.

Why did the project have to be completed?

--- in order to become a member

--- because the projects were to be displayed

--- in order to go on the trip

How had Ann felt about completing her project?

enthusiastic   indifferent   indignant

G

As he strolled home through the park, John smiled to himself at the thought of his heated dispute with Garry before lunch.

What happened first?

the walk home   lunch   the disagreement

How had John felt when talking to Garry?

amused   bewildered   angry

How did he feel as he walked home?

amused   bewildered   angry

H

Diligence is the mother of good luck.

Which saying below has most nearly the same meaning?

--- The only sure thing about luck is that it will change.

--- A man in earnest finds means, or if he cannot find, creates them.

--- An ounce of performance is worth more than a pound of preachment.

A

Cross out the silent consonants.

design	knoll	salmon
sheriff	hymn	ghastly
wrestling	fright	rhubarb

Cross out the silent vowels.

domain	guidance	besiege
recite	maneuver	rogue
leash	drainage	troupe

Cross out both silent consonants and vowels.

challenge	wholesale	thoroughfare
dough	campaign	scene
pneumonia	writhe	rhinestone

B

Underline c if it has the s sound.

sacrifice   vacancy   disconcerting   capacity

Underline c if it has the k sound.

consequence   licorice   circumstance   practice

Underline s if it has the z sound.

resist   prisms   disposition   sarcasm

Underline g if it has the j sound.

engage   geologist   baggage   gorgeous

C

Put S or L to show whether the vowel sound in the accented syllable is short or long.

com pel′ ___	hin′der ___	es teem′ ___
re fine′ ___	cli′ent ___	sen′a tor ___
to′ken ___	sub mit′ ___	re frain′ ___
muz′zle ___	fu′tile ___	vi′ ta min ___
at tain′ ___	a buse′ ___	leg′ end ___

D

Mark the accented syllable of each word.

check er	de cline	fur row
re proach	a light	mot tle
bu gle	chan nel	freck les
en camp	un clasp	ex pire

E

Draw a line between the syllables of each word.

burlap	disgruntle	beckon
donate	urchin	luminous
ankle	opponent	wheedle
daffodil	leisure	exclusive

F

Write the number of syllables you hear in each word on the line following the word.

interpret___	architecture___	unison___
representative___	characteristic___	imperative___
constitutional___	employees___	diameter___

G

Underline the words in each row that are formed by adding a prefix to an English root word.

subway   substitute   subtitle   subject   subnormal

behave   belittle   benefit   belabor   besiege

mischief   misshapen   missile   mistrial   misinform

prehistoric   premium   preview   prepaid   precise

H

Write the English root word beneath each one.

absurdity	irregularity	preoccupied
exhilaration	imaginative	intercolonial
reassuringly	congratulatory	harmonize

I

In each word below, the root word was changed before an ending was added.

Put 1 if the final consonant was doubled.

Put 2 if the final e was dropped.

Put 3 if the final y was changed to i.

___ witty	___ swarthiness	___ propeller
___ recital	___ metallic	___ complication
___ pitiable	___ justifiable	___ merciless
___ security	___ enclosure	___ snobbery

J

Underline the word in each sentence that is related in meaning to the word above the sentence.

rest

The restful nap restored Becky's energy.

fury

When the furrier examined the damaged coat, he was furious with the owner.

sea

During the fishing season, boats of all sizes and descriptions headed seaward.

A

Underline words in which you hear the sound the underlined letters stand for in the key word.

h<u>a</u>t	<u>a</u>ge	f<u>ar</u>	l<u>e</u>t
ranch	mantel	heart	attend
page	snail	father	many
calf	replace	pair	delight
plaid	happen	sharp	people

t<u>er</u>m	<u>i</u>t	<u>o</u>pen	<u>oi</u>l
season	thin	adorn	ahoy
pearl	busy	throat	doing
journey	grief	although	voice
burn	bright	profit	joyous

<u>ou</u>t	c<u>u</u>p	<u>u</u>se	lem<u>o</u>n
house	full	beauty	complete
crowd	trouble	fewer	lonely
bough	does	fatigue	moment
now	mood	yule	cautious

B

Underline words in which you hear the sound the underlined letters stand for in the key word.

<u>f</u>at	<u>n</u>o	<u>w</u>ill	<u>y</u>es
laugh	manner	wrap	opinion
phrase	hymn	choir	berry
ghost	knife	quick	stay
effort	gnash	wide	hallelujah

<u>sh</u>oe	<u>ch</u>ild	<u>th</u>in	so<u>ng</u>
scheme	reach	bath	tongue
ocean	chemist	breathe	ingrown
machine	question	thank	hinge
mission	future	there	ink

C

Number the words in each list alphabetically.

.... heather		.... printer
.... skillet		.... prose
.... dissolve		.... praise
.... hurricane		.... principal
.... moisture		.... produce
.... southern		.... prime

D

Which definition of the word fits the sentence? Draw a line under that definition.

im pet u ous (im pech′ü əs), **1.** moving with great force or speed: *the impetuous rush of water over Niagara Falls.* **2.** acting hastily, rashly, or with sudden feeling: *Boys are more impetuous than old men.*

When land was sighted, the *impetuous* sailor leaped in the air and yelled joyfully.

re treat (ri trēt′), **1.** go back; move back; withdraw: *The enemy retreated.* **2.** act of going back or withdrawing: *The army's retreat was orderly.* **3.** signal for retreat: *The drums beat a retreat.* **4.** signal on a bugle or drum, given in the army at sunset. **5.** a safe, quiet place; place of rest or refuge.

The animal's hasty *retreat* into the forest was caused by the appearance of the automobile.

slight (slīt), **1.** not much; not important; small. **2.** not big around; slender. **3.** frail; flimsy: *a slight excuse.* **4.** treat as of little value; pay too little attention to; neglect: *This maid slights her work.* **5.** slighting treatment; act of neglect.

Some schools *slight* the teaching of grammar.

en trance¹ (en′trəns), **1.** act of entering: *The actor's entrance was greeted with applause.* **2.** place by which to enter; door, passageway, etc. **3.** freedom or right to enter; permission to enter.

en trance² (en trans′), **1.** put into a trance. **2.** fill with joy; delight; charm.

A sign was placed over the subway *entrance*.

E

What entry word would you look for in the dictionary?

The farmer praised the work John had done and called him a *hustler*.

Hunger *impelled* the timid dog to enter the store.

Susan chose the *daintiest* flowers she could find for the corsage she was making.

Ed was *distributing* the samples to the students.

The company policy was changed *radically*.

Don was amazed at the *flimsiness* of the sails.

A

Ted lay on the ground, doubled up with pain. The third quarter had hardly begun when the Elm City center had driven his elbow into Ted's stomach. Groans arose from the Union rooters. Mrs. Bowers jumped up, ready to rush to her son. But her husband gripped her coat and pulled her back into her seat. "Better stay here," he said. "Ted wouldn't want you on the field."

During what kind of sports event did this happen?
baseball game   football game   wrestling match

Where was Mrs. Bowers?
among the spectators   on the field   at home

On what team was Ted playing?
Elm City   Union

What did Mrs. Bowers want to do?
go to Ted   go home   get Ted's attention

To whom was Mr. Bowers speaking?
the Elm City center   Mrs. Bowers   Ted

How far along was the game?
just starting   almost finished   half over

B

As Ken rushed from the cabin into the moonlit night, the zero air brought tears to his eyes. He ran toward the trail, only to find that snow had obliterated it. He started off in what he thought was the right direction but soon realized that he was lost. Looking frantically about for a familiar object, Ken saw the Big Dipper in the sky. That would guide him through the woods to the village —and help. And he *had* to get help quickly. His cheeks tingled as he hurried along. Suddenly a mass of clouds covered the sky. Ken's heart sank, but he dared not stop.

What three things did Ken see?
birds   shadows   water   stars   trees   grass

How did Ken feel as he started out?
reckless   weary   anxious   cautious

What caused Ken's cheeks to tingle?
fear   cold   grief   anger

How did Ken feel when the clouds appeared?
outraged   fretful   defiant   dismayed

What is the general mood of this passage?
urgency   amusement   gloom   indignation

C

Modern automobiles have many safety features. "Wrap-around" windshields and large windows give the motorist a wide field of vision. Turn signals and back-up lights inform fellow motorists of a driver's intentions. These and many other devices have increased the safety of highway travel, but it is still true that the driver rather than the vehicle is responsible for most accidents.

Small glass areas decrease safety because____
the glass is not shatterproof.
the driver may not see all approaching cars.
there is more space for upholstery.

Signal lights on a car reduce accidents because____
they tell motorists what a driver plans to do.
they are expensive to install.
they signal right and left turns.

Cars are not accidentproof because____
the necessary materials are not available.
automobiles are a relatively new invention.
most accidents are due to human errors.

D

"I'd have felt better if Mrs. Hughes had given me a good scolding," said Tom. "But when she saw the broken window, she just helped me pick up the pieces and went in to call about a new one."

"She knew the door was locked and that you broke in when you heard cries for help. I know you didn't realize that it was just her daughter practicing for the school play," said Uncle Jim. "But after this, I think you'll agree that it's best to investigate a situation before acting on impulse."

Which sentence best describes Tom's feelings?
He travels fastest who travels alone.
He must be pure who would blame another.
Silence is sometimes the severest criticism.

Which best characterizes Mrs. Hughes' reaction?
Empty barrels make the most noise.
Don't cry over spilled milk.
People in glass houses shouldn't throw stones.

Which best describes Uncle Jim's attitude?
Discretion is the better part of valor.
Not failure, but low aim is crime.
If a thing is worth doing, it's worth doing well.

Books You May Like

Have you ever started to read a book just because it had a catchy title, and then been disappointed when the book was not what you had expected it to be? As you've probably discovered, you can't always tell from the title alone whether a book will interest you. Some books with eye-catching covers and interesting titles may, unfortunately, be dull or difficult to read. To choose a book you will like, you need to know more than just the title or even the author. You often need to know something about the story and the characters or maybe something about the subject and the facts you can learn.

Here is a list of books that have been read and enjoyed by many teen-agers. The reviews of the books will help you decide which ones you want to read. In each book review, one or more of these questions are answered for you: Who is in this book? What is the book about? Where and when does the story take place? Why should I read this book?

The books are arranged by interests in fourteen groups—"Air Travel and Outer Space," "Animals," "Careers," to name the first three groups. This is done to help you quickly find a book about something you are especially interested in. For example, if you want to know whether flying saucers are real or imaginary, there are books in the first section, "Air Travel and Outer Space," you'll want to read. Are you interested in speed? Do you know who has thrown the fastest baseball? How fast can a rocket or jet go? How can you "soup up" your hot rod? To find books that will answer such questions, read the reviews under the heading "Love of Speed." If you're a worrier, there are books in "Tips for Teens" that give answers to such questions as: What can I do with my free time? How can I improve my appearance? Why can't I be as popular as the next person?

To help you decide whether a book is easy or hard to read, there is a simple key. If you see the name of a book without a star in front of it, that means the book is easy. The books with one star are a little harder. But don't be scared, try some of them. A book with two stars may be a real challenge to you. If it's about something that's near to your heart, why not try it anyway? You may surprise yourself.

Of course, there are many books besides these that you will enjoy. So you might try exploring the library on your own. You may find a good book there that is not on this list. If you do, try your hand at writing a review of it. Then pass on your comments about the book to your classmates. Your remarks may be just the right thing to help someone else find a book that he will have fun reading, too.

Air Travel and Outer Space

The Earth Satellite. John Lewellen. (Alfred A. Knopf[1]) It isn't a secret anymore. You can find out for yourself how we put a satellite into space and made it spin around the earth in less time than it takes you to finish a morning in school. If you were in it, would you get dizzy? freeze? fall? Is it safe? This book has some answers to these questions and many others you must have about the world of space.

You and Space Travel. John Lewellen. (Childrens Press) Maybe it will be you. Maybe you will be the first one to land on the moon. If not you, it will be somebody in your lifetime. That's what the scientists tell us. If you were sitting in a rocket ship right now, ready to take off, you might be wondering, "How fast will I go? How will I feel? How long will it take? What will I find there? How can I get back home?" These questions and more will be answered in this book.

You may also want to read *Your Trip into Space*, by Lynn Poole (Whittlesey House), and **Going into Space*, by Arthur C. Clarke (Harper).

All about the Stars. Anne Terry White. (Random House) If you were on a quiz show and the subject were "Stars," how many of these questions could you answer? What's a "hairy" star?

---

[1]The name in parentheses after each book is the name of the publisher. It sometimes helps to know the publisher's name when you are trying to find a book.

How many stars can you see on a clear night with your own two eyes? Is there life on Mars? If there really are billions of stars spinning around in the sky, why aren't there more crack-ups and accidents between them? Will we ever go to a star? The answers are in this book.

The Worlds Around Us. Patrick Moore. (Abelard-Schuman) Flying saucers do not come from other planets. When we reach the moon we'll find it a dead world. There are no men on Mars. If you want proof, this book can help you.

We. Charles A. Lindbergh. (Grosset and Dunlap) It is nighttime and pitch black. You are flying alone over the Atlantic Ocean. If you can make it from New York to Paris, nonstop, you'll be the first one in the whole world who ever did it. You'll even collect $25,000.

This is the story of Charles Lindbergh. It tells how he became a great flier and the first man to cross the Atlantic Ocean in a plane.

All about Rockets and Jets. Fletcher Pratt. (Random House) The rocket is now part of your life. There are rockets that can take off thousands of miles from where you live and still hit your house. There's a rocket that can find anything in the sky it looks for and bring it down. There may be a rocket someday that will shoot a man to the moon. This book takes you inside rockets and shows you what makes them go.

If you liked this book, try **The Complete Book of Jets and Rockets*, by D. N. Ahnstrom (World). You may also enjoy *New Era of Flight, Aeronautics Simplified*, by Lewis Zarem and Robert H. Maltby (E. P. Dutton), and *Helicopters: How They Work*, by John Lewellen (Thomas Y. Crowell).

**Flying Saucers from Outer Space.* Major Donald E. Keyhoe. (Henry Holt) "There's no such thing as a flying saucer," people say. The man who writes this book thinks there is. He thinks these saucers come from another planet and that they can be dangerous to us. Does he prove it? Can you believe him? Make up your mind after reading this book.

**Sabre Pilot.* Stephen W. Meader. (Harcourt, Brace) Kirk loved jet planes, but he thought he would never get a chance to fly one. He did get his chance, though, in the Air Force during the Korean War. And he made the most of it. After forty missions he was hit and forced to bail out in enemy territory. He came closer to losing his life on land and in the water than in the air.

**Space Tug.* Murray Leinster. (Shasta) Joe Kenmore is an American assigned to carry supplies to our man-made satellite. He does, but only after beating his country's enemies 4000 miles up in space. If you wonder who can fight you up there, and how, and what you use to defend yourself, you'll find the story in this book.

**Star Ship on Saddle Mountain.* Atlantis Hallam. (Macmillan) Maybe there is, maybe there isn't human life on other planets. Nobody really knows. But Charlie Holt and his horse Navajo found out when they were kidnaped and taken by space ship to another planet. They tried to escape; it was no use. Finally they were allowed to return to earth. Then Charlie decided to go back up again. Why? Because there was something he liked about the way they lived there. Maybe you will or maybe you won't agree with his decision after you read this book.

You'll also like **Space Cadet*, **Between Planets*, and **The Rolling Stones*, by Robert Heinlein (Charles Scribner).

Animals

Insect Engineers; The Story of Ants. Ruth Bartlett. (William Morrow) When you step on an ant, you may be killing an important member of an ant community—a carpenter or a farmer, a nurse or a cleaning woman. Or, you may be destroying a nuisance—a thief or a beggar. This book explains that ants live and work much like human beings. They even have armies that can eat a wounded elephant or a sleepy snake.

Panuck, Eskimo Sled Dog. Frederick Machetanz. (Charles Scribner) When an Eskimo has to get someplace fast, he can't take a jeep or a truck or a plane. He has only his dog and sled. This is the story of an Eskimo dog that ran for twenty hours through a blizzard to help save a life.

Another story about a dog that served his master well is **Juneau, the Sleigh Dog*, by West Lathrop (Grosset and Dunlap).

Tim, a Dog of the Mountains. Margaret S. Johnson and Helen L. Johnson. (Harcourt, Brace) Tim, a foreign dog, is not very happy in the United States because he finds everything so strange. One day he saves his master from being burned to death in a forest fire. He proves that no matter where a dog lives, he'll do anything in the world for a master he loves.

Other interesting books by the same authors and publisher are *Barney of the North; Vickie, a Guide Dog; Rolf, an Elkhound of Norway;* and *Rex of the Coast Patrol.* You might also try *Inki*, by Elizabeth P. Heppner (Macmillan).

Amos, the Beagle with a Plan. John Parke. (Pantheon Books) This is all about Amos, a beagle, that did something amazing. When his master left him and moved hundreds of miles away, Amos found him. How? That's the story.

Another dog story is *Old Yeller*, by Fred Gipson (Harper). *The True Story of Fala*, by M. L. Suckley and Alice Dalgliesh (Charles Scribner), tells about the dog President Roosevelt loved.

Training You to Train Your Dog. Blanche Saunders. (Doubleday) This book explains how you can be a good master and make your dog obey because he loves and respects you. You'll learn how to watch your language, your voice, and your hands when you're training your dog. You'll also find 21 rules on dog training that will help you avoid some bad mistakes.

If you want to turn your dog into a professional performer, read **The Story of Lassie, His Discovery and Training from Puppyhood to Stardom*, by John H. Rothwell and Rudd B. Weatherwax (Duell, Sloan and Pearce). This book also tells about war dogs in World War II. For other stories about a war dog, get **Awol: K-9 Commando* and **Awol the Courier*, by Bertrand Shurtleff (Bobbs-Merrill).

All about the Insect World. Ferdinand C. Lane. (Random House) Which insect do many people tie to a bedpost at night so they can get a night's sleep? Which insects are so important to our own lives that we raise them by the millions in incubators, just as we do chickens? Which insect makes paper out of wood? Will a scorpion's sting poison you? This book gives the answers to these and hundreds of other questions you may have about the world of insects.

My Life with the Big Cats. Alfred Court. (Simon and Schuster) You may have wondered why anybody wants to endanger his life by going into a cage full of lions, tigers, and jaguars; how a man can have the courage to put his head into a lion's mouth; how a person could kiss an angry jungle tiger on the nose without having his own nose clawed off. If you think the animals are doped or hypnotized, you're wrong. You have to like these cats and know how to talk to them. You have to show them *you're* the boss, even when it seems they are. There are worried moments and tragic moments but there is never a dull moment in life with the big cats.

You'll also like *Adventures with Animals*, selected by Mary Yost Sandrus (Scott, Foresman), and **They Never Talk Back*, by Henry Trefflich as told to Bayard Kendrich (Appleton-Century-Crofts). If you're especially interested in snakes, read *Snakes*, by Herbert S. Zim (William Morrow), and **Adventures with Reptiles; The Story of Ross Allen*, by C. J. Hylander (Julian Messner).

The Black Stallion. Walter Farley. (Random House) He was a black stallion and as wild as the wildest mustang. You couldn't ride him; he'd throw you. You couldn't get friendly with him; he wanted to be alone. You never knew what he would do next. This story tells how Alec, a teen-ager who loved the Black, got to know him, survived a shipwreck with him, learned to ride him, and won a wild horse race with him.

Other books by the same author and publisher are: **Son of the Black Stallion, **The Island Stallion, **The Black Stallion and Satan, **The Black Stallion Revolts*, and **The Island Stallion Races.*

Big Red. Clarence W. Anderson. (Macmillan) The author of *Big Red* is a man who loves race horses and understands them just as if they were members of his own family. In this book he tells about Man O'War, a horse that many think was the greatest that ever lived and ran.

Other books by the same author and publisher are: *Tomorrow's Champion*, which gives some answers to the question "What makes a champion racer?"; **Deep Through the Heart**, which tells about brave race horses like Humorist who became a champion in spite of the fact that he had only one lung; and **Sketchbook**, which gives good hints on how to draw horses. If you want to find out something about one of Man O'War's grandsons, read *Little Vic*, by Doris Gates (Viking Press).

Careers

Young Ike. Alden Hatch. (Julian Messner) Maybe you do need some "breaks" to become a five-star general and the President of the United States, but you need something special inside, too. Dwight Eisenhower had it almost from the day he was born. You'll want to read about him.

You may also enjoy *The Story of Dwight D. Eisenhower*, by Arthur J. Beckhard (Grosset and Dunlap). To find out about another President, read **Abe Lincoln: Log Cabin to White House**, by Sterling North (Random House).

Zoo Doctor. William Bridges. (William Morrow) Being a zoo doctor is harder in many ways than being a doctor for human beings. Sick animals can't explain what hurts them, and they often fight help. When a bear gets a running nose, you've got to give him more than a "hankie" and a pill. When a monkey slips on a banana peel and breaks his leg, do you shoot him or set the broken bone? In this book you'll find out how animals at the Bronx Zoo are kept healthy.

Leatherneck. C. B. Colby. (Coward-McCann) "My rifle is my best friend. . . . It is my life. I must master it as I must master my life. . . ." This is only one of the promises a marine-in-training makes to himself. In this book you'll find the full story of what a marine goes through to become the great fighting man he is.

Other books written by Major Colby include *Air Drop* and *Frogmen* (Coward-McCann). Should you be interested in the life of a West Point Cadet and in some of the great generals who have been West Pointers, get *The West Point Story*, by Colonel Red Reeder and Nardi Reeder Campion (Random House).

Armed with Courage. May McNeer and Lynd Ward. (Abingdon Press) The seven heroes in this book have become famous because of the work they have done. Albert Schweitzer, for instance, could have been a successful doctor in a rich community, but instead, he opened up his office in the African jungle. Jane Addams was a rich woman, who shared all she had with the poor. George Washington Carver, born a slave, left a job in a large college to work in one of the poorest in the country.

If you want to learn more about one of these people, read **Dr. George Washington Carver; Scientist**, by Shirley Graham and George D. Lipscomb (Julian Messner).

The F. B. I. Quentin Reynolds. (Random House) The FBI does an important job for everyone in our country. Sometimes when the police can't solve a crime, the FBI helps find the criminal. This book tells how the FBI investigator, or G-man, becomes so good at his job.

You may also want to read **Our F.B.I.; An Inside Story** and **Men Against Crime**, both by John J. Floherty (J. B. Lippincott); **The F.B.I. Story**, by Don Whitehead (Random House); and *The Story of the Secret Service*, by Ferdinand Kuhn (Random House).

The Story of the Texas Rangers. Walter Prescott Webb. (Grosset and Dunlap) This is the true story of how the Texas Rangers have caught bank robbers and fought Indians, outlaws, and cattle rustlers. This book will also tell you how a ranger is chosen, what weapons he needs, and even how he rides.

Another good book is **The Texas Rangers**, by Will Henry (Random House).

Baseball Is Their Business. Edited by Harold Rosenthal. (Random House) If baseball is the sport you love, you may want to earn your living at it. If you're good enough, you could do it as a player. If you can't make the grade as a player, don't give up. You could be one of the scouts who travels over the country searching for another Mickey Mantle. You could be a coach, or a radio and TV sportscaster.

There's much more to baseball than the players. For every playing job, there are many non-playing jobs where you can make good money. You can find out about these jobs in this book.

Television Works Like This. Jeanne and Robert Bendick. (Whittlesey House) TV is growing up fast. More and more workers—cameramen, engineers, stagehands, as well as writers, actors, producers—are needed every year. If you want to know how a TV show gets rolling and what goes on behind your screens, get this book.

You might also like **Your Place in TV; A Handy Guide for Young People*, by Edwin B. Broderick (David McKay). For a story about a girl who gets a job in TV, try *TV Girl Friday*, by Ruth Milne (Little, Brown).

Forest Patrol. Jim Kjelgaard. (Holiday House) If you're thinking of becoming a forest ranger because you believe it's a quiet, easy life in the woods, you'll change your mind after reading this book. The life of a ranger is as much war as peace—war against forest fires, killer bears and wolves, hunters who do the wrong things and have to be warned. This is the story of a nineteen-year-old boy who learned about the life of a ranger.

Another book about forest rangers is **The Real Book about Our National Parks*, by Nelson Beecher Keyes (Garden City).

**Reporters Around the World*. Frank K. Kelly. (Little, Brown) A great reporter will go into the jungles and suffer from disease and heat, yet find the man he is looking for and send the story back to his newspaper. A great reporter will endanger his own life getting a murderer to surrender to the FBI. A great reporter will live with soldiers in muddy trenches to report exactly how they feel and what they suffer, even if it means getting killed while doing it. This is the story of seventeen such great reporters.

**The Betty Betz Career Book*. Betty Betz. (Grosset and Dunlap) Here are some important tips on getting a job and making good on it: (1) don't *write* your letter of application for a job, *type* it; (2) don't make personal phone calls on your business phone; (3) don't discuss your salary with other workers; (4) don't be afraid to start at the bottom—it's the way to get to the top.

These are just four of the many commandments you'll read about in this book. There's even a more important one—"Don't wait around for lucky breaks!" Hard work is the secret of many famous people in sports, fashion, photography, and other fields. Let them tell you how you can succeed, too.

**Angel of Mercy; The Story of Dorothea Lynde Dix*. Rachel Baker. (Julian Messner) You may say to yourself as you read this book, "Why did she do it?" She could have had a soft, easy life. Instead, she gave her whole life to improving conditions in prisons, insane asylums, and hospitals. She wanted to give hope to anyone who was sick, poor, or in trouble. Why *does* a woman give up her own pleasures to help others?

These books tell about two other outstanding women: **Clara Barton*, by Mildred Mastin Pace (Charles Scribner), and **The First Woman Doctor; The Story of Elizabeth Blackwell, M.D.*, by Rachel Baker (Julian Messner).

**Star for a Compass*. D. S. Halacy, Jr. (Macmillan) His father wanted him to stay in school, but Rod had other ideas. So he stowed away on his father's tuna ship and found out what deep-sea fishing was like. The trip proved to be quite exciting, especially when Rod jumped into the water to save a man from a shark.

You may also like *Let's Take a Trip to a Fishery*, by Sarah R. Riedman (Abelard-Schuman), and *Meat from Ranch to Table*, by Walter Buehr (William Morrow).

Journeys and Discoveries

A World Full of Homes. William A. Burns. (Whittlesey House) "A man's home is his castle," you have heard people say. It's the place where he likes to feel safe and sound. So you may wonder, when you read this book, why people have built homes in trees, on cliffs, on stilts, and why they have settled near live volcanoes or rivers that often overflow. Since history began, every type of home has had a reason for being built. It's all explained here.

You'll also enjoy *Man and His Tools*, by William A. Burns (Whittlesey House).

The Conquest of the North and South Poles; Adventures of the Peary and Byrd Expeditions. Russell Owen. (Random House) You may wonder why a man will suffer terrible cold and hunger and risk his life just to get to the North Pole. You may wonder even more when you learn that this man had a wife and child and a comfortable home. You'll find out his reasons when you read about Admiral Peary.

You may ask why a man would risk crashing a plane into a mountain of ice and snow 10,000 feet high and want to live in cold so fierce that his breath freezes right in front of him. You'll find out when you read about Admiral Byrd and why he went to the South Pole.

Cave of Riches: The Story of the Dead Sea Scrolls. Alan Honour. (Whittlesey House) This is a true story of two teen-age Arab boys who accidentally discovered a great treasure in a cave. When the boys first found it, they called it "old rubbish." What they had found, though, were scrolls written over 2000 years ago. People who study Biblical times are especially interested in these scrolls. What was written on them? The book tells you.

Another book on the same subject is *The Great Discovery; The Story of the Dead Sea Scrolls*, by Azriel Eisenberg (Abelard-Schuman).

To California by Covered Wagon. George R. Stewart. (Random House) When you see a movie about pioneers crossing the country in covered wagons, you may say to yourself, "It's just a movie. It really couldn't have been that bad." As you read this true story of the first party to reach California by covered wagon, you'll be amazed that they ever got there.

You might also try *We Were There in the Klondike Gold Rush*, by Benjamin Appel (Grosset and Dunlap), and *Henry Hudson*, by Ronald Syme (William Morrow).

**The Caves of the Great Hunters*. Hans Baumann. (Pantheon Books) One day when four French boys and their dog, Robot, were walking through a forest, the dog got lost. The boys looked for Robot, but he had disappeared. He had found a hole and begun to dig for food. But it wasn't food Robot reached; it was a cave. On the walls of the cave were painted pictures of animals that had lived in this same forest 10,000 years ago. The story of why hunters, who lived thousands of years ago, painted animals on the walls of their caves will really surprise you.

**Kon-Tiki*. Thor Heyerdahl. (Rand McNally) This is the hard-to-believe, but true, story of six men who got on a raft and let the wind and current take them 4000 miles on a 101-day trip to a South Sea island. Once they caught a dolphin by hand. They worried because they thought a whale that was following them might smash the raft to bits. Often they wondered why they were even on this raft. You may wonder, too, until you reach the end of this bold and eventful journey.

Just Good Stories

Teen-Age Tales, Book One. Edited by Ruth Strang and Ralph Roberts. (D. C. Heath) Stories about these three people and many others are in this book:

(1) Every baby sitter in town had trouble with Ronnie, a child who bit. One night a baby sitter really fixed him. Ronnie never bit anyone again!

(2) Pete was a teen-ager without a driver's license. Yet it was his driving that helped catch a bank robber.

(3) Thomas Edison, the great inventor, was said to have been stupid in school. Then how

was it he invented the electric light, the phonograph, and many things you use every day?

If you liked the stories in this book, read *Teen-Age Tales, Book Two*, also edited by Ruth Strang and Ralph Roberts (D. C. Heath).

When Boy Dates Girl; Boy-Girl Stories for the Teens. Compiled by Aurelia Stowe. (Random House) It happened to two boys in this book: One boy wanted to impress his girl whom he had taken to the drugstore. But some headache tablets played havoc and he couldn't take her home. Another boy in this book warned his best friend that he was going to steal the friend's girl.

You might also like *Double Date, by Rosamond du Jardin (J. B. Lippincott); **Seventeenth Summer*, by Maureen Daly (Dodd, Mead); and **Trish*, by Margaret Maze Craig (Thomas Y. Crowell).

Behind the Ranges. Stephen W. Meader. (Harcourt, Brace) Put yourself in Dick's place. He goes on a hunt high up in the Olympic Mountains, looking for a rare animal, the whistling marmot. But he meets a human being that is much more rare, a killer caveman. We know cavemen lived thousands of years ago; yet here's a man who looks and acts like one. Who is he? How did he get here? Is he captured? That's the story.

Mike Fink. James Cloyd Bowman. (Little, Brown) In the old days when keel boats carried goods up and down American rivers, you had to be a brave man to get a job on the crew. This is the story of how Captain Mike Fink, the king of the river, and his crew (Mickey Thunderbolt, the Mocker, and others) fought and shot their way out of scrapes with all kinds of enemies.

Shane. Jack Schaefer. (Houghton Mifflin) When he came near, most people moved away and some even ran away. Everyone felt there was dynamite in him that could explode any minute. Yet he wouldn't hurt a fly if he didn't have to. He even hated guns.

In this story you learn why he had to break a man's arm in one fight, why he left four cowboys in a bloody mess, and why he shot it out with two men and killed them both. This was Shane, the strong, silent cowboy who did these things because he was loyal to a family he liked.

Also try **Heroes, Heroes, Heroes: Stories of Rescue, Courage, and Endurance*, selected by Phyllis R. Fenner (Franklin Watts); and **The Edge of Danger: True Stories of Adventure*, selected by Margaret Scoggin (Alfred A. Knopf).

**Celestial Space, Inc.* Charles Coombs. (Westminster Press) One day a Super Sabre jet zoomed low over Eddie Winston's chicken yard, frightening all the chickens and killing one. Eddie got mad, went into partnership with his friend, Brick, and started something unusual. Before long they were in a big business, and their town, Riverdale, was on the map. It all happened when they decided to sell *Space*—not the kind you buy in a newspaper, but the kind you find all around you.

Love of Speed

Where Speed Is King. Margaret O. and Edwin Hyde. (Whittlesey House) Where do you like your speed? in track? You can meet some of the record holders in this book and even get some tips from them. No matter where you like your speed—on a bicycle, a bobsled, a boat, a horse, a motorcycle, a pair of skis—this book will give you the records as well as tips on how the record holders do it.

If you like stories about speedy racing cars, hot rods, speedboats, submarines, space ships, and PT boats, you'll enjoy **Speed, Speed, Speed*, edited by Phyllis R. Fenner (Franklin Watts).

Driving Today and Tomorrow. Margaret O. Hyde. (Whittlesey House) You've heard about the "road hog" who thinks he owns the road. In this book you'll meet the rest of the Driver's Zoo—the "turtle," "antelope," "sheep," "goose," "eager beaver," "mouse," "monkey," and "lion." Together they are responsible for killing 300,000 and injuring 10,000,000 people in the last ten years.

Many older people say teen-agers are too young, too wild, or too careless to drive. No one who reads this book will want to be wild or careless. You find out how important it is to be an alert driver. You also learn how to avoid an accident or what to do if you have one.

**Hot Rod It—And Run for Fun.* Fred Horsley. (Prentice-Hall) You have a second-hand car and you want to "soup it up." Then read the chapter in this book called "How to Make It Hot." If you want to be a top driver, though, read the safety rules, too. And if there's a word in "hot rod" lingo you can't find in the dictionary, chances are you'll find it here.

**Hot Rod.* Henry Gregor Felsen. (E. P. Dutton) Bud Crayne loved speed. He raced against any car in town, including ambulances and police cars. Once, though, when he beat a police car in a race, he was really sorry. If you love your car the way Bud loved his, you'll go thundering down the road with him in this book.

Another book by the same author is **Street Rod* (Random House).

**Sport and Racing Cars.* Raymond F. Yates and Brock W. Yates. (Harper) There are two kinds of hot rodders. One kind is so speed-mad he doesn't care what he drives, or where, or how fast. The other is the boy who loves speed, but respects safety and takes pride in his driving. This book is for the second kind of hot rodder.

You may also like **Mexican Road Race,* by Patrick O'Connor (Ives Washburn).

**Faster and Faster; The Story of Speed.* Raymond F. Yates (Harper) Every year a few baseball players are "beaned" by a pitcher. Some of these players are badly hurt. You can understand why when you know that a baseball can travel more than ninety miles an hour. Bobby Feller once threw one that went 98.6 and Mack Koenig one that went 127 miles an hour. You can find these and many other figures about all kinds of speed records in this book.

Today, jet planes go over a thousand miles an hour. Tomorrow, engineers dream of much faster planes. That's how much we're learning about speed. That's what this book is all about.

Men and War

The Pirate Lafitte and the Battle of New Orleans. Robert Tallant. (Random House) This is the true story of a famous pirate who had a big smuggling business in Louisiana. When the governor put a price on his head, he turned around and offered $1500 for the governor's capture. When a group of his men mutinied, he killed the leader on the spot. As bad as he was, though, he and his "dirty shirts" helped save New Orleans for America during the War of 1812.

Another account of Lafitte is **Black Falcon,* by Armstrong Sperry (John C. Winston). You might also try *Pirates, Pirates, Pirates; Stories of Cutlasses and Corsairs, Buried Treasure and Buccaneers, Ships and Swashbucklers,* compiled by Phyllis R. Fenner (Grosset and Dunlap).

The Story of D-Day: June 6, 1944. Bruce Bliven, Jr. (Random House) It was D-day, June 6, 1944—the day General Eisenhower and his staff had long planned for. It was the day on which the invasion of France and the attack against Hitler were to begin. This is the story of one of the most important battles in history, and the men whose heroic deeds won that battle.

If you liked this book, you may also want to get *We Were There at the Normandy Invasion,* by Clayton Knight (Grosset and Dunlap). This is the story of a boy, his family, and his dog who helped the Americans capture some Nazi soldiers near the Normandy beach. Or read *The Battle of Britain,* by Quentin Reynolds (Random House).

We Were There at the Battle for Bataan. Benjamin Appel. (Grosset and Dunlap) In this book you are there when Eddie, his sister Diana, and their father, Captain Belden, get caught in the fighting against the Japanese during World War II.

Another exciting book is **Submarine Rendezvous; Pacific Adventures in World War II,* by Joseph B. Icenhower (John C. Winston).

Guadalcanal Diary. Richard Tregaskis. (Random House) It took six months for the marines to prepare for and capture this island, foot by foot, yard by yard, mile by mile. We had to learn how to fight an enemy who preferred to die rather than surrender. This was one of our important battles because it was a turning point in World War II.

*Thirty Seconds over Tokyo. Ted W. Lawson, edited by Bob Considine. (Random House) This story begins: "I helped bomb Tokyo on the Doolittle raid of April 18, 1942. I crashed in the China Sea. I learned the full, deep meaning of the term 'United Nations' from men and women whose language I couldn't speak. I watched a buddy of mine saw off my left leg. And finally I got home to my wife after being flown, shipped and carried around the world."

You might also read **Battle Stations: True Stories of Men in War, by Margaret Scoggin (Alfred A. Knopf).

*The Real Book about Spies. Samuel Epstein and Beryl Williams. (Garden City) You will read about the spy who stole our secret of the atom bomb and gave it to the Russians. You'll also read about other spies, living and dead, who do this dangerous work. You may dislike most of them but you'll admire some because they risk their lives for their country.

**Dawn at Lexington. Norma Wood James. (Longmans, Green) If your country was fighting for its life, you'd want to be in the thick of the battle. That's just how fifteen-year-old Jeremiah Cutler felt in Revolutionary War days. He had more exciting experiences than he had expected, too. He met General Washington, got involved with the traitor Benedict Arnold, and saw Major André, the British spy, hanged. This is American history through the eyes of a teen-ager.

Other books about the United States, its history, and its heroes are: *Early American, the Story of Paul Revere, by Mildred Mastin Pace (Charles Scribner); **Young Nathan, by Marion Marsh Brown (Westminster Press); **Six Feet Six; the Heroic Story of Sam Houston, by Bessie Rowland James and Marquis James, adapted from The Raven, by Marquis James (Bobbs-Merrill); and **James Bowie and His Famous Knife, by Shannon Garst (Julius Messner).

Music Makers

Tune Up: Presenting the Instruments of the Orchestra. Harriet E. Huntington. (Doubleday) *Making an Orchestra. Dorothy Berliner Commins. (Macmillan) Most of the musical instruments we use today had interesting beginnings. If it hadn't been for the bow and arrow, we might never have had the violin. The French horn was used by the French kings for hunting calls. These two books tell you something about the instruments and their beginnings.

*Trumpeter's Tale: The Story of Young Louis Armstrong. Jeanette Eaton. (William Morrow) They call him "Satchmo," which is short for "Satchel-Mouth." It's the nickname for Louis Armstrong, one of the greatest jazz trumpeters who has ever lived. Yet for many years while he was playing in bands, he couldn't read a note. He got away with it because he had something that other musicians would like to have. This is the story of Louis Armstrong.

**The Story of George Gershwin. David Ewen. (Henry Holt) "I'm sorry . . . you haven't any talent . . . forget all about music." That's what a violinist said to George Gershwin when he was just beginning to play the piano. If someone said that to you, would you quit? George didn't. Instead he went on to write songs we still hear today. This book tells the story of his short life and the great jazz he wrote.

**The Story of Irving Berlin is by the same author and publisher. Also try **Men and Melodies, by Leonard A. Paris (Thomas Y. Crowell).

Science

More Power to You: A Short History of Power from the Windmill to the Atom. Herman and Nina Schneider. (William R. Scott) If you are interested in finding out what makes things move, read this book. For instance, how does a steam engine run? You can prove how it runs by experimenting in your own kitchen. All you need to find out for yourself is the top of an oatmeal box, a piece of metal foil, a snap fastener, a needle, a pencil with an eraser, a spool, eight paper clips, and a teakettle.

If you want to understand how a jet plane flies without propellers, all you need is a toy balloon and some wind from your lungs. Why could a jet never reach the moon? Why could a rocket do it someday? This book explains.

You may also want to get *The Story of Power*, by Edward Stoddard (Garden City).

Everyday Weather and How It Works. Herman Schneider. (Whittlesey House) You could become a popular and useful man in your neighborhood by reading this book. It tells how to be your own weatherman and make your own instruments for very little money. For example, you can make a barometer with a milk carton, an empty tin can, a piece of balloon, and such things as clips, thumbtacks, and a broom straw.

Should your mother's club have that picnic tomorrow? You could tell her. Should your ball game be postponed? You could tell your friends. "Suppose I predict wrong?" you ask. So does the weatherman, once in a while.

All about Strange Beasts of the Past. Roy Chapman Andrews. (Random House) Once there lived horses that were no bigger than cats, saber-toothed tigers that could bite through the toughest hide, and beasts that were bigger than two school buses piled one on top of the other. This is no fairy tale. This is the truth. And the man who writes this book can prove it to you.

To find out what America was like millions of years ago, read *Prehistoric America*, by Anne Terry White (Random House).

All about Our Changing Rocks. Anne Terry White. (Random House) Thousands of feet below where you are sitting or standing or lying down, there is a terrifically hot, liquid substance called magma, which isn't sitting or standing or lying still at all. It's on the move! This magma can do many wonderful or terrible things. It can pour gold, silver, or diamonds into some of the earth's cracks. It can cause an earthquake, too—one of the million small earthquakes that happen every year, or one of those dozen or more big ones that can destroy

an entire city. This book tells about rock formations and what they do.

Other good books include *Rocks, Rivers, and the Changing Earth; A First Book about Geology*, by Herman and Nina Schneider (William R. Scott), and **Restless Earth*, by Rose Wyler and Gerald Ames (Abelard-Schuman).

The First Book of Electricity. Sam and Beryl Epstein. (Franklin Watts) There are many facts about science that are *not* deep, dark secrets. They're all around you—for example, in your own kitchen. You can understand science, if like scientists in their laboratories, you will stop, look, and listen. This book will help you.

You may also want to get *Through the Magnifying Glass*, by Julius Schwartz (Whittlesey House), and *Everyday Machines and How They Work*, by Herman Schneider (Whittlesey House). Or you may like **First Electrical Book for Boys*, ***The Boys' Book of Engines, Motors and Turbines*, and ***First Chemistry Book for Boys and Girls*, by Alfred Morgan (Charles Scribner).

Microbes at Work. Millicent E. Selsam. (William Morrow) Microbes are tiny things, and they are everywhere—in the air, in the ground, in your food, on your hands. Most of them won't hurt you; some will help you. Others, though, can kill you quickly. This book tells which microbes are your friends and which are not.

***Magic Bullets*, by Louis Sutherland (Little, Brown), tells how we have found the "bullets" with which to "shoot" many killer-microbes.

The Wonders Inside You. Margaret Cosgrove. (Dodd, Mead) You are a city. Your heart is the pumping station; your brain and nervous system the government. You have an air-conditioning system, a plumbing department, and sanitation workers—all inside you. In social studies you learn how to keep the city you live in clean and healthy. This book can help you learn how to do the same for the city that lives in you.

You'll also like *How Your Body Works*, by Herman and Nina Schneider (William R. Scott), and ***Wonders of the Human Body*, by Anthony Ravielli (Viking Press).

All about Radio and Television. Jack Gould. (Random House) We have sent a message to the moon. It happened in 1946 when a radar signal made a round trip to the moon. This book explains some of the wonders that occur in the air waves—for example, why you can flip a radio or TV dial and hear or see what's happening thousands of miles away.

If you're interested, also try **The Boys' First Book of Radio and Electronics*, and **The Boys' Second Book of Radio and Electronics*, by Alfred Morgan (Charles Scribner).

Science the Super Sleuth. Lynn Poole. (Whittlesey House) The criminal who tries to commit the perfect crime is up against not only the police and the FBI but also something equally important— Science. For instance, a man killed somebody and left no fingerprints or clues. If it hadn't been for a piece of wax in his ear that proved he was the killer, he might be free today. Science caught this murderer as it catches others—through a speck of dirt, a drop of blood, or even a thread.

**The World We Live In.* By the editorial staff of *Life* and Lincoln Barnett; text especially adapted by Jane Werner Watson from the original version. (Simon and Schuster) The world we live in, they say, began five billion years ago. How do we know that? How long did it take for life to start in water and on land? What's the proof? How did life change, little by little, over billions of years until it is what it is today? How can we tell? What will the world be like five billion years from now? You'll have a better idea how to answer when you've read this book.

**The Boy Scientist.* John Lewellen. (Simon and Schuster) Many people don't bother to ask why or how things happen. Why does an electric light burn? Why does an apple fall down, not up? How does the moon keep from smashing into the earth? How does the X ray work?

This is the story of famous scientists who couldn't rest until they found answers to the "Why's" and "How's" that bothered them. Many suffered because they asked questions. But they kept on until they found the answers.

Sports

The Ted Williams Story. Gene Schoor and Henry Gilfond. (Julian Messner) He gets more money a year than any man ever got playing baseball. You'll understand why when you look at his record and read about the games Ted Williams has won with his slugging.

If you liked this book, you may enjoy *The Mickey Mantle Story*, by Mickey Mantle as told to Ben Epstein (Henry Holt); *The Pee Wee Reese Story*, by Gene Schoor (Julian Messner); *Lou Gehrig: A Quiet Hero*, by Frank Graham (G. P. Putnam); *Born to Play Ball*, by Willie Mays as told to Charles Einstein (G. P. Putnam); *The Babe Ruth Story*, as told to Bob Considine (E. P. Dutton); and *Yankee Bat Boy*, by Joe Carrieri as told to Zander Hollander (Prentice-Hall).

Casey Stengel; Baseball's Greatest Manager. Gene Schoor and Henry Gilfond. (Julian Messner) They called him "nuts" when he was an outfielder in the minor leagues. He'd catch a fly ball, return it to the infield, throw his glove a few feet away, and then practice sliding into it until the next batter was up. He wasn't "nuts"; he was using every free minute to become a better player. When he got too old to play, he became the greatest manager in the big leagues. Was he luckier or smarter than other managers? You'll find out when you read the story of Casey Stengel.

You may also want to get *Mighty Men of Baseball*, by Charles Spain Verral (Aladdin Books).

Winning Baseball (Revised Edition). Ethan Allen. (Ronald Press) You become a better baseball player not only by playing a lot, but also by playing correctly. Here are Ted Williams, Willie Mays, and dozens more to teach you the right way to bat, bunt, field, throw, and slide.

Two good baseball stories are *Rookie of the Year* and *The Kid from Tomkinsville*, by John R. Tunis (Harcourt, Brace).

Fighting Five. William Heuman. (William Morrow) This is the story of a college basketball player who was a snob at first. He didn't like the "hick college" he went to, the old gym he had to play in, or the old uniform he had to wear. In time, though, he learned to respect not only things but also people, and he helped his team get to the national play-offs.

Another good story is *Basketball Clown*, by C. P. and O. B. Jackson (Whittlesey House). Or you may like **Basketball Illustrated*, by Howard A. Hobson (Ronald Press).

Center Ice. Philip Harkins. (Holiday House) Some of the best ice-hockey players are Canadians. Pete Grenville found this out when he tried to become a "pro" on the New York Rangers. Should he quit? fight a losing battle? or go back to a semipro team for more experience? What would you do?

Ice Hockey, by Eddie Jeremiah (Ronald Press), tells about building good players.

Weight Lifting and Progressive Resistance Exercise. Jim Murray. (Ronald Press) This book can help you build a better body. You'll read, too, about famous sports figures who have lifted heavy weights to keep in trim.

Another good book is *Boy's Book of Body Building*, by Stanley Pashko (Grosset and Dunlap).

**The Jim Thorpe Story; America's Greatest Athlete*. Gene Schoor and Henry Gilfond. (Julian Messner) The King of Sweden called him the most wonderful athlete in the world. He was voted the greatest football star of the twentieth century. He was a top professional baseball player for many years. He won the decathlon in the Olympic games. This is the story of Jim Thorpe—an all-around athlete, the best we ever had.

Iron Duke, by John R. Tunis (Harcourt, Brace), tells about a college student who breaks the record for the two-mile race. For general information, try *Pictorial History of American Sports*, by John Durant and Otto Bettmann (A. S. Barnes).

**In This Corner*. Adrien Stoutenburg. (Westminster Press) Ted Smith wasn't big and strong, but he accidentally K.O.'d Bruce Tate, who was the town's muscle man. Ted didn't mean to.

He just wanted to forget it, but no one would let him. Judo and body building rescued him.

Another good story is **The Challenger*, by Frank Waldman (World). Or read *The Joe Louis Story*, by Joe Louis (Grosset and Dunlap).

**Larry Koller's New Hunting Annual*. Larry Koller. (Bobbs-Merrill) If you're out hunting a buck, a male deer, look for "rubs" on saplings. That could mean your buck is nearby and you've a good chance to "bag" him. This is only one of many hints you'll get in this book about finding, shooting, and skinning the animals you hunt.

Stories We All Should Know

Famous Mysteries. Edited by Mary Yost Sandrus. (Scott, Foresman) Make believe you could wish for anything you wanted, and that, before you knew it, you got your wish. That's what happened to a farmer and his wife in one of the mysteries in this book. There are other exciting stories, too—one about a boy who trapped his father's kidnaper, one about a doctor who was both a killer and a kind soul, and seven more.

You may also like *Eight Treasured Stories*, adapted by Mary Yost Sandrus, Gertrude Moderow, and Ernest Noyes (Scott, Foresman).

20,000 Leagues Under the Sea. Jules Verne, adapted by Gertrude Moderow. (Scott, Foresman) When you look into the skies these days, do you wonder what's coming next? This is a story about people who wondered, too, when they saw something in the ocean that moved fast and gave out a strange light. What was it? It was something unbelievable for people who lived over a hundred years ago.

Another version of this story is **Twenty Thousand Leagues Under the Sea*, by Jules Verne (Charles Scribner).

Moby Dick. Herman Melville, adapted by Verne B. Brown. (Scott, Foresman) This is the story of an around-the-world whale hunt. The object of the hunt is Moby Dick, a white whale that had chewed off Captain Ahab's leg. The one-legged captain swears he will get revenge, no matter how many of his crew suffer, no matter if he has to die—just so long as he can kill the whale he hates more than anything in the world.

Another version is *The Story of Moby Dick, the White Whale*, adapted and retold by Frank L. Beals from *Moby Dick*, by Herman Melville (Benj. H. Sanborn). If you'd like an exciting story about fishing in the days of the sailing ships, get *Captains Courageous*, by Rudyard Kipling and adapted by Lou P. Bunce (Scott, Foresman).

The Story of Lemuel Gulliver in Lilliput Land. Adapted and retold by Frank L. Beals from *Gulliver's Travels* by Jonathan Swift. (Benj. H. Sanborn) A sportswriter reporting on a boxer said, "He punches like a Lilliputian." He meant the boxer's punches were small and weak.

The word *Lilliputian* comes from the story of Lemuel Gulliver who was shipwrecked on the island of Lilliput where the people were only five or six inches tall. If you want to know how it felt to be a giant with the power to rule an entire country of small people, you'll like this book.

Robinson Crusoe, by Daniel Defoe and adapted by Verne B. Brown (Scott, Foresman), is the story of another man who was shipwrecked.

The Odyssey of Homer and *The Iliad of Homer.* Retold by Alfred J. Church. (Macmillan) A teen-ager named his jalopy "Penelope" because she was so faithful. A reporter wrote about a boxer who had been K. O.'d by a sock on the jaw, "The beaten boxer had his Achilles heel in his jaw." The names *Penelope* and *Achilles* come from the story of the Trojan War. Penelope was a woman who waited faithfully for many years for her husband to return from that war. Achilles was a Greek hero who had one weak spot—his heel. These books will introduce you to the famous names in that famous war.

You can learn about many other names we use today by reading *Adventures with the Gods, *Adventures with the Giants*, and *Adventures with the Heroes*, by Catherine F. Sellew (Little, Brown).

Around the World in Eighty Days. Jules Verne, adapted by Gertrude Moderow. (Scott, Foresman) Today, you could zoom around the world in eighty hours or less in a jet. In 1872, when this story takes place, even eighty days was considered impossible. Phileas Fogg was willing to bet $100,000 he could do it, though. And the race everybody bet that he would lose started.

You'll also enjoy *The Last of the Mohicans*, by James Fenimore Cooper and adapted by Verne B. Brown and edited by Gertrude Moderow; *Tom Sawyer*, by Mark Twain and adapted by A. O. Berglund; and *Huckleberry Finn*, by Mark Twain and adapted by Verne B. Brown (Scott, Foresman). **The Call of the Wild*, by Jack London (Macmillan), tells about a wild dog.

Paul Bunyan. Esther Shephard. (Harcourt, Brace) This is a story about one of America's first supermen. When he was three weeks old, he rolled around so much in his sleep he knocked down four square miles of timber. When he became a man, he was such a giant he could walk across a state with a few steps.

Paul Bunyan Swings His Axe, by Dell J. McCormick (Caxton Printers), is also good.

**Julius Caesar in Modern English.* Adapted from Shakespeare's play by Elsie M. Katterjohn. (Scott, Foresman) About 2000 years ago there was a man named Julius Caesar, whom many people thought was a dictator. Some leaders, like Brutus, wanted to get rid of him for the sake of the country. Others, like Cassius, wanted to murder him for their own selfish reasons. You'll wonder, as you read this famous play, "Does violence ever really pay?"

Time on Your Hands

Keen Teens: Or 101 Ways to Make Money. Stookie Allen. (Emerson Books) Albert Boomer, a smart fourteen-year-old, had an idea that really paid off. He got some frogs and ducks and put them in a pond. Then he put an electric light over the pond. The bugs came; the frogs ate well; the ducks got fat. And Al went into business selling frogs' legs and ducks to restaurants. Keen? This book tells about 250 such keen teens as these: a boy who bought a second-hand diving suit and made $20,000 in one year bringing up lost logs at a lumber mill; a girl who made $25,000 in one year designing purses.

Not everyone has an idea that can be turned into money, but everyone has ideas. You can match yours against those in this book.

Never Too Young to Earn: 101 Part Time Jobs for Girls, by Adrian A. Paradis (David McKay), gives tips on how to hunt for a part-time job and describes dozens of jobs you can get. It also tells about things you can do, if you prefer to work at home.

The Real Book about Real Crafts. C. C. Roberts. (Garden City) Suppose you'd like to have a model of a certain building. You *can* make it yourself. Suppose you'd like to give some junior puppeteer a puppet theater, but you can't afford to buy it. You *can* make it. Suppose you'd like to have a pair of moccasins. You *can* make them. This book shows how to use leather, wood, metal, or paper to make many things you'll enjoy giving to others or keeping.

Other good books are *Fun with Wire, *Fun with Wood*, and *Fun with Clay*, by Joseph Leeming (J. B. Lippincott). Also get *The Boys' Book of Tools*, by Raymond F. Yates (Harper).

Home-Made Zoo. Sylvia S. Greenberg and Edith L. Raskin. (David McKay) You don't have to envy the zoo keeper, who can spend a lot of time with animals. You can, too, and right in your own home. This book tells where to buy, how to feed, and how to house animals, reptiles, birds, or fish. If your hamster gets a toothache, it tells you how to be his dentist. If your frog faints from the heat, there's a way to help him.

These books may also prove helpful: *How to Make a Miniature Zoo*, by Vinson Brown (Little, Brown); *Tank Menagerie*, by Theodore McClintoch (Abelard-Schuman); *Tropical Fishes and Home Aquaria*, by Alfred Morgan (Charles Scribner); and **First Aid for Pets*, by Leon F. Whitney (Vanguard Press).

The Junior Book of Camping and Woodcraft. Bernard S. Mason. (Ronald Press) Camping outdoors can be lots of fun. It can also be dangerous if you don't know how to protect yourself against many things that could happen to you. In this book an expert discusses tents, packing, sleeping, clothing, cooking, and so on. If you are interested in camping, get this book.

You might also read *Let's Go Camping and **Let's Fish*, by Harry Zarchy (Alfred A. Knopf).

Tricks Any Boy Can Do. Joseph Leeming. (Appleton-Century-Crofts) The hand is quicker than the eye. Magicians have learned that, and they can amaze an audience with their tricks. This book takes you right into their secrets. You'll see how they do almost 200 tricks with cards, handkerchiefs, matches, and coins, and you can learn how to do these tricks yourself.

Photography for Teen-Agers. Lucile Robertson Marshall. (Prentice-Hall) You can double, even triple, the money you make baby-sitting. How? Take your camera along and snap the baby, a pet, or anything the owner of the house would like to see in a picture. This book also suggests many other ways to make money with this hobby. It tells, too, how to become a better photographer and how to develop pictures.

If you're a stamp collector, get **So You're Collecting Stamps*, by Mannel Hahn (Dodd, Mead).

The Betty Betz Teen-Age Cookbook. Betty Betz. (Henry Holt) Name a dish, from peanut brittle to southern-fried chicken, that you want to make for fun or for a party. This book has it. It shows you, among other things, how to be a smart shopper and how to set a table correctly.

**First Rifle: How to Shoot It Straight and Use It Safely*. C. B. Colby. (Coward-McCann) When you want to kill a pest around your neighborhood —a rat, a woodchuck, a red squirrel—you use a rifle. If you want to be sure to get the pest with your first shot, *First Rifle* will tell you exactly what kind of bullet you need and what part of the body to aim at. The author also tells you how to have fun with your rifle and how to use it carefully and safely.

You may also like **Six Shooter: Pistols, Revolvers, and Automatics Past and Present*, by the same author and publisher.

How to Make a Home Nature Museum. Vinson Brown. (Little, Brown) If you are interested in keeping specimens of the life about you—animal tracks, rocks and minerals, snakeskins, and so on—you'll want to read this book. It will even tell you how to shoot an animal for your museum without letting it suffer.

Tips for Teens

Teen Talk. Marion Glendining. (Alfred A. Knopf) Do you have money troubles? Do you worry about not being popular? Do you have pesky brothers and sisters? Are there other things that bother you? You'll get some ideas on how to help yourself by reading this book.

Betty White's Teen-Age Dance Etiquette. Betty White. (David McKay) Are you always sure of what to do when you go to a dance? If you're the young man, you may wonder when to pay the cloakroom tip for your girl and when not to; or when to walk into the entrance before your girl and when not to. If you're the young woman, you may wonder when it's all right to dance with a stag, or how often you can say "no" to an invitation to dance. You can stop wondering. The answers are in this book.

Questions Boys Ask. David W. Armstrong. (E. P. Dutton) Hundreds of the questions that teen-agers ask are answered in this book. Here are a few of these questions: Do you have to have money to be popular? Why am I shy? Why does my teacher seem to "have it in for me"? What about smoking and drinking? Are "Dutch treats" OK? What can I do about pimples?

Plain Talk for Men under 21! Allen Ludden. (Dodd, Mead) In this book you'll get one man's opinion on these and other subjects: (1) how much to tip in a restaurant; (2) how to know when you're ready to go steady; (3) how to pick the job you want for the rest of your life; (4) how to become a better dancer.

You'll also want to read **Blondes Prefer Gentlemen; Brunettes, Too—Redheads Included!** by Sheila John Daly (Dodd, Mead).

Questions Girls Ask. Helen Welshimer; new edition revised by Elizabeth L. O'Neill. (E. P. Dutton) Is it all right to call a boy on the telephone? How late is "late"? What kind of hairdo is right for school? How do you run a good party? How can I develop my talents? In this book you'll find one woman's answers.

Other good books are *Betty Cornell's Glamour Guide for Teens* and *Betty Cornell's Teen-Age Popularity Guide*, both by Betty Cornell (Prentice-Hall); *Teen-Age Glamor*, by Adah Broadbent (Doubleday); **What's Your P.Q. (Personality Quotient)?** by Maureen Daly (Dodd, Mead); and **Seventeen Book of Young Living**, by Enid A. Haupt (David McKay).

Fun with Skits, Stunts, and Stories. Helen and Larry Eisenberg. (Association Press) With this book at your side there should never be a dull moment at your parties. In the section called "Can You Do This?" you'll find lots of suggestions to keep your friends active—having a Ping-pong ball contest, swinging a bell without ringing it, threading a needle while you balance on one knee.

You may also want to get *Riddles of Many Lands*, by Carl Withers and Sula Benet (Abelard-Schuman); *Riddles, Riddles, Riddles*, selected by Joseph Leeming (Franklin Watts); *A Dillar, A Dollar: Rhymes and Sayings for the Ten-O'Clock Scholar*, compiled by Lillian Morrison (Thomas Y. Crowell); and *Jokes, Jokes, Jokes*, selected by Helen Hoke (Franklin Watts).

Superstitious? Here's Why! Julie Forsyth Batchelor and Claudia De Lys. (Harcourt, Brace) When you knock on wood for good luck, you're doing something that people have done for thousands of years. Once people believed that gods lived in trees. If you wanted a favor from a god, you tapped on the tree; when you got it, you tapped again to thank him. If you want to know how other superstitions started, read this book.

Underwater—for Science, Sport, Survival

Diving for Science. Lynn Poole. (Whittlesey House) There are many divers who dive not only for fun but also for money. They are paid to find out if there's oil, gold, silver, and other minerals in the ocean. And there is—more than you ever dreamed.

Divers are not so much afraid of living things in the water as they are of mistakes they can make—for example, coming out of deep water too fast and getting the bends that may cripple a man. Diving for science is thrilling, but you've got to "be on the ball" every minute.

*Underwater Adventure. Willard Price. (John Day) Put yourself in this diver's place. He's running away from a tiger shark and takes shelter in an underwater cave. Then a deadly moray eel grabs him by the wrist, and draws blood. The shark smells the blood. How does this diver come out alive? In this adventure book, death comes close many times and it strikes twice.

You might also read **The Silent World, by J. Y. Cousteau and Frédéric Dumas (Harper).

**Treasures in the Depths. Robert Uhl. (Prentice-Hall) Believe it or not, about 260 billion dollars' worth of treasure is buried under water. That's enough to give every person in this country almost $1400 apiece—if we could ever dig it up.

This is the story of three boys who hear about a Spanish ship that may have more than $1400 apiece for each of them and their mother. They go after the treasure and get into lots of trouble.

**Up Periscope. Robb White. (Doubleday) This is the story of Ken Braden who went to the Underwater Demolition School during World War II and was given the job of getting a code that had been stolen from us. While his submarine waits for him, he swims under water to the island where the code is. He gets the code, but not without being seen by the enemy. Ken manages, however, to get back to his submarine. Then the submarine is surrounded and bombed.

Acknowledgments

For permission to adapt and use copyrighted materials, grateful acknowledgment is made to the following:

To the author for "When the Bleachers Rocked" by Vincent Edwards; reprinted from Forward; copyright, 1955, by W. L. Jenkins; used by permission. To the author and publishers for "Danger Detectives" by Lawrence Lader; adapted and reprinted from Coronet, December 1953; copyright © 1953, by Esquire, Inc. To the publishers for "Cooled with Kerosene"; adapted from an article in The Lamp; copyright, 1956, by Standard Oil Company (New Jersey). To the publishers for "A Fish Story"; adapted from "It Rains Trout in the Sawtooths" by S. Dale Hamilton in Travel; copyright, 1942, by Robert M. McBride & Company, Inc. To the author and publishers for "The First Basketball Game"; adapted from "I Played in the First Basketball Game" by Raymond P. Kaighn; from Boys' Life; by permission of the author and Boys' Life; published by the Boy Scouts of America. To the publishers for "Thirteen" by William E. Dodge, a student in Grover Cleveland High School, Caldwell, New Jersey; reprinted from Junior Scholastic; copyright, 1956, by Scholastic Magazines, Inc. To the author and publishers for "The Giants of the Galápagos"; adapted from "Strange Reptiles of the Galápagos" by Rolf Blomberg in Natural History; copyright, 1951, by The American Museum of Natural History. To the author and publishers for "It's the Ham in Them"; adapted from an article by Joseph S. Stocker; from Boys' Life; by permission of the author and Boys' Life; published by the Boy Scouts of America. To the publishers for "Old Threetoes"; from "The Citadel in the Swamp" in Trails by William H. Bunce; copyright, 1935, by The Broadman Press. To the author for "Rose of the West" by Trumbull Reed; reprinted from Venture; copyright, 1955, by W. L. Jenkins; used by permission. To the author for "Two-Legged Fish" by Charles Coombs; adapted by permission of the author; from Boys Today. To the author for excerpts from "Hatty" by Audrey Harvey; adapted from a story in Collins Magazine. To the publishers for an excerpt from The Sea Around Us by Rachel Carson; copyright, 1951, by Oxford University Press, Inc. To the estate of the author for an excerpt from The Cruise of the Snark by Jack London. To the publishers for "Across Four Continents on Two Cylinders" by Jacques Cornet as told to Richard Dempewolff; from Popular Mechanics; copyright, 1955; adapted by permission of the publishers. To the author for "Malemute Mail" by Charles Coombs; adapted by permission of the author; from Boys Today. To the publishers for an excerpt from "The Silver Outrigger" adapted from Night Boat and Other Tod Moran Mysteries by Howard Pease; copyright, 1938, by Howard Pease; reprinted by permission of Doubleday & Company, Inc. To the estate of the author for an excerpt from "To Build a Fire" by Jack London. To the publishers for an excerpt from "That Infinite Capacity for Taking Pains"; from On Safari by Theodore J. Waldeck; copyright, 1940, by Theodore J. Waldeck; reprinted by permission of The Viking Press, Inc., New York. To the author and publishers for "What It Takes" by Burr Leyson; from Boys' Life; adapted by permission of the author and Boys' Life; published by the Boy Scouts of America. To the publishers for "Oklahoma Wasn't 'Civilized' " by Marquis James; adapted from Chapter 2 of The Cherokee Strip by Marquis James; copyright, 1945, by The Viking Press, Inc. To the publishers for an excerpt from Palomino and Other Horses by Wesley Dennis; copyright, 1950, by The World Publishing Company. To the author and publishers for "On Ice" by Denzil Batchelor; adapted from an article in Collins Magazine. To the publishers for "The Accident That Couldn't Happen"; adapted from "Man Failure" in Newsweek; copyright © 1956, by Weekly Publications, Inc. To the publishers for "Mystery Voice"; adapted from Senior Scholastic by permission; copyright, 1957, by Scholastic Magazines, Inc.